THE BIAS BENEATH THE FACTS
Education in a Democratic Society

FIRST EDITION

By Debra L. Clark

Kent State University

cognella
San Diego, CA

Bassim Hamadeh, CEO and Publisher
Christopher Foster, General Vice President
Michael Simpson, Vice President of Acquisitions
Jessica Knott, Managing Editor
Kevin Fahey, Cognella Marketing Manager
Jess Busch, Senior Graphic Designer
Sarah Wheeler, Project Editor
Stephanie Sandler, Licensing Associate

First published in the United States of America in 2013 by Cognella, Inc.

Trademark Notice: Product or corporate names may be trademarks or registered trademarks, and are used only for identification and explanation without intent to infringe.

15 14 13 12 11   1 2 3 4 5

Printed in the United States of America

ISBN: 978-1-62131-146-1

www.cognella.com 800.200.3908

TABLE OF CONTENTS

INTRODUCTION

In the classes I teach, I take my students on a journey from an extremely teacher-centered classroom to an extremely student-centered classroom. At the beginning of the semester, I am the all-knowing authority figure in the class. I tell students what to know, how to learn it, what to do, and when to do it. I make all of the decisions in the class. By the end of the semester, the students are in charge of the class and make all class decisions. This book is organized around this pedagogical focus.

Though I start my classes as the all-knowing authority figure, I quickly involve students in questioning my authority. This begins with the topic of educational history (Chapter One of this text). When reading about history, a false assumption is that what is being read actually occurred. Granted, all historians try to present the facts of the past, but everyone is biased. To help students understand this, I explain in Chapter One the difference between constitutional history and cultural history—the two primary lenses through which historians examine the past. I also make the point that history traditionally was written by men. Thus, because I am a woman, Chapter One is her-story. This may seem like simply a play on words, but gender, as with all dimensions of diversity, creates a lens through which scholars examine topics.

The key to understanding this text is that the goal is to assist pre-service teachers in finding their own professional voices. To accomplish this, I believe it is imperative that all professors in teacher education programs open ourselves up and allow students to see us *not* as all-knowing authority figures, but as life-long scholars, questioning what we know. The students need to understand how professors make pedagogical decisions, that we make mistakes, that we are biased. Students need to see professors as the teacher they hope to be one day. For this reason, in my class and in this text, I invite students to determine my partiality beneath the facts I present. This begins in Chapter One with discussion questions at the end of the chapter, which invite students to check my sources and examine the argument presented. Determining my bias is the first step in discovering their own professional voices. Additional discussion questions, activities, and online resources will assist pre-service teachers in creating knowledge, as well as consuming it.

In Chapter Two, additional information regarding educational history is provided, but in this chapter it is by two other authors. The first article was selected because the bias—Marxism—is rather obvious. The second article allows students to gain a clearer picture of what is meant by cultural history. The history presented in most history textbooks is constitutional history or history about the great leaders of the past. The second article in Chapter Two provides a picture of how history looks different from the perspective of "common people." Again, via discussion questions, activities, and online resources, readers are invited to identify the biases of the authors, and examine the implications of bias and the lens through which an author writes.

Chapter Three is the first of four chapters in which educational law is introduced. Perhaps more than any other topic, law is something viewed as "just is," or something to not question. The opposite of this is my goal in the chapters regarding education law. I want pre-service teachers to understand that laws are fluid and can and should change. In my students' futures they will have power, via teachers' unions and professional associations, to influence and change laws. But first they must understand the dynamic nature of educational law.

In Chapter Three, readers are introduced to the structure of our legal system, the significance of the First and Fourteenth Amendments to the U.S. Constitution, and case laws pertaining to freedom of speech, religion in schools, and equality of access. In Chapter Four, I include articles regarding religion and student speeches, the right to privacy and student athletes, and the evolution/creationism issue. The articles selected for this chapter are due to the timeliness of the issues discussed, as well as the academic discipline of the authors. The academic disciplines of law and education are both represented, which allow students to see how the lens of one's academic discipline shapes the partiality of authors. With Chapters Three and Four, readers are again invited to identify the biases of the authors, but the "examining implications" part changes. Instead of simply identifying bias and its implication, pre-service teachers must apply their knowledge of case laws to common activities found in most public schools via discussion questions, activities, and the online sources provided.

In Chapter Five, the educational law discussion shifts from case law to educational policy. Case laws tend to be right/wrong or good/bad legal decisions; educational policy tends to be "how-to" laws. By focusing on No Child Left Behind (NCLB) and the Individuals with Disability Education Act (IDEA), readers begin to see how educational policy shapes the structure and organization of schools; however, the changes to schools are always in a historical or traditional context. Thus, before introducing NCLB and IDEA, I explain the historical structure of schools, which has been paternalistic and patriarchal at the same time as it is democratic and decentralized. I then explain how the two educational polices are changing and/or reinforcing these characteristics in schools.

In Chapters Five and Six, I am much more open about my own biases, just as I am in my own classroom when I discuss educational policies. In Chapter Six, articles are provided regarding NCLB and IDEA by other authors, and again, readers are guided in understanding the prejudices of the authors, but with this chapter the emphasis is on the publisher; where an article is published shapes the bias of the article written. Also, the educational policies chapters introduce readers to the politics of education. Through discussion questions, activities, and online resources, the political nature of education in our nation becomes apparent.

In Chapter Seven, the focus of the book shifts. No longer are readers guided on identifying biases; instead, the focus becomes naming biases or giving a professional language to the process of critical reading. Often, students in my classes are able to identify that an author or speaker is biased; identifying the belief system behind the bias is much more difficult. Chapter Seven introduces the reader to labeling prejudices and tying those biases to belief systems. To do so, I utilize traditional theories of education often discussed in teacher education programs. Teachers need a professional language to become engaged in the political nature of education if they are to be viewed as professional experts. That language exists and has for many years, but has been disregarded as irrelevant. In Chapter Seven, not only are belief systems identified, but the power of understanding and using them is discussed.

Chapter Eight begins the process of applying information included in the first seven chapters of this text. My writing voice changes as I guide pre-service teachers in discovering their own professional voices via activities, which help them analyze the topic of teacher professionalization. Ultimately, as indicated above, my goal is for my students to begin developing a professional voice. For this reason, when we get to the topic of teacher professionalization in Chapter Eight, I dramatically begin withholding my professional opinions.

In Chapter Nine, my professional voice further diminishes as students are guided through two activities, which examine the topic of human diversity. The purpose of the first activity is for students to gain an understanding of their own cultural identities. The second activity gives students a broader understanding of differences in the definition of childhood in our nation and abroad.

The last step in the journey from a teacher-centered classroom to a student-centered classroom is an extensive small-group activity; each semester this activity changes. In Chapter Ten, I share with the reader two activities done in my course in previous semesters.

I have always dreamed of writing a book and could not have done so without the help of many teachers. I dedicate this book to my teachers …

My parents and first teachers, Mr. and Mrs. Gordon (Ike) and Carole Clark, who taught me the blessing of being able to learn, the significance of seeking truth, and the values of work and generosity;

Those who taught me not only how to read and write, but to also enjoy both skills — Mrs. Stevens, Mr. Kovacs, Ms. Mumaw, and Mrs. Ucchino;

Those who taught me to question truth — Dr. William Coleman, Dr. Averil McClelland, and Dr. Natasha Levinson;

And those outside of the classroom — who taught me, by example, the value of hard work and generosity of time and energy — Mrs. Dorothy Allen and Mr. Crawford Jackson.

Last, but definitely not least, this book would not be possible without the assistance, proofreading, advice, and support of Ms. Nancy Robitaille.

CHAPTER ONE
EDUCATIONAL HISTORY: AN OVERVIEW

WHY DO I NEED TO KNOW THIS?

D o you know your ancestry? Are you interested? Your family history helps define your identity. It might not help you avoid the mistakes of your parents, but it does define you (how so will be explained further in a later chapter). Understanding the history of your chosen profession will help define your professional identity.

Schools in the United States, as you will see in the following sections, played a key role in defining and strengthening our nation. Yet, educational history is not commonly known. We know what Abraham Lincoln did for this nation, as well as Harriet Tubman, Susan B. Anthony, and Amelia Earhart. We know famous personalities of the past, some who changed our nation, some who were less influential, but popular. However, most people have never heard of Horace Mann, who did more to shape this nation than most U.S. presidents. Most have not heard of Emma Willard, who was instrumental in promoting female education. Many have no idea who Booker T. Washington or W. E. B. Du Bois were, and why they played a key role in defining the education of blacks, well before the famous *Brown v. Board of Education* decision.

One cannot get a clear picture of the history of the United States without an understanding of educational history, yet it is rarely mentioned in social studies classes. Is it not as interesting as the history of wars? I view it as more compelling. Is it less inspirational than the stories of other famous people in our history? I think that it is full of extremely motivating stories. Is it not as sensational, or perhaps as ugly, as other pieces of history? Brutality and violence existed in this history also.

I cannot say why educational history is not well known. I do believe, however, that once you understand educational history, you will be amazed at the role it played in defining our nation. I also believe that understanding this history will bring a sense of professionalism to teaching, because professionals know their history. Building on the shoulder of giants, or those who came before us is key to being a professional. We cannot do so if we do not know our shared history.

WHAT IS EDUCATIONAL HISTORY?

History is perhaps the most accurate word in the English language, because traditionally, history is *his*-story. History was primarily written by men about men. The reason for this tradition is twofold. First, higher education was not open to women; thus, historians have primarily been men. Second was the belief that if we understand the lives of those who ruled, we will understand the past. Because men primarily ruled and men were primarily historians, history has traditionally been his-story. That form of history is referred to as constitutional history; however, not all constitutional history has been written about men. For example, to understand England, you must know that Queen Elizabeth I ruled in the 16th century, and thus would have been studied by constitutional historians.

In the 1960s and 1970s, as universities opened to men and women, a new breed of historian arose who argued that if we want to understand our past, knowing about the lives of those who ruled is not enough. We need to understand the lives of the common people as well. This branch of history is commonly referred to as cultural history. A cultural historian would argue that understanding the lives of the people who tilled the land of royal families and the soldiers who fought their battles is as important, if not more important, than understanding the lives of royalty.

Many newer academic disciplines evolved from the efforts of cultural historians—African American History, Women's History, Native American History, to name just a few. Educational history is a combination of cultural and constitutional history, because both perspectives are necessary in gaining a clearer picture of our past. The following examples demonstrate the different perspectives:

> To understand the history of the Catholic faith, a constitutional historian would study the lives and writings of popes; cultural historians would study the lives of the Knights Templars, soldiers of the Catholic faith during the Crusades.
>
> To understand the history of knowledge, constitutional historians would study the governing structure of ancient Greece, as well as the writings of philosophers such as Plato and Aristotle; cultural historians, in contrast, would study the lives of boys in training in Sparta or the role of mythologies in the lives of Greeks.
>
> To understand the empire of Great Britain, understanding the role of the royal family would be critical for a constitutional historian; for a cultural historian, understanding how Jack the Ripper evaded capture would be much more telling.
>
> For the Civil War, Lincoln, as well as Lee and Grant, must be clearly examined by constitutional historians; for cultural historians, the lives of slaves and freed men and women, as well as infantry men (and the women who disguised themselves as such) are much more interesting.

Clearly, both sides give part of the story of what happened in our past; however, the work of constitutional historians is easier due to the writings of those who governed, and the contemporary writings of those who wrote about those who governed. For cultural historians, a significant challenge is trying to determine a means for understanding common people, given the reality that most common people could not write.

For example, above I made the claim that Christianity did not play as central a role in the foundation of our nation as some would like us to believe, but did Christianity play a central role in schooling? A cultural historian might approach this question via an examination of textbooks.

A hornbook was a wooden paddle with a parchment stretched across it and was used by children in colonial America, often in dame schools found in Puritan Massachusetts. The Lord's Prayer can be easily seen as having prominence in this text. The next popular textbook was the New England Primer.

horn book

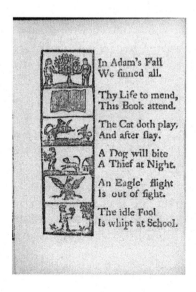

As can be seen in this text, religion continued to play a prominent role in the schools that utilized this text. However, by the 19th century, the first Reader of the McGuffey Reader was the most popular school textbook, and it made no mention of religion.[1]

This simplified review of textbooks only gives a snapshot of the story of religion and schools, but it exemplifies how a cultural historian might approach the topic. In contrast, a constitutional historian would examine laws in place and the writing of educational officials such as Horace Mann.

My argument is that both perspectives are necessary to understand history, but both perspectives are also biased due to their approach in answering research questions. What follows is also biased. One could argue that what follows is actually *her*-story, or my bias regarding educational history. As you read the following, know that I am leaving out key pieces that many in my field would find objectionable. For example, I do not discuss John Dewey (I will introduce him in Chapter Seven). I do not include John Dewey in her-story, because I believe his significance is much more relevant in the history of teacher education than in the history of K–12 schooling. I also do not include him in this chapter, because he does not play a role in what I believe is the main message of educational history in our nation. See if you can identify this message before I outline it at the end of this chapter.

HER-STORY

Colonial America

Education existed before we were a nation, as did schooling in some colonies. Though the education of children was widespread, schooling was not. To understand this, one must recognize

---

1   Retrieved July 4, 2011, from School: The Story of American Education, Public Broadcasting Services http://www.pbs.org/kcet/publicschool/evolving_classroom/books.html

that family, children, parents, and marriage were not viewed then as they are now. Families were communities in themselves. No stores existed for buying food or clothes. No switches existed for turning on lights or heating homes. No water flowed within a home from a faucet and there were no indoor toilets. Every necessity of survival had to come from the family. The success of a family literally meant the survival of everyone in that family. [handwritten: families]

Children were necessary for that survival, but the survival of children was not a given. Many more mothers and babies died in child birth than they do today, and if the child did survive, chances were not great that the child would make it past the age of five.[2] However, children were necessary to maintain the family farm, harvest the crops, tend the animals, make the fabric for clothes, created the candles for light, etc. Children, bluntly put, were a commodity. The more children who survived, the more likely the parents would also survive. [handwritten: kids]

Marriage was business also. If a wife died while giving birth, it was critical for the survival of the family that another wife was found. She was necessary for all of the tasks in the home, as well as the potential survival of the commodity of children. This is not to say parents did not love their children then as they do now. Children, however, were much more valuable.[3] [handwritten: Kids] [handwritten: than they are now]

The education of children was the purview of the parents or another adult family member. Remember that parents, for the most part, also did not attend school, nor were they able to read or write. Thus, what they taught their children were the skills of maintaining the community of the family, as well as passing down cultural beliefs. [handwritten: school]

This pattern of education was particularly true in the Middle Atlantic Colonies, where, one could argue, the purpose of education was accumulation of wealth.[4]

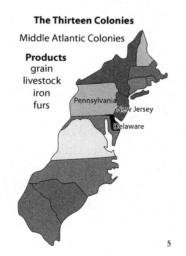

The Thirteen Colonies

Middle Atlantic Colonies

Products
grain
livestock
iron
furs

Pennsylvania
New Jersey
Delaware

5

[handwritten: purview =
the range of
operation, authority,
control, concern, etc.]

2   Retrieved July 4, 2011, from *Childbirth in Early America*, Department of History and College of Education, University of Houston, http://www.digitalhistory.uh.edu/historyonline/childbirth.cfm
3   Gerda Learner, *The Creation of Patriarchy*. 1986. New York: Oxford University Press.
4   Max Sugar, *Regional Identity and Behavior*. 2002. New York: Plenum Publishers.
5   Retrieved July 4, 2011, from http://www.mce.k12tn.net/colonial_america/middle_colonies.htm

Exceptions to this pattern, of course, existed. Towns did develop, and in those towns were families that ran the local tavern, maintained the local place of worship or served in some governing capacity, sometimes all in the same building. Eventually, schoolhouses were also built, but much later than in areas north of these colonies.[6]

The Southern Colonies, in contrast, were colonized by the second, third, fourth, etc., son of royalty in Europe.[7] At this time only the oldest son inherited the title and most, if not all, of the land of his father. Other sons of royal families were valuable to the family primarily if the oldest son died. Thus, other sons had to find other means for survival and success. One way that developed, after Europeans began living on this continent, was to relocate here and try to recreate what the oldest brother inherited back in Europe.

Created their own kingdoms.

The Thirteen Colonies
Southern Colonies

Products
tobacco
indigo
rice
farm products
furs

Maryland
Virginia
North Carolina
South Carolina
Georgia

8

Schools in the South

For this to occur, cheap labor was necessary. Initially, bonded servants were used who agreed to work in exchange for passage to this country and life's necessities upon arrival. Eventually, as we know, the institution of slavery became much more lucrative. Thus, three separate educational systems developed in the Southern Colonies. The children of parents who could not own bonded servants or slaves were the property of their parents and were educated much like children in the Middle Colonies. Children of slaves were educated to serve the interests of their parents' master, who also owned them. As such, they could be sold to another slave owner or given a role to serve the plantation. In contrast, the children of the plantation owners were educated to become proper ladies and gentlemen. Reading and writing was less valuable than how to interact with those from the opposite gender. Thus, they were taught how to dance, fence, embroider hankies, etc.

---

6   Ian S. Hornsey, *A History of Beer and Brewing*. 2003. Cambridge: The Royal Society of Chemistry.

7   Retrieved July 4, 2011, from http://www.libraryindex.com/history/pages/cmxyrcnycr/colonial-settlement-colony-virginia.html

8   Retrieved July 4, 2011, from http://www.mce.k12tn.net/colonial_america/southern_colonies.htm

Though education was primarily in the hands of parents and slave masters, forms of schooling did exist, but they were not viewed favorably in the middle and southern colonies, except for dame schools. Widowed women and/or orphaned girls who did not have a husband or father who owned them survived by providing a necessary service, not the "oldest profession," though I suspect that existed also. Instead, they survived by watching children not old enough to work on the family farm. Remember, farming can be quite dangerous and labor intensive. The value of children came to fruition when they could work. Thus, all family members who could work needed to do so, and the potential workers needed to stay alive, if possible. Dame schools became a solution to the problem. The education that children received in these schools varied greatly and was contingent on the knowledge of the woman in charge. Some did learn letters and numbers; many began learning the skills necessary to maintain the family farm.[9]

dame schools

DAME SCHOOL[10]

In the Northern Colonies, the tradition of formal schooling began, more specifically in Puritan Massachusetts. A common myth is that the Puritans came to this land to fight for religious freedom. Well, no, they came to impose their religious beliefs. Their goal was to replicate their successes in Ireland, that failed in England. In Ireland, Puritans were very successful in outlawing the Catholic faith, as well as taking the land and punishing Catholics in a variety of ways, including limiting the education of Catholic children,[11] much like slave owners in this country limited the education of slaves. However, when they tried to do the same in England, they were much less

9   David Tyack and Elisabeth Hansot, *Learning Together*. 1990. London: Yale University Press New Haven.
10   Retrieved July, 4, 2011, from http://faculty.mdc.edu/jmcnair/Joe28pages/Schooling,%20Education,%20and%20Literacy%20in%20Colonial%20America.htm
11   Conversations with Batt Burns, professional storyteller and tour guide, April 2009. During a trip where I took 11 undergraduate students to Ireland for a comparative analysis of education in democratic societies, I had the pleasure to have multiple conversations about the history of Ireland. Much of my knowledge of Ireland came from those

Puritan history

successful. They were, however, quite resilient, and pushed their beliefs to the point where they were no longer tolerated. As a result, in England, in an effort to limit the Puritans' influence, they became the persecuted. For that reason, they came to this land in an effort to create their own theocracy—a land governed by their religious beliefs.

Anne Hutchinson

Failure to abide by the rules of the Puritan faith was quite harshly punished. The story of Anne Hutchinson exemplifies the severity of the punishment. Hutchinson was a woman who believed that God spoke to her heart and she began Bible studies for other women. Initially, this was of little concern to those in charge of the colony, but eventually wives began taking their husbands to the religious meetings and this could not be tolerated. Religious orthodoxy was the purview of men; women had not such authority. So what was the punishment for Hutchinson? A metal bore was put in a fire and then placed in her mouth, burning out the offending tongue. Then she and her children were exiled from the colony, which resulted in loss of resources and measures of safety. She and her children were eventually murdered by Indians.[12]

laws

Another effort to make sure that the rules of the faith were followed was the indoctrination of the youth. In this effort, they wrote a law in 1642 which required parents to teach their children to read, so that they could read the Bible and understand the law. This law, however, was not enforceable because most parents at that time could not read. In 1647 a second law, commonly referred to as the Old Deluder Satan Act, was enacted, which required towns with 50 or more people to hire a schoolmaster and towns with 100 or more people to build a school building. So began the tradition of public schooling, but not free schooling.[13]

Puritan schools

These schools, referred to as English or Latin grammar schools, were primarily open to boys of parents who could afford to pay the schoolmaster and maintain the school building. That is not to say that girls did not attend school—they did so to a lesser extent and usually when boys were not present—on weekends or during harvest season. The children not welcome in these schools may have considered themselves quite fortunate, because the life of children in these schools was quite brutal by today's standards. As explained by Elphalet Nott, "If I was not whipped more than three times a week, I considered myself for the time peculiarly fortunate." Six-year-old James Sims was sent to a boarding school where new boys were always flogged, usually "until the youngster vomited or wet his breeches."[14]

---

conversations; Moran, Patrick Francis, *Historical Sketch of the Persecutions Suffered by the Catholics of Ireland under the Rule of Cromwell and the Puritans.* 1907. Dublin: M. H. Gill and Son, Ltd.

12   Gerda Lerner, *Creation of Feminist Consciousness.* 1993. Oxford: Oxford University Press.

13   Old Deluder Satan Law, retrieved July 15, 2011, from http://www.lawlib.state.ma.us/docs/DeluderSatan.pdf; Massachusetts Education Laws of 1642 and 1647, retrieved July 15, 2011, from http://www.nd.edu/~rbarger/www7/masslaws.html

14   Kaestle, *Pillars of the Republic: Common Schools and American Society, 1780–1860*, p. 19.

SCHOOLS AND THE FOUNDING OF OUR NATION

Anyone who uses the Founding Fathers to argue anything about what occurs in schools likely does not understand them—because for the most part, the Founding Fathers did not see a role for schools in our nation, at least not a role for public schooling. The reason for this is because of the prevailing ideology of Calvinism.[15]

A commonly held belief today is that the rich are richer because they work harder and the poor are poorer because they are lazy. Most have not been given the opportunity to explore the commonly held beliefs about wealth and poverty in our nation. Numerous reasons exist as to why this opportunity for contemplation has not occurred, but I believe its origins can be found in the ideology that governed this land when we became the nation of the United States of America—Calvinism.

Simply put, Calvinists in the 1700s believed that the rich were rich because God liked them and the poor were poor because God did not like them so much. In other words, your station in life was preordained by the will of God. Who is man to interfere with God's plan? Schooling for all children would be interfering with God's efforts to reward the rich and punish the poor.[16]

Not all of the Founding Fathers, however, excluded schooling as a means for creating a national identity or strengthening our fledgling democracy. Thomas Jefferson, in the Bill for the More General Diffusion of Knowledge Act,[17] proposed that the sons of fathers who did not own land (initially only landowners were considered citizens in this country) or the sons of fathers who had the means to pay for the schooling be permitted to attend school also. Jefferson argued against what he referred to as the "Artificial Aristocracy," and for the "Natural Aristocracy."[18] A highly educated man himself, Jefferson believed that if this democracy were to prevail, schools should be used to identify the natural aristocracy, those male children with the most intelligence. These male children would eventually become our elected officials instead of following the assumption that the sons of the wealthy would fulfill those roles. Jefferson lost the argument and the bill did not pass. Calvinism prevailed.

---

15 Thomas Jefferson, "A Declaration by the Representatives of the United States of America, in General Congress assembled," in Adrienne Koch and William Peden (eds.), *The Life and Selected Writings of Thomas Jefferson*, (New York: Modern Library, 1972), p. 22, as cited in Urban and Wagoner, p. 69.

16 Thomas Jefferson, "A Declaration by the Representatives of the United States of America, in General Congress assembled," in Adrienne Koch and William Peden (eds.), *The Life and Selected Writings of Thomas Jefferson* (New York: Modern Library, 1972), p. 22, as cited in Urban and Wagoner, p. 69.

17 Library of Congress, retrieved July 15, 2001, from http://www.loc.gov/exhibits/jefferson/jeffrep.html

18 Thomas Jefferson, "To Peter Carr, with enclosure," in Gordon Lee, *Cursed against Ignorance: Thomas Jefferson on Education*, Gordon Lee (ed.), (New York: Teachers College Press, 1961), pp. 145–146 as cited in Spring, 2001, p. 64.

Thomas Jefferson

Benjamin Rush went even further than Jefferson. He argued that girls as well as boys should be taught the principles of democracy in public schools so that future mothers could educate their children regarding these principles and assist their husbands as they fulfilled their role as citizens of this nation. Rush's beliefs became known as Republican Motherhood, and the idea did take root to some extent, but not to the point of establishing public schools for boys and girls.[20] Calvinism prevailed.

Benjamin Rush

Benjamin Franklin, a particularly unique founding father, went so far as to start his own school. Franklin believed that in this new nation, schooling should not reflect education that existed in Latin or English schools. Rather, schooling should have a more practical focus. To achieve this

19 Retrieved December 7, 2011, from http://commons.wikimedia.org/wiki/File:Reproduction-of-the-1805-Rembrandt-Peale-painting-of-Thomas-Jefferson-New-York-Historical-Society_1.jpg

20 Benjamin Rush, "Thoughts upon Female Education, Accommodated to the Present State of Society, Manners, and Government in the United States," in Fredrick Rudolph, (ed.), *Essays on Education in the Early Republic*, (Cambridge: Harvard University Press, 1965), pp. 230, 27–40 as cited in Tyack and Hansot, p. 33.

21 Retrieved December 7, 2011, from http://commons.wikimedia.org/wiki/File:Benjamin_Rush_Painting_by_Peale_1783.jpg

goal, Franklin began his own school, but it failed because parents did not enroll their children in his school. Calvinism prevailed.

Benjamin Franklin

THE ORIGINS OF PUBLIC SCHOOLING

Prior to the 1800s, teachers did not exist in the United States. The head of the class was the schoolmaster, a male not trained to be a teacher. Instead, schoolmasters were trained to be religious leaders and they held the position of schoolmaster only temporarily, often until they got their own parish. That practice began to change because of women such as Emma Willard, Catherine Beecher, and Mary Lyons.

In the 1800s through the early part of the 20th century, it was believed that the brain of a human female was comparable to that of a gorilla. It made as much sense to put resources into the education of females than it would to put resources into the education of monkeys. Emma Willard and other women argued that such an argument was circular. The belief that women were less educable than men was indefensible, because women, for the most part, had not received an education. Thus, the position of these women was that, until women commonly receive an education, no conclusions could be made regarding their ability to learn. How is it possible that such women could exist if girls were, for the most part, not welcome in schools?[23]

The daughters of the wealthy were often tutored alongside their brothers throughout history. Thus, educated women have existed throughout history, though schooling for women has not. However, upon receiving this education, the expectation that these daughters assume the role

---

22   Retrieved December 7, 2011, from http://commons.wikimedia.org/wiki/File:BenFranklinDuplessis.jpg
23   Tyack and Hansot, *Learning Together*, 1990; Catherine Beecher, *A Treatise on Domestic Economy*, (New York: Schocken Books, 1977), p. 2, as cited in Jane Roland Martin, *Reclaiming a Conversation*, (New Haven: Yale University Press, 1985), p. 105.

of a wife and mother prevailed. As a result, they often did not have any opportunity for further education or intellectual pursuits upon leaving girlhood. Though many women bristled at these constraints, until the early 1800s, very few women, outside of religious orders, had success in changing the status quo.

Catherine Beecher and other women did so by creating female seminaries and finding male backers for their schools. Some families sent their daughters to these schools; some daughters escaped their families and found the schools. Regardless of how they got there, the girls in these schools received an education to make them better mothers and wives via a curriculum similar to that in universities for men. Though female seminaries started before the establishment of common schools, they eventually played a significant role in their success.

Female Seminary, Washington, Pennsylvania.

Horace Mann is my hero, and I believe he is the most significant American to ever live, because he is the father of public education and teacher education. He certainly accomplished a feat that affected most Americans living today. Can the same be said for any U.S. president?

Initially, when offered the position of secretary of education for the state of Massachusetts, Mann was reluctant. No such position previously existed, nor did a system of public schools—so Horace Mann went on holiday to Boston to contemplate this offer.[24] Only after attending a temperance meeting, fleeing his hotel after it was set on fire, and witnessing an anti-Catholic riot did he decide to accept the position. Mann believed that public schools could become the great equalizer. He believed that the evils caused by men abusing alcohol—wife beating, children starving, etc., could be avoided if boys and girls attended school. He believed crime could be averted if all children received an education. And if little Catholic children sat next to little Protestant children on the schoolhouse bench, they would be less likely to grow up and try to kill each other.

---

24   Joel Spring, *The American School, 1642–1996*, fourth ed., New York: McGraw-Hill Companies, Inc., 1997.

In his journal, on the day that he accepted the position he wrote, "Henceforth, so long as I hold this office, I devote myself to the supremest welfare of mankind upon earth ... I have faith in the improvability of the race."[25]

26

Horace Mann

Though setting about in his new position with lofty goals, Mann's challenge often led him to unpleasant locations. But he was, above all else, determined. Riding his horse from town to town, he inspected and reported on the conditions of the schools that existed. What he discovered often dismayed him—children were learning in schools with little heat, light, or cleanliness. In his travels, he also engaged his skills as the consummate politician, promoting his idea of a common school for all children. To the Workingman's Party, he explained that if common schools existed for all children, their children would have more opportunities to prosper; to rich industrialists he explained that schools for all children would result in workers arriving to work on time. To Protestants he made the claim that their Bible would be used to teach children how to read; to Catholics he explained that, yes the Protestant Bible would be utilized to teach reading (it was the most commonly published book), but teachers would not use it to promote their own faith.[27]

His efforts were quite fruitful in the establishment of common schools (what we refer to today as public schools), but this created a new problem. As common schools sprouted across the nation, the first teaching shortage developed. Remember, at this time men were schoolmasters, and that position was temporary. The solution to this problem was at least partially seen among the graduates of female seminaries. Mann argued that women were natural nurturers, and besides they could be paid one third of what men were paid. The public, however, was still wary of

25 Mann, 1907, pp. 80–81, as cited in Spring, p. 111.
26 Retrieved December 7, 2011, from http://commons.wikimedia.org/wiki/File:Horace_Mann.jpg
27 Spring.

females at the head of the classroom, but Mann had a solution for that also—the creation of teacher education programs, which were called normal schools.[28]

Mann's ideas did not result in the far-reaching goals he set forth, but they did begin a process which eventually led to the establishment of public school systems nationwide. In 1852 Massachusetts enacted the first compulsory school attendance law.[29] By 1857, two years before Mann's death, Boston had 213 one-room primary common schools.[30] By 1880, 32 of 38 states had urban common schools, which were open for more than 180 days each year.[31] By 1883 three fourths of all children in rural areas were attending some form of common school. By the turn of the century, over 13 million children attended primary school in approximately 224, 500 school buildings.[32]

One outcome that Mann may not have foreseen, however, is the degree to which the balance in the education of girls and boys would shift. In 1790 twice as many men as women were considered literate; by 1870 girls began surpassing boys "in their rates of literacy and academic achievement."[33] By 1870 women also outnumbered men as public school teachers (59 percent), with the largest number located in the common schools of the North Atlantic states.[34]

AMERICANIZATION

Though we may like to view ourselves as the land of immigrants and our nation continues to be a refuge for many around the world looking for a better life, we are not a nation that welcomes immigrants with open arms. Rather, we tend to look at new arrivals suspiciously and with contempt. Today in arguments regarding the illegal immigration issue, the voices of those who believe that immigrants will negatively influence our culture are often heard. "They will take our jobs." "Our wages will be lowered because they are willing to work for less." "If they want to come here they had better learn English." These arguments are not new.

William Torrey Harris, superintendent of the St. Louis school system, 1868–1880, described immigrant children in the following manner:

> Living in narrow, filthy alleys, poorly clad and without habits of cleanliness, "the divine sense of shame,: which Plato makes to the foundation of civilization, is very little developed. Self respect is the basis of character and virtue: cleanliness of person and clothing is a sine qua non for its growth in the child. The child, who passes his years in the

28 John L. Rury, "Vocationalism for Home and Work: Women's Education in the United States, 1880–1930." *History of Education Quarterly*, spring 1984.

29 Robert F. McNergney, and Joanne M. Herbert, *Foundations of Education.* Boston: Allyn and Bacon, 1998.

30 Tyack and Hansot, *Learning Together*; Gutek, *Cultural Foundations of Education.*

31 Tyack and Hansot, *Learning Together.*

32 Ibid.

33 Tyack and Hansot, *Learning Together*, p. 46.

34 Rury, "Vocationalism for Home and Work: Women's Education in the United States, 1880–1930,"p. 99.

misery of the crowded tenement house or alley, becomes early familiar with all manner of corruption and immortality.[35]

The following political cartoons show how Irish immigrants were particularly viewed as problematic.

THE IRISH FRANKENSTEIN. [36]

Contempt for foreigners led to Americanization policies and led to school practices that we often take for granted today. For example, school lunchrooms were created to teach immigrants to eat like Americans. Good Americans bought their bread from a local store and it came wrapped in a brown paper bag; dirty foreigners ate filthy homemade bread. Playgrounds were established to keep children away from their foreign parents because it was believed that the children of immigrants could be saved, but only if their parents had as little influence as possible. School nurses were hired to inspect the dirty immigrant children to make sure they did not bring a disease with them to school. Swimming pools and showers were established to clean the dirty immigrant children.

For Native American children, Americanization policies were much harsher. Children as young as five years old were taken from their parents and sent to Indian Boarding Schools. Upon arriving at their new school, they were stripped of their cultural garb, their hair was cut, and they were given a school uniform. Below is a picture of Apache children on the day of their arrival at school. Take note of their dress, hair, and facial expressions. They were forced to discard their

---

35   Troen, *The Public Schools: Shaping the St. Louis System, 1838–1920*, as cited in Spring, p. 232.

36   Retrieved July 5, 2011, from http://www.nlm.nih.gov/frankenstein/escaping.html

original tribal dress, their hair was cut if male and pulled back and up if female, and the expressions on their faces appear to be that of stunned individuals.

EDUCATING THE INDIAN RACE.   GRADUATING CLASS OF CARLISLE, PA.

Children in these schools were forbidden to practice their culture or religion, or speak their native language. The punishment for infractions of the rules was quite harsh—they were placed in solitary confinement and beaten.[37]

Children in Indian boarding schools were not permitted to return to their tribe until the age of 17, if they survived until that age. Though forced to attend the schools, there was no guarantee of food. Instead, children worked eight hours or more each day harvesting food for the school. If they had a bad harvest, the children starved. In the summers, the children were given to white families for the supposed purpose of learning how to become white. Their treatment was contingent on the families' view of Indians. Many of the children were viewed as summer slaves. The harsh treatment of children in the Indian boarding school system helps explain two phenomena. One, many of the children actually died of homesickness. Two, you will know when you are driving by what was once an Indian boarding school. It is the school with the cemetery.[38]

---

37   South Dakota, Zitkala-Sa. Excerpts from *The School Days of an Indian Girl*; Barbara Landis, the Carlisle Indian Industrial School; Ronald D. ChrisJohn, *Key Issues and Challenges*, compiled from *The Circles Game*, submitted October 1994, retrieved July 5, 2001, from http://www.english.illinois.edu/maps/poets/a_f/erdrich/boarding/index.htm
38   Ibid.

WARS AND SCHOOLS

The contempt for most things foreign did not improve when our soldiers encountered foreign cultures during World Wars I and II, even though many of the soldiers returned impressed with what they saw. In 1919 the American Legion, whose organizers "were U.S. Army officers who were fearful that members of the U.S. military forces in Europe were being exposed to radical political belief,"[39] set about establishing rules which would promote 100 percent Americanism. In this effort, the National Americanization Commission of the American Legion was established with the following goals:

1. "Combat all anti-American tendencies, activities and propaganda.
2. Work for the education of immigrants, prospective American citizens and alien residents in the principles of Americanism.
3. Inculcate the ideals of Americanism in the citizen population, particularly the basic American principle that the interests of all people are above those of any special interest or any so-called class or section of the people.
4. Spread throughout the people of the nation information as to the real nature and principles of American government.
5. Foster the teaching of Americanism in all schools."[40]

From the 1920s to the 1950s, proponents of the Protestant ethic dictated moral guidelines in movies, on the radio, and especially in schools. Academic scholars developed theories which supported the Protestant ethic.[41] Teachers, especially English teachers, welcomed the findings of these scholarly reports, and recommended that children's movie watching be closely supervised.[42] The Bureau of Educational Research of Ohio State University published a textbook for use in public schools, entitled *How to Appreciate Motion Pictures: A Manual of Motion Picture Criticism Prepared for High School Students*.[43] In 1934 the National Council of Teachers of English began advocating movie attendance.[44]

At the same time that movies were being advocated by teachers, the National Education Association (NEA) was involved in ensuring that the "right" movies be made. Under the threat of censorship, the film industry established the Motion Picture Producers and Distributors of America (MPPDA).[45] The first president of MPPDA, Will Hays, was invited to speak at the annual meeting of the NEA. His speech sheds light on the degree to which the entertainment industry, in conjunction with schools, came to promote the Protestant ethic during this era:

---

39 Spring, *The American School, 1642–2000*, p. 333.
40 Gellerman, "The American Legion as Educator", p. 68, as cited in Spring, *The American School, 1642–2000*, p. 333.
41 Spring, *The American School, 1642–2000*.
42 Ibid.
43 Ibid, p. 340.
44 Ibid.
45 Ibid.

We accept the challenge in the righteous demand of the American mother that the entertainment and amusement of ... youth shall be worthy of their value as a potent factor in the country's future ... I am against political censorship, of course, because political censorship will not do what is hoped for in the last analysis ... but there is one place and one place only where evils can be eliminated ... and that is the point where and when pictures are made ... Right is right and wrong is wrong, and men know right from wrong, the correction can be made, real evil can and must be kept out, the highest standards of art, taste, and morals can be achieved, and it is primarily the duty of producers to do it. [46]

Hays was true to his word, and helped establish and enforce a self-regulatory code ensuring that only movies deemed as morally, socially, or politically righteous were produced.[47]

Teachers were also subject to censorship at this time. In 1933 teachers in eight states were required to take loyalty oaths. Within two years, 20 states required teachers to take similar oaths.[48] These practices continued until after World War II, when American Legion members continued to "weed subversion from schools."[49] Teachers and administrators suspected of unpatriotic beliefs were fired. In addition, textbooks became the target of patriotic groups.[50]

In 1940 the Daughters of Colonial Wars declared that textbooks "tried to give the child an unbiased viewpoint instead of teaching him real Americanism."[51] Backed by the American Legion, Orlen K. Armstrong brought the following charges against textbooks written by Harold Rugg, a professor at Teachers College:

1. To present a new interpretation of history in order to "debunk" our heroes and cast doubt upon their motives, their patriotism and their service to mankind.
2. To cast aspersions upon our Constitution and our form of government, and shape opinions favorable to replacing them with socialistic control.
3. To condemn the American system of private ownership and enterprise, and form opinions to collectivism.
4. To mould opinions against traditional religious faiths and ideas or morality, as being parts of an outgrown system.[52]

Armstrong's attack of Rugg's textbooks basically consisted of accusing Rugg of not supporting pro-American ideals. In doing so, Armstrong gained the support of school officials. Rugg's

---

46   Moley, the Hays Office, as cited in Spring, *The American School, 1642–2000*, pp. 334–335.
47   Ibid.
48   Ibid., p. 333.
49   Ibid., p. 334.
50   Ibid., p. 334.
51   *Book Learning*, p. 65, as cited in Kliebard, *The Struggle for The American Curriculum, 1893–1958*, p. 206.
52   Armstrong, "Treason in Textbooks," *The American Legion Magazine*, as cited in Kliebard, *The Struggle for The American Curriculum, 1893–1958*, p. 207.

textbooks, which had previously obtained a circulation rate of 1,317,960 with an additional 2,687,000 workbooks, were never revised and began to disappear from classrooms.[53]

The 1950s saw the introduction of a new type of curriculum in public schools. Under the rubric of life adjustment courses, schools added to the responsibilities of teachers one more component of moral agency. In these courses, students were instructed in everything from "the problem of improving one's personal appearance" to the "problem of developing and maintaining wholesome boy-girl relationships."[54] One of the best examples of the implementation of life adjustment courses was a guide provided by the Illinois Secondary Schools Curriculum Program, which identified the needs of youth as follows:

> Tools of communication; strong body; sound attitude toward it; Satisfactory Social Relationships; Competence in and appreciation of improved family living; Knowledge of, practice in, and zeal for democratic processes; sensitiveness to importance of group action; Effectiveness as consumers; Adjustment to occupation; and Development of meaning for life.[55]

Though not all schools had as an extensive program of life adjustment courses, many, at least in part, provided such courses. For some, schools came to be viewed as an American institution which not only supported wholesome values, but also as the moral glue keeping this country together. For many employed teachers during this era, their moral agency reached what might be viewed as the highest level. This was true in that few dared question the values expounded.

This level of social clout began to crumble with the launch of the satellite *Sputnik* on October 5, 1957.[56] Urban and Wagoner explain how the launching of *Sputnik* triggered the involvement of the federal government into affairs of the public schools:

> The most significant educational consequence of *Sputnik*, even more important in the long run than the attention paid to academic studies, was the impetus it gave to federal financing of public education. The battle over the issue of federal aid to education in the United States had been going on since before the birth of the nation ...[57]

In 1958 the National Defense Education Act was enacted, and a link between the schools and the federal government was established.[58] No longer were schools viewed as simply a state issue.

In addition to the National Defense Education Act, one other link between the federal government and schools was instituted in the 1950s. This link occurred three years prior to the launching

---

53 Kliebard, *The Struggle for The American Curriculum, 1893–1958*.

54 Bestor, *Educational Wastelands*, pp. 36–38, as cited in Spring, *The American School, 1642–2000*, p. 367.

55 Houston, Sanford, and Trump, *Guide to the Study of Curriculum in Secondary Schools*, p. 23, as cited in Kliebard, *The Struggle for The American Curriculum, 1893–1958*, p. 251.

56 Ibid., p. 274.

57 Ibid., pp. 279–280.

58 Ibid., pp. 281–283.

of Sputnik and with much less fanfare, but would become instrumental and symbolic of the cultural wars that followed. In 1954 the Supreme Court of the United States reversed the *Plessy v. Ferguson* decision and declared segregated schools as unconstitutional.[59]

While in many respects, the 1950s were the years in which teachers reached the zenith of their moral authority, it was also the decade in which their social status began to show signs of weakness. During the "the Red Scare," a time in which believing communist belief was considered a crime, the moral agency of schools was a conservative agenda that proclaimed "foreign" ideas as evil. Of particular concern were any ideas that hinted at supporting communism or socialism. For teachers, not supporting such xenophobic beliefs was a job requirement. Many teachers did so willingly and enjoyed the level of status they obtained.

The Renewal of Interest in Religiously Based Moral Education and Its Critics

Throughout the 1960s and 1970s, conservatives balked at laws which limited the promotion of the Protestant ethic in schools and made schools more inclusive for minorities. Spring argues that much headway in this direction occurred during the presidencies of Reagan and Bush:

In the 1980 and 1984 elections, President Ronald Reagan appealed to the religious right and conservatives by supporting school prayer, educational choice and a restoration of moral values in public schools. Also, he promised to limit federal involvement in education … During the 1980 and 1984 presidential elections, each political party appealed to a particular educational constituency. The Democrats appealed to the two major teachers [sic] unions, members of dominated cultures, and liberals favoring increased federal aid to local schools. Republicans appealed to the religious right and conservatives. These clear differences between the two parties meant that education was now a national issue with clearly defined national constituencies.[60]

During Reagan's tenure, federal reports such as "A Nation at Risk" also began to surface with alarmist statements such as the following:

If an unfriendly foreign power had attempted to impose on America the mediocre educational performance that exists today, we might well have viewed it as an act of war.[61]

"A Nation at Risk" was the first of many reports that sounded an alarm regarding the quality of public school education.[62] According to Webb and Sherman, these reports, which are often referred to as excellence reports, tend to fall into one of the following four categories, with each category representing a different interest group: 1) economic and technical excellence reports; 2) academic excellence reports; 3) institutional excellence reports; and 4) excellence and equity

---

59 Kliebard, *The Struggle for The American Curriculum, 1893–1958*; Spring, *The American School, 1642–2000*; Urban and Wagoner, *American Education: A History*.
60 Spring,, *The American School, 1642–2000*, p. 396.
61 "A Nation at Risk."
62 Ibid.

reports.[63] According to Cross, though the various excellence reports represent different interest groups and provide somewhat opposing solutions, the excellence reports are united in their criticism of teachers.[64]

One outcome of these reports was a polarization of beliefs regarding the purpose and process of public schools. Teachers were placed, often unwillingly, at the center of these battles. Twenty years later, these battles continue and teachers are still standing in a vulnerable position. Furthermore, teachers have been deemed by many as unable to teach academic subjects effectively. As moral agents, teachers have also come to be viewed by some groups as potentially dangerous.

CONCLUSIONS

Though I am ending my overview of the history of education in the United States for now, I will return to this topic throughout this text. Educational law, belief systems and education, teacher professionalization, and human diversity in education, the topics of other chapters in this text, are all tied to educational history. The above are simply those pieces I view as most significant in understanding the history of the purpose of schooling in the United States. If you have not noticed yet, I did not include key pieces such as IQ testing or school segregation, or notable people such as John Dewey, Booker T. Washington, or W. E. B. Du Bois. The reasons for those exclusions in this chapter are twofold. One, though very significant events or people, they fit in another chapter better. Two, they do not fit as well in my argument regarding the overall message of the history of education as the pieces I included.

In the next chapter are readings in educational history. They focus on a specific population, time period, or region. That is the nature of research articles. For an overview of any topic, such as the history of education, you must seek out a textbook. For that I recommend three authors: Joel Spring, Wayne Urban, and Jennings Wagoner (Urban and Wagoner are co-authors). I have met Joel Spring as well as Wayne Urban and also heard them speak. Each time I walked away impressed with their scholarship.

DISCUSSION QUESTIONS:

1. Did you notice the footnotes at the bottom of each page? In school you were taught that footnotes and a bibliography are necessary to avoid plagiarism. However, they also have an equally, if not more, important purpose. Footnotes and bibliographies are the evidence of an author's argument. What about the evidence for my arguments? Are they valid pieces of evidence? Should I have used other sources, and if so, does that weaken my argument? How

---

63 Webb and Sherman, *Schooling and Society.*
64 Cross, "The Rising Tide of School Reform Reports."

does one determine if a source is valid? In Chapter Nine I will outline how to evaluate online sources.

2. What is my bias regarding educational history? The above is by no means a comprehensive history of education in the United States. I was selective in what I included. I only discussed those parts of educational history that I thought were significant and my decisions regarding what was significant were driven by my bias. Two themes exist in the above argument, but they are only themes that support my belief regarding the main message of educational history. The themes are, who should be taught and what should be taught? However, that is not what I believe is the overarching message of the history of education in the United States. If you and your class would like to check if you are correct regarding my bias, please feel free to contact me at dlclark@kent.edu. Please put "student from (your college)" or I might accidently delete your e-mail as spam.

3. What was the purpose of education during the different periods of educational history? What is the purpose of public schooling today?

ACTIVITIES

1. Create two mission statements for the high school you attended, not using the one that already exists. Instead, write the first based on your experience in school. The second mission statement should focus on what could or should be the purpose of education and should not be limited by your own experiences. Use the following restrictions:
   a. No mention of test scores, graduation, or dropout rates, or anything that would lead to higher test scores, graduation rates, or lower dropout rates.
   b. The mission of the school may not in any way be tied to the economy, the workforce, or college entry.
   c. Your mission should be tied to something that would make our nation greater.

2. Using the online resources in the following section, identify what you believe are the five most important events or people in the history of education in the United States. At least three items on your list should be items I did not discuss. What does your choice say regarding your bias of the history of education?

ONLINE RESOURCES

1. History of Education: A Web Project, http://www.nd.edu/~rbarger/www7/
2. A History of Teaching in America by Those Who Know, http://www.wakingbear.com/archives/a-history-of-teaching-in-america-as-told-by-those-who-know.html

3. <u>PBS: Only a Teacher</u>, http://www.pbs.org/onlyateacher/
4. <u>History of African American Education</u>, http://andromeda.rutgers.edu/~natalieb/afroamed. htm
5. <u>Indian Boarding Schools</u>, http://www.english.illinois.edu/maps/poets/a_f/erdrich/boarding/index.htm
6. <u>The Academic Side of Asian American History</u>, http://www.asian-nation.org/academic.shtml
7. <u>School Violence Time Line</u>, http://www2.indystar.com/library/factfiles/crime/school_violence/school_shootings.html
8. <u>History of Compulsory Education</u>, http://www.hslda.org/courtreport/V16N5/V16N501.asp?PrinterFriendly=True
9. <u>Beyond Affliction: The Disability History Project</u>, http://www.straightaheadpictures.org/beyond-affliction/intr_pre.html
10. <u>History of Bilingual Education</u>, http://www.pbs.org/kcet/publicschool/roots_in_history/bilingual.html
11. <u>PBS: Faith and Reason</u>, http://www.pbs.org/faithandreason/

CHAPTER TWO
EDUCATIONAL HISTORY SCHOLARSHIP

WHY DO I NEED TO KNOW THIS?

Chapter One of this book was written with first-semester pre-service teachers[1] in mind. As you progress through your college years, you will encounter fewer and fewer textbooks, especially ones with pictures. Some professors will give you articles to read, as well as scholarly books. The readings in this chapter are a selection of such readings. While reading these articles, examine their use of evidence versus my use of evidence in Chapter One. Which author provides the strongest evidence, and what is the source of the strength of that evidence? If you concluded that the evidence I provided in Chapter One is strong, you will see in these articles that it was actually lacking. I quoted others who actually did research on the topic. These scholars did their own research. Also, being a scholar does not negate bias. Thus, though the evidence provided by these authors is stronger than the evidence I provided, they were still guided by their own scholarly bias, which can be initially seen in the topics they chose to study, but will also be evident in how they organized their articles. What is the bias of these authors?

WHAT IS EDUCATIONAL HISTORY SCHOLARSHIP?

Unlike the overview provided in Chapter One, educational history scholarly articles focus on one specific piece of educational history (i.e., Horace Mann's writings, the education of freed slaves)

---

1   Preservice teachers is the phrase given to those studying to be a teacher. Unlike college students studying to be a doctor, lawyer, business executive, etc., students learning to be teachers begin their professional training the first semester on campus. Whereas future doctors, lawyers, religious leaders, and politicians are given the freedom to explore their early adult lives in college and make mistakes (the 43rd president of the United States has a drunk-driving violation on his record from after his college graduation), future teachers dare not make similar mistakes or they will likely be denied a teacher's license. Preservice teachers are in professional training starting on the day they declare a major in education. Why this is the case will be discussed further in Chapter Five.

within a specific time period (i.e., 1796–1859, the Reconstruction Era). This narrow focus on a specific topic and time period allows us to see more clearly that piece of history.

One could argue that professors write for other professors, not the general public. Such is the nature of academia. A process called peer review determines if an article is published in a scholarly journal. Scholars (professors) do research and write articles and then submit those articles to journals for publication. Experts on the topic (professors) evaluate the articles to determine if they are worthy of publication. The criteria for determining if an article is worthy of publication is the method of research utilized, as well as the topic of the research. Many articles do not pass this criterion. Do not be mistaken, however, in believing that everything found in research journals is superior to other sources of knowledge. Politics plays a role in whom and what is published. For example, a professor writing an article supporting teaching intelligent design (creationism) would be hard pressed to find any scholarly journal to publish the article.

So why do professors write articles that may never be published? Part of the reason is simply a quest for more knowledge. In doctoral programs, candidates are socialized to build upon the knowledge of those who went before them. Another, perhaps more significant, reason is job security. Professors are granted tenure based on the number of articles they publish, as well as the status of the journals that publish their articles. Professors are also granted tenure based on the number and amount of grants they receive, which financially support the university where they teach. Grant applications are partially evaluated on the number of previous articles published, as well as whether or not one has received a previous grant. Unlike receiving a scholarship to attend college, once a professor receives one grant he or she is more likely to receive another grant. In other words, politics governs the application and awarding of grants also.

The politics of getting published and/or receiving a grant, of course, influences what professors study. As such, the process in itself initiates bias, coupled with the individual bias of an author or authors (many articles are written by more than one author). The process, however, also provides the illusion of objectivity. Thus, the challenge in reading scholarly articles is overcoming the belief that what one is reading is truth. That is not to say that authors of scholarly articles set out to mislead their readers. Nothing could be further from the truth. Scholars follow rigorous methodologies in an effort to get as close as possible to the truth (i.e., the scientific method), but bias is present in everything. The difference between scholarly bias and other biases is that the process of publication shapes that bias. In this way, an understanding of the journal or book in which the following pieces were published, as well as the governing professional association of the author (the National Educational History Association) will assist in determining biases.

Schooling in a Capitalist America
by Samuel Bowles and Herbert Gintis[2]

I chose each of these readings for a specific reason. The first reading is what is commonly referred to as a seminal text, a groundbreaking book, and one that all students in the sociology of education should read. Bowles and Gintis wrote the book "Schooling in a Capitalist America" in 1976, and did so from the theoretical perspective of Marxist political theory. They also introduced correspondence theory—the belief that schools reproduce the values, beliefs, and practices of capitalism, which in turn allows for controlling of the workforce by owners of corporations. Thus, Marxism is clearly their bias. A clear bias does not negate the significance of a reading; it simply helps the reader understand the lens through which an author views a topic. Keep that in mind when reading this and other select readings. Also, repeatedly challenge authors to prove their argument by evaluating critically the evidence they provide.

EDUCATION AND INEQUALITY

Universal education is the power, which is destined to overthrow every species of hierarchy. It is destined to remove all artificial inequality and leave the natural inequalities to find their true level. With the artificial inequalities of caste, rank, title, blood, birth, race, color, sex, etc., will fall nearly all the oppression, abuse, prejudice, enmity, and injustice, that humanity is now subject to.

Lester Frank Ward, *Education* c. 1872

A review of educational history hardly supports the optimistic pronouncements of liberal educational theory. The politics of education are better understood, in terms of the need for social control in an unequal and rapidly changing economic order. The founders of the modern U.S. school system understood that the capitalist economy produces great extremes of wealth and poverty, of social elevation and degradation. Horace Mann and other school reformers of the antebellum period knew well the seamy side of the burgeoning industrial and urban centers. "Here," wrote Henry Barnard, the first state superintendent of education in both Connecticut and Rhode Island, and later to become the first U.S. Commissioner of Education, "the wealth,

---

2   Samuel Bowles and Herbert Gintis, *Schooling in Capitalist America: Educational Reform and the Contradictions of Economic Life*, pp. 26–37, 124–131 (Basic Books,1976).

enterprise and professional talent of the state are concentrated … but here also are poverty, ignorance, profligacy and irreligion, and a classification of society as broad and deep as ever divided the plebeian and patrician of ancient Rome."[1] They lived in a world in which, to use de Tocqueville's words, "… small aristocratic societies … are formed by some manufacturers in the midst of the immense democracy of our age [in which] … some men are opulent and a multitude … are wretchedly poor."[2] The rapid rise of the factory system, particularly in New England, was celebrated by the early school reformers; yet, the alarming transition from a relatively simple rural society to a highly stratified industrial economy could not be ignored. They shared the fears that de Tocqueville had expressed following his visit to the United States in 1831:

> When a work man is unceasingly and exclusively engaged in the fabrication of one thing, he ultimately does his work with singular dexterity; but at the same time he loses the general faculty of applying his mind to the direction of the work. … [While] the science of manufacture lowers the class of workmen, it raises the class of masters. … [If] ever a permanent inequality of conditions … again penetrates into the world, it may be predicted that this is the gate by which they will enter.[3]

While deeply committed to the emerging industrial order, the far-sighted school reformers of the mid-nineteenth century understood the explosive potential of the glaring inequalities of factory life. Deploring the widening of social divisions and fearing increasing unrest, Mann, Barnard, and others proposed educational expansion and reform. In his Fifth Report as Secretary of the Massachusetts Board of Education, Horace Mann wrote:

> Education, then beyond all other devices of human origin, is the great equalizer of the conditions of men—the balance wheel of the social machinery. … It does better than to disarm the poor of their hostility toward the rich; it prevents being poor.[4]

Mann and his followers appeared to be at least as interested in disarming the poor as in preventing poverty. They saw in the spread of universal and free education a means of alleviating social distress without redistributing wealth and power or altering the broad outlines of the economic system. Education, it seems, had almost magical powers.

> The main idea set forth in the creeds of some political reformers, or revolutionizers, is, that some people are poor because others are rich. This idea supposed a fixed amount of property in the community … and the problem presented for solution is, how to transfer a portion of this property from those who are supposed to have too much to those who feel and know that they have too little. At this point, both their theory and

their expectation of reform stop. But the beneficent power of education would not be exhausted, even though it should peaceably abolish all the miseries that spring from the coexistence, side by side of enormous wealth, and squalid want. It has a higher function. Beyond the power of diffusing old wealth, it has the prerogative of creating new.[5]

The early educators viewed the poor as the foreign element that they were. Mill hands were recruited throughout New England, often disrupting the small towns in which textile and other rapidly growing industries had located. Following the Irish potato famine of the 1840s, thousands of Irish workers settled in the cities and towns of the northeastern United States. Schooling was seen as a means of integrating this "uncouth and dangerous" element into the social fabric of American life. The inferiority of the foreigner was taken for granted. The editors of the influential *Massachusetts Teacher*, a leader in the educational reform movement, writing in 1851, saw "… the increasing influx of foreigners …" as a moral and social problem:

> Will it, like the muddy Missouri, as it pours its waters into the clear Mississippi and contaminates the whole united mass, spread ignorance and vice, crime and disease, through our native population?
>
> If … we can by any means purify this foreign people, enlighten their ignorance and bring them up to our level, we shall perform a work of true and perfect charity, blessing the giver and receiver in equal measure. …
>
> With the old not much can be done; but with their children, the great remedy is education. The rising generation must be taught as our own children are taught. We say must be because in many cases this can only be accomplished by coercion.[6]

Since the mid-nineteenth century the dual objectives of educational reformers—equality of opportunity and social control—have been intermingled, the merger of these two threads sometimes so nearly complete that it becomes impossible to distinguish between the two. Schooling has been at once something done for the poor and to the poor.

The basic assumptions which underlay this comingling helps explain the educational reform movement's social legacy. First, educational reformers did not question the fundamental economic institutions of capitalism: Capitalist ownership and control of the means of production and dependent wage labor were taken for granted. In fact, education was to help preserve and extend the capitalist order. The function of the school system was to accommodate workers to its most rapid possible development. Second, it was assumed that people (often classes of people or "races") are differentially equipped by nature or social origins to occupy the varied economic and social levels in the class structure. By providing equal opportunity, the school system was to elevate the masses, guiding them sensibly and fairly to the manifold political, social, and economic roles of adult life.

Jefferson's educational thought strikingly illustrates this perspective. In 1779, he proposed a two-track educational system which would prepare individuals for adulthood in one of the two classes of society: The "laboring and the learned."[7] Even children of the laboring class would qualify for leadership. Scholarships would allow "… those persons whom nature hath endowed with genius and virtue …"to"… be rendered by liberal education worthy to receive and able to guard the sacred deposit of the rights and liberties of their fellow citizens."[8] Such a system, Jefferson asserted, would succeed in "… raking a few geniuses from the rubbish."[9] Jefferson's two-tiered educational plan presents in stark relief the outlines and motivation for the stratified structure of U.S. education which has endured up to the present. At the top, there is the highly selective aristocratic tradition, the elite university training future leaders. At the base is mass education for all, dedicated to uplift and control. The two traditions have always coexisted although their meeting point has drifted upward over the years, as mass education has spread upward from elementary school through high school, and now up to the post-high-school level.

Though schooling was consciously molded to reflect the class structure, education was seen as a means of enhancing wealth and morality which would work to the advantage of all. Horace Mann, in his 1842 report to the State Board of Education, reproduced this comment by a Massachusetts industrialist:

> The great majority always have been and probably always will be comparatively poor, while a few will possess the greatest share of this world's goods. And it is a wise provision of Providence which connects so intimately, and as I think so indissolubly, the greatest good of the many with the highest interests in the few.[10]

Much of the content of education over the past century and a half can only be construed as an unvarnished attempt to persuade the "many" to make the best of the inevitable.

The unequal contest between social control and social justice is evident in the total functioning of U.S. education. The system as it stands today provides eloquent testimony to the ability of the well-to-do to perpetuate in the name of equality of opportunity an arrangement which consistently yields to themselves disproportional advantages, while thwarting the aspirations and needs of the working people of the United States. However grating this judgment may sound to the ears of the undaunted optimist, it is by no means excessive in light of the massive statistical data on inequality in the United States. Let us look at the contemporary evidence.

We may begin with the basic issue of inequalities in years of schooling. As can be seen in figure 2-1, the number of years of schooling attained by an individual is strongly associated with parental socioeconomic status. This figure presents the estimated distribution of years of schooling attained by individuals of varying socioeconomic backgrounds. If we define socioeconomic background by a weighted sum of income, occupation, and educational level of the parents, a child from the ninetieth percentile may expect, on the average, five more years of schooling than a child in the tenth percentile.[11]

A word about our use of statistics is in order. Most of the statistical calculations which we will present have been published with full documentation in academic journals. We provide some of

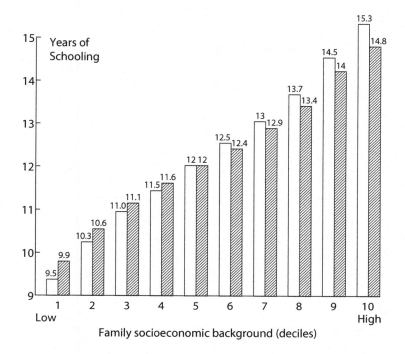

Notes: For each socioeconomic group, the left-hand bar indicates the estimated average number of years of schooling attained by all men from that group. The right-hand bar indicates the estimated average number of years of schooling attained by men with IQ scores equal to the average for the entire sample. The sample refers to "non-Negro" men of "non-farm" backgrounds, aged 35-44 years in 1962.17 source: Samuel Bowles and Valerie Nelson, "The 'Inheritance of IQ.' and the Intergenerational Transmission of Economic Inequality," *The Review of Economics and Statistics*, Vol. LVI, No. 1, February 1974. Reprinted by permission of the President and Fellows of Harvard College.

Figure 2-1. Educational Attainments Are Strongly Dependent on Social Background Even for People of Similar Childhood I.Q.s

the relevant technical information in our footnotes and Appendix. However, those interested in gaining a more detailed understanding of our data and methods are urged to consult our more technical articles.

The data, most of which was collected by the U.S. Census Current Population Survey in 1962, refers to "non-Negro" males, aged 25–64 years, from "non-farm" background in the experienced labor force.[12] We have chosen a sample of white males because the most complete statistics are available for this group. Moreover, if inequality for white males can be documented, the proposition is merely strengthened when sexual and racial differences are taken into account.

Additional census data dramatize one aspect of educational inequalities: The relationship between family income and college attendance. Even among those who had graduated from high school in the early 1960s, children of families earning less than $3,000 per year were over six times as likely not to attend college as were the children of families earning over $15,000.[13] Moreover, children from less well-off families are both less likely to have graduated from high school and more likely to attend inexpensive, two-year community colleges rather than a four-year B.A. program if they do make it to college.[14]

Not surprisingly, the results of schooling differ greatly for children of different social backgrounds. Most easily measured, but of limited importance, are differences in scholastic achievement. If we measure the output of schooling by scores on nationally standardized achievement tests, children whose parents were themselves highly educated outperform the children of parents with less education by a wide margin. Data collected for the U.S. Office of Education Survey of Educational Opportunity reveal, for example, that among white high school seniors, those whose parents were in the top education decile were, on the average, well over three grade levels in measured scholastic achievement ahead of those whose parents were in the bottom decile.[15]

Given these differences in scholastic achievement, inequalities in years of schooling among individuals of different social backgrounds are to be expected. Thus one might be tempted to argue that the close dependence of years of schooling attained on background displayed in the left-hand bars of Figure 2-1 is simply a reflection of unequal intellectual abilities, or that inequalities in college attendance are the consequences of differing levels of scholastic achievement in high school and do not reflect any additional social class inequalities peculiar to the process of college admission.

This view, so comforting to the admissions personnel in our elite universities, is unsupported by the data, some of which is presented in Figure 2-1. The right-hand bars of Figure 2-1 indicate that even among children with identical IQ test scores at ages six and eight, those with rich, well-educated, high-status parents could expect a much higher level of schooling than those with less-favored origins. Indeed, the closeness of the left-hand and right-hand bars in Figure 2-1 shows that only a small portion of the observed social class differences in educational attainment is related to IQ differences across social classes.[16] The dependence of education attained on background is almost as strong for individuals with the same IQ as for all individuals. Thus, while Figure 2-1 indicates that an individual in the ninetieth percentile in social class background is likely to receive five more years of education than an individual in the tenth percentile; it also indicated that he is likely to receive 4.25 more years schooling than an individual from the tenth percentile with the same IQ. Similar results are obtained when we look specifically at access to college education for students with the same measured IQ. Project Talent data indicates that for "high ability" students (top 25 percent as measured by a composite of tests of "general aptitude"), those of high socioeconomic background (top 25 percent as measured by a composite of family income, parents' education, and occupation) are nearly twice as likely to attend college than students of low socioeconomic background (bottom 25 percent). For "low ability" students (bottom

25 percent), those of high social background are more than four times as likely to attend college as are their low social background counterparts.[18]

Inequality in years of schooling is, of course, only symptomatic of broader inequalities in the educational system. Not only do less well-off children go to school for fewer years, they are treated with less attention (or more precisely, less benevolent attention) when they are there. These broader inequalities are not easily measured. Some show up in statistics on the different levels of expenditure for the education of children of different socioeconomic backgrounds. Taking account of the inequality in financial resources for each year in school and the inequality in years of schooling obtained, Jencks estimated that a child whose parents were in the top fifth of the income distribution receives roughly twice the educational resources in dollar terms as does a child whose parents are in the bottom fifth.[19]

The social class inequalities in our school system, then, are too evident to be denied. Defenders of the educational system are forced back on the assertion that things are getting better; the inequalities of the past were far worse. And, indeed, there can be no doubt that some of the inequalities of the past have been mitigated. Yet new inequalities have apparently developed to take their place, for the available historical evidence lends little support to the idea that our schools are on the road to equality of educational opportunity. For example, data from a recent U.S. Census survey reported in Spady indicate that graduation from college has become no less dependent on one's social background. This is true despite the fact that high-school graduation is becoming increasingly equal across social classes.[20] Additional data confirm this impression. The statistical association (coefficient of correlation) between parents' social status and years of education attained by individuals who completed their schooling three or four decades ago is virtually identical to the same correlation for individuals who terminated their schooling in recent years.[21] On balance, the available data suggest that the number of years of school attained by a child depends upon family background as much in the recent period as it did fifty years ago.

Thus, we have empirical reasons for doubting the egalitarian impact of schooling. But what of those cases when education has been equalized? What has been the effect? We will investigate three cases: The historical decline in the inequality among individuals in years of school attained, the explicitly compensatory educational programs of the War on Poverty, and the narrowing of the black/white gap in average years of schooling attained.

Although family background has lost none of its influence on how far one gets up the educational ladder, the historical rise in the minimum legal school-leaving age has narrowed the distance between the top and bottom rungs. Inequality of educational attainments has fallen steadily and substantially over the past three decades.[22] And has this led to a parallel equalization of the distribution of income? Look at Figure 2-2. The reduction in the inequality of years of schooling has not been matched by an equalization of the U.S. income distribution.[23] In fact, a recent U.S. Labor Department study indicates that as far as labor earnings (wages and salaries) are concerned, the trend since World War II has been unmistakenly away from equality. And it is precisely inequality in labor earnings which is the target of the proponents of egalitarian school reforms.[24] But does the absence of an overall trend toward income equality mask an equalizing thrust of schooling

Figure 2-2. Equalization of Education Has Not Been Associated with Equalization of Income

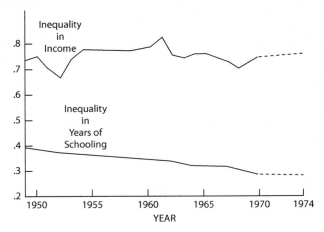

Notes: The upper line shows the trend over time in the degree of inequality of income, as measured by the standard deviation of the natural logarithm of annual income of males aged twenty-five or older. The lower line shows the trend over time in the degree of inequality of years of schooling, as measured by the coefficient of variation (the standard deviation divided by the mean) of the years of schooling attained by males aged twenty-five and older. Data for 1970 to 1974 are estimates based on U.S. Census data.

Source: Barry Chiswick and Jacob Mincer, "Time Series Changes in Personal Income Inequality in the U.S.," *Journal of Political Economy*, Vol. 80, No. 3, Part II (May–June 1972).

that was offset by other disequalizing tendencies? Perhaps, but Jacob Mincer and Barry Chiswick of the National Bureau of Economic Research, in a study of the determinants of inequality in the United States, concluded that the significant reduction in schooling differences among white male adults would have had the effect—even if operating in isolation—of reducing income inequality by a negligible amount.[25]

Next, consider that group of explicitly egalitarian educational programs brought together in the War on Poverty. In a systematic economic survey of these programs, Thomas Ribich concludes that with very few exceptions, the economic payoff to compensatory education is low.[26] So low, in fact, that in a majority of cases studied, direct transfers of income to the poor would have accomplished considerably more equalization than the educational programs in question. The major RAND Corporation study by Averch came to the same conclusion.

Lastly, consider racial inequalities. In 1940, most black male workers (but a minority of whites) earned their livelihoods in the South, by far the poorest region; the education gap between nonwhites and whites was 3.3 years (38 percent of median white education).[27] By 1972, blacks had moved to more affluent parts of the country, and the education gap was reduced to 18 percent (4 percent for young men aged 25-34 years).[28] Richard Freeman has shown that this narrowing of the education gap would have virtually achieved black/white income equality had blacks received the same benefits from education as whites.[29] Yet the income gap has not closed substantially: The income gap for young men is 30 percent, despite an education gap of only 4 percent.[30] Clearly as blacks have moved toward educational (and regional) parity with whites, other mechanisms—such as entrapment in center-city ghettos, the suburbanization of jobs, and perhaps increasing segmentation of labor markets—have intensified to maintain a more-or-less constant degree of racial income inequality. Blacks certainly suffer from educational inequality, but the root of their exploitation lies outside of education, in a system of economic power and privilege in which racial distinctions play an important role.

The same must be concluded of inequality of economic opportunity between men and women. Sexual inequality persists despite the fact that women achieve a level of schooling (measured in years) equivalent to men.

We conclude that U.S. education is highly unequal, the chances of attaining much or little schooling being substantially dependent on one's race and parents' economic level. Moreover, where there is a discernible trend toward a more equal educational system—as in the narrowing of the black education deficit, for example—the impact on the structure of economic opportunity is minimal at best. As we shall presently see, the record of the U.S. school system as a promoter of full human development is no more encouraging.

EDUCATION AND PERSONAL DEVELOPMENT: THE LONG SHADOW OF WORK

> Every child born into the world should be looked upon by society as so much raw material to be manufactured. Its quality is to be tested. It is the business of society, as an intelligent economist, to make the best of it.
>
> Lester Frank Ward, *Education*, c. 1872

It is not obvious why the U.S. educational system should be the way it is. Since the interpersonal relationships it fosters are so antithetical to the norms of freedom and equality prevalent in American society, the school system can hardly be viewed as a logical extension of our cultural heritage. If neither technological necessity nor the bungling mindlessness of educators explain the quality of the educational encounter, what does?

Reference to the educational system's legitimation function does not take us far toward enlightenment. For the formal, objective, and cognitively oriented aspects of schooling capture only a fragment of the day-to-day social relationships of the educational encounter. To approach an answer, we must consider schools in the light of the social relationships of economic life. In this chapter, we suggest that major aspects of educational organization replicate the relationships of dominance and subordinancy in the economic sphere. The correspondence between the social relation of schooling and work accounts for the ability of the educational system to produce an amenable and fragmented labor force. The experience of schooling, and not merely the content of formal learning, is central to this process.

In our view, it is pointless to ask if the net effect of U.S. education is to promote equality or inequality, repression or liberation. These issues pale into insignificance before the major fact: The educational system is an integral element in the reproduction of the prevailing class structure of society. The educational system certainly has a life of its own, but the experience of work and the nature of the class structure are the bases upon which educational values are formed, social justice assessed, the realm of the possible delineated in people's consciousness, and the social relations of the educational encounter historically transformed.

In short, and to return to a persistent theme of this book, the educational system's task of integrating young people into adult work roles constrains the types of personal development which it can foster in ways that are antithetical to the fulfillment of its personal developmental function.

REPRODUCING CONSCIOUSNESS

> … children guessed (but only a few and down they forgot as up they grew autumn winter spring summer)…
>
> e e cummings, 1940

Economic life exhibits a complex and relatively stable pattern of power and property relationships. The perpetuation of these social relationships, even over relatively short periods, is by no means automatic. As with a living organism, stability in the economic sphere is the result of explicit mechanisms constituted to maintain and extend the dominant patterns of power and privilege. We call the sum total of these mechanisms and their actions the reproduction process.

Amidst the sundry social relations experienced in daily life, a few stand out as central to our analysis of education. These are precisely the social relationships which are necessary to the security of capitalist profits and the stability of the capitalist division of labor. They include the patterns of dominance and subordinacy in the production process, the distribution of ownership of productive resources, and the degrees of social distance and solidarity among various fragments of the working population—men and women, blacks and whites, and white- and blue-collar workers, to mention some of the most salient.

What are the mechanisms of reproduction of these aspects of the social relations of production in the United States? To an extent, stability is embodied in law and backed by the coercive power of the state. Our jails are filled with individuals who have operated outside the framework of the private-ownership market system. The modern urban police force as well as the National Guard originated, in large part, in response to the fear of social upheaval evoked by militant labor action. Legal sanction, within the framework of the laws of private property, also channels the actions of groups (e.g., unions) into conformity with dominant power relationships. Similarly, force is used to stabilize the division of labor and its rewards within an enterprise: Dissenting workers are subject to dismissal and directors failing to conform to "capitalist rationality" will be replaced.

But to attribute reproduction to force alone borders on the absurd. Under normal conditions, the effectiveness of coercion depends at the very least on the inability or unwillingness of those subjected to it to join together in opposing it. Laws generally considered illegitimate tend to lose their coercive power, and undisguised force too frequently applied tends to be self-defeating. The consolidation and extension of capitalism has engendered struggles of furious intensity. Yet instances of force deployed against a united and active opposition are sporadic and have usually given way to detente in one form or another through a combination of compromise, structural change, and ideological accommodation. Thus it is clear that the consciousness of workers—beliefs, values, self-concepts, types of solidarity and fragmentation, as well as modes of personal behavior and development—are integral to the perpetuation, validation, and smooth operation of economic institutions. The reproduction of the social relations of production depends on the reproduction of consciousness.

Under what conditions will individuals accept the pattern of social relationships that frame their lives? Believing that the long-term development of the existing system holds the prospect of fulfilling their needs, individuals and groups might actively embrace these social relationships. Failing this, and lacking a vision of an alternative that might significantly improve their situation, they might fatalistically accept their condition. Even with such a vision they might passively submit to the framework of economic life and seek individual solutions to social problems if they believe that the possibilities for realizing change are remote. The issue of the reproduction of consciousness enters each of these assessments.

The economic system will be embraced when, first, the perceived needs of individuals are congruent with the types of satisfaction the economic system can objectively provide. While perceived needs may be, in part, biologically determined, for the most part needs arise through the aggregate experiences of individuals in the society. Thus the social relations of production are reproduced in part through a harmony between the needs which the social system generates and the means at its disposal for satisfying these needs.

Second, the view that fundamental social change is not feasible, unoperational, and utopian is normally supported by a complex web of ideological perspectives deeply embedded in the cultural and scientific life of the community and reflected in the consciousness of its members. But fostering the "consciousness of inevitability" is not the office of the cultural system alone. There must also exist mechanisms that systematically thwart the spontaneous development of social experiences that would contradict these beliefs.

Belief in the futility of organizing for fundamental social change is further facilitated by social distinctions which fragment the conditions of life for subordinate classes. The strategy of "divide and conquer" has enabled dominant classes to maintain their power since the dawn of civilization. Once again, the splintered consciousness of a subordinate class is not the product of cultural phenomena alone, but must be reproduced through the experiences of daily life.

Consciousness develops through the individual's direct perception of and participation in social life.[31] Indeed, everyday experience itself often acts as an inertial stabilizing force. For instance, when the working population is effectively stratified, individual needs and self-concepts develop in a correspondingly fragmented manner. Youth of different racial, sexual, ethnic, or economic characteristics directly perceive the economic positions and prerogatives of "their kind of people." By adjusting their aspiration accordingly, they not only reproduce stratification on the level of personal consciousness, but bring their needs into (at least partial) harmony with the fragmented conditions of economic life. Similarly, individuals tend to channel the development of their personal powers—cognitive, emotional, physical, aesthetic, and spiritual—in directions where they will have an opportunity to exercise them. Thus the alienated character of work, for example, leads people to guide their creative potentials to areas outside of economic activity: Consumption, travel, sexuality, and family life. So needs and need-satisfaction again tend to fall into congruence and alienated labor is reproduced on the level of personal consciousness.[32]

But this congruence is continually disrupted. For the satisfaction of needs gives rise to new needs. These new needs derive from the logic of personal development as well as from the evolving structure of material life, and in turn undercut the reproduction of consciousness. For this reason the reproduction of consciousness cannot be the simple unintended by-product of social experience. Rather, social relationships must be consciously organized to facilitate the reproduction of consciousness.

Take, for instance, the organization of the capitalist enterprise discussed in Chapter Three. Power relations and hiring criteria within the enterprise are organized so as to reproduce the workers' self-concepts, the legitimacy of their assignments within the hierarchy, a sense of the technological inevitability of the hierarchical division of labor itself, and the social distance among groups of workers in the organization. Indeed, while token gestures towards workers' self-management may be a successful motivational gimmick, any delegation of real power to workers becomes a threat to profits because it tends to undermine patterns of consciousness compatible with capitalist control. By generating new needs and possibilities, by demonstrating the feasibility of a more thoroughgoing economic democracy, by increasing worker solidarity, an integrated and politically conscious program of worker involvement in decision-making may undermine the power structure of the enterprise. Management will accede to such changes only under extreme duress of worker rebellion and rapidly disintegrating morale, if at all.

But the reproduction of consciousness cannot be insured by these direct mechanisms alone. The initiation of youth into the economic system is further facilitated by a series of institutions, including the family and the educational system, that are more immediately related to the formation of personality and consciousness. Education works primarily through the institutional relations to which students are subjected. Thus schooling fosters and rewards the development of certain capacities and the expression of certain needs, while thwarting and penalizing others. Through these institutional relationships, the educational system tailors the self-concepts, aspirations, and social class identifications of individuals to the requirements of the social division of labor.

The extent to which the educational system actually accomplishes these objectives varies considerably from one period to the next. We shall see in later chapters that recurrently through U.S. history these reproduction mechanisms have failed, sometimes quite spectacularly. In most periods—and the present is certainly no exception—efforts to use the schools to reproduce and extend capitalist production relations have been countered both by the internal dynamic of the educational system and by popular opposition.

In earlier chapters we have identified the two main objectives of dominant classes in educational policy: The production of labor power and the reproduction of those institutions and social relationships which facilitate the translation of labor power into profits. We may now be considerably more concrete about the way that educational institutions are structured to meet these objectives. First, schooling produces many of the technical and cognitive skills required for adequate job performance. Second, the educational system helps legitimate economic inequality. As we argued in the last chapter, the objective and meritocratic orientation of U.S. education, reduces discontent over both the hierarchical division of labor and the process through which individuals attain position in it. Third, the school produces, rewards, and labels personal characteristics relevant to the staffing of positions in the hierarchy. Fourth, the educational system, through the pattern of status distinctions it fosters, reinforces the stratified consciousness on which the fragmentation of subordinate economic classes is based.

What aspects of the educational system allow it to serve these various functions? We shall suggest in the next section that the educational system's ability to reproduce the consciousness of workers lies in a straight-forward correspondence principle: For the past century at least, schooling has contributed to the reproduction of the social relations of production largely through the correspondence between school and class structure.

Upon the slightest reflection, this assertion is hardly surprising. All major institutions in a "stable" social system will direct personal development in a direction compatible with its reproduction. Of course, this is not, in itself, a critique of capitalism or of U.S. education. In any conceivable society, individuals are forced to develop their capacities in one direction or another. The idea of a social system which merely allows people to develop freely according to their "inner natures" is quite unthinkable, since human nature only acquires a concrete form through the interaction of the physical world and preestablished social relationships.

Our critique of education and other aspects of human development in the United States fully recognizes the necessity of some form of socialization. The critical question is: What for? In the United States the human development experience is dominated by an undemocratic, irrational, and exploitative economic structure. Young people have no recourse from the requirements of the system but a life of poverty, dependence, and economic insecurity. Our critique, not surprisingly, centers on the structure of jobs. In the U.S. economy work has become a fact of life to which individuals must by and large submit and over which they have no control. Like the weather, work "happens" to people. A liberated, participatory, democratic, and creative alternative can hardly be imagined, much less experienced. Work under capitalism is an alienated activity.

To reproduce the social relations of production, the educational system must try to teach people to be properly subordinate and render them sufficiently fragmented in consciousness to preclude their getting together to shape their own material existence. The forms of consciousness and behavior fostered by the educational system must themselves be alienated, in the sense that they conform neither to the dictates of technology in the struggle with nature, nor to the inherent developmental capacities of individuals, but rather to the needs of the capitalist class. It is the prerogatives of capital and the imperatives of profit, not human capacities and technical realities, which render U.S. schooling what it is. This is our charge.

DISCUSSION QUESTIONS

1. How has Jefferson's proposed "two-track" system endured in modern education?
2. Do you think mandatory college attendance, hypothetically, would narrow the income gap between rich and poor citizens. Why or why not?

NOTES

1. Henry Barnard, *Papers for the Teacher: 2nd Series* (New York: F. C. Brownell, 1866), pp. 293–310.
2. Alexis de Tocqueville, as quoted in Jeremy Brecher, *Strike!* (San Francisco: Straight Arrow Books, 1972), pp. xi, xii.
3. *Ibid*, p. 172.
4. Horace Mann as quoted in Michael Katz, ed., *School Reform Past and Present* (Boston: Little Brown and Company, 1971), p. 141.
5. *Ibid.*, p. 145.
6. *The Massachusetts Teacher* (October 1851), quoted in Katz (1971), *loc. cit.*, pp. 169-170.
7. David Tyack, *Turning Points in American Educational History* (Waltham, Mass.: Blaisdell, 1967), p. 89.
8. *Ibid.*, p. 109.
9. *Ibid.*, p. 89.
10. Mann, quoted in Katz (1971), *loc. cit.*, p. 147.
11. This calculation is based on data reported in full in Samuel Bowles and Valerie Nelson, "The 'Inheritance of IQ' and the Intergenerational Transmission of Economic Inequality," *The Review of Economics and Statistics,* Vol. LVI, No. 1, February 1974. It refers to non-Negro males from non-farm backgrounds, aged 35–44 years. The zero-order correlation coefficient between socioeconomic background and years of schooling was estimated at 0.646. The estimated standard deviation of years of schooling was 3.02. The results for other age groups are similar.
12. See Appendix A, footnote 14, in Chapter Four and the following sources: Bowles and Nelson (1974), *op. cit.;* Peter Blau and Otis D. Duncan, *The American Occupational Structure* (New York: John Wiley, 1967); Otis D. Duncan, D. C. Featherman, and Beverly Duncan, *Socioeconomic Background and Occupational Achievement, Final Report*, Project No. S-0074 (EO-191) (Washington, D.C.: Department of Health, Education and Welfare, Office of Education, 1968); Samuel Bowles, "Schooling and Inequality from Generation to Generation," *The Journal of Political Economy*, Vol. 80, No. 3, Part II, May–June 1972.

13. These figures refer to individuals who were high-school seniors in October, 1965, and who subsequently graduated from high school. College attendance refers to both two- and four-year institutions. Family income is for the twelve months preceding October 1965. Data is drawn from U.S. Bureau of the Census, *Current Population Reports*, Series P-60, No. 183, May 1969.

14. For further evidence, see U.S. Bureau of the Census (1969), *op. cit.;* and Jerome Karabel, "Community Colleges and Social Stratification," *Harvard Educational Review*, Vol. 424, No. 42, November 1972.

15. Calculation based on data in James S. Coleman *et al., Equality of Educational Opportunity* (Washington, D.C.: U.S. Government Printing Office, 1966), and Bowles and Gintis (1972), *loc. cit.*

16. The data relating to IQ are from a 1966 survey of veterans by the National Opinion Research Center; and from N. Bayley and E. S. Schaefer, "Correlations of Maternal and Child Behaviors with the Development of Mental Ability: Data from the Berkeley Growth Study," *Monographs of Social Research in Child Development*, 29, 6 (1964).

17. This figure is based on data reported in full in our Appendix A and in Bowles and Nelson (1974), *op. cit.* The left-hand bars of each pair were calculated using the estimated correlation coefficient between socioeconomic background and education of 0.65. The results for other age groups were similar: 0.64 for ages 25–34 and 44–54, and 0.60 for ages 55–64 years. The right-hand bars were calculated from the normalized regression coefficient on socioeconomic background from an equation using background and early childhood IQ to predict years of schooling, which was estimated at 0.54. The results for other age groups were similar: 0.54 for ages 25–34 and 45–54, and 0.48 for ages 55–64.

18. Socioeconomic background is defined as normalized sum of father's education, father's occupational status, and parents' income. The mean and standard deviation of years of schooling were estimated at 11.95 and 3.02, respectively.

19. Based on a large sample of U.S. high-school students as reported in: John C. Flannagan and William W. Cooley, *Project Talent, One Year Follow-up Study*, Cooperative Research Project, No. 2333, University of Pittsburgh: School of Education, 1966.

20. Christopher Jencks *et al., Inequality: A Reassessment of the Effects of Family and Schooling in America* (New York: Basic Books, 1972), p. 48.

21. William L. Spady, "Educational Mobility and Access: Growth and Paradoxes," in *American Journal of Sociology*, Vol. 73, No. 3, November 1967; and Blau and Duncan, *op. cit.* (1967). More recent data support the evidence of no trend toward equality. See U.S. Bureau of Census (1969), *op. cit.*

22. Blau and Duncan (1967), *op. cit.* See the reported correlations in Appendix A.

23. We estimate the coefficient of variation of years of schooling at about 4.3 in 1940 (relying on Barry Chiswick and Jacob Mincer, "Time Series Changes in Personal Income Inequality in the U.S.," *Journal of Political Economy*, Vol. 80, No. 3, Part II [May–June 1972], Table 4 for the standard deviation of schooling and the Decennial Census for the mean), and at 2.95 in 1969 (relying on Chiswick and Mincer [1972], Table B10).

24. Calculated from Table B1 and Table B10 in Chiswick and Mincer (1972), *op. cit.*

25. Peter Henle, "Exploring the Distribution of Earned Income," *Monthly Labor Review*, Vol. 95, No. 12, December 1972. Inequalities in income (profit, rent interest, and transfer payments plus labor earnings) may also have increased if the unmeasured income from capital gains and other tax shelters for the rich are taken

into account. See Jerry Cromwell, "Income Inequalities, Discrimination and Uneven Development," unpublished Ph.D. dissertation, Harvard University, May 1974.

26. Chiswick and Mincer (1972), *loc. cit.*

27. Thomas I. Ribich, *Education and Poverty* (Washington, D.C.: Brookings Institution, 1968).

28. United States Bureau of the Census, *Current Population Reports*, Series P-60, October 1970, Table 75, p. 368.

29. *Ibid* (November 1972), Table 1, p. 14.

30. Michael Reich, *Racial Discrimination and the Distribution of Income*, Ph.D. dissertation, Harvard University, May 1973.

31. Herbert Gintis, "Welfare Criteria with Endogenous Preferences: The Economics of Education," *International Economic Review*, June 1974; Alfred Schutz and Thomas Luckmann, *The Structure of the Life-World* (Evanston, Illinois: Northwestern University Press, 1973); and Peter L. Berger and Thomas Luckmann, *The Social Construction of Reality: A Treatise in the Sociology of Knowledge* (Garden City, L.I., N.Y.: Doubleday and Co., 1966).

32. For an extended treatment of these issues, see Herbert Gintis, "Alienation and Power," in *The Review of Radical Political Economics*, Vol. 4, No. 5, Fall 1972.

The Way We Learned: African American Students' Memories of Schooling in the Segregated South[3]
by Linda Coats

In my overview of the history of education, I compared and contrasted constitutional and cultural history. What is found in history textbooks is often constitutional history. The following is an example of purely cultural history. As you will see in reading this article, the experiences of segregated schools from a cultural historian's perspective is quite different than that of a constitutional historian. From constitutional history, we hear about the Brown v. Board of Education Supreme Court decision. We hear about Governor Faubus's enlistment of the state's National Guard to keep the Little Rock Nine from entering a newly desegregated school. We come to understand President Eisenhower's decision to bring federal troops to Little Rock, Arkansas, and Governor Wallace standing at a university door to prevent a black student from entering.

With cultural history, like the article that follows, we gain a very different perspective. We hear about the teachers in the black segregated schools and their commitment to the children in those schools. We discover that many, if not most, of those teachers were highly educated. We gain information that helps us today close the achievement gap between ethnic minorities and white children. In this cultural history, blacks are not victims; rather, they are heroes from whom we can learn.

With the increasing diversity of students who make up public school classrooms and the lack of diversity of classroom teachers, additional research on teaching methods that appear to be effective with one or more minority groups is essential to identify ways to equalize the academic performance of minority students with that of their European American counterparts. The purpose of this research study was to uncover the types of learning experiences and teachers' behaviors that students who attended southern rural segregated schools during the 1940s–1960s valued, and in their opinion, contributed to their academic achievement and career success.

RESEARCH QUESTIONS

The research questions that guided this study are what memories of school have lasting impact on students and what are some distinguishing teacher behaviors that impact students' academic and career success?

---

3   Linda Coats, "The Way We Learned: African American Students' Memories of Schooling in the Segregated South." *Journal of Negro Education*; Winter 2010; 79; 1; ProQuest Direct Complete, p. 6.

HISTORICAL SIGNIFICANCE

This study is informed by the literature that reports, analyzes, and describes the history of de jure segregation of African American schools in the South. The literature that recaptures segregated education in the South paints contrasting views—inferior education due to societal injustices (Ashmore, 1954; Clift, Anderson, & Hullfish, 1962; Johnson, 1941) and treasured education resulting from a "cultural form of teaching and learning" (Fultz, 1995a; Walker, 2000, p. 234). This research study follows the latter view and adds definition to the historical picture painted through the scholarship that has uncovered a more positive treatment of the knowledge imparted to students in segregated schools (Anderson, 1988; Bullock, 1967; Fairclough, 2004; Fultz, 1995a, 1995b; Riley, 1998; Walker, 2000). Specifically, the findings from this study provide a clearer understanding of the behaviors of African American teachers who taught in segregated schools during 1940–1969 through the eyes of their students.

Additionally, this study is linked to the scholarship that describes students' perceptions of African American teachers. Stanford (1997) claimed successful urban African American teachers possessed characteristics that support "community solidarity, community of learners, focus on the whole child, and personal accountability" (p. 108). In Howard's (2002) study, African American students' perceptions of their teachers' pedagogy and the impact of the teachers' pedagogy on the students' academic and social success demonstrated the teachers' ability to foster a family, community environment, to display "culturally connected caring," and talk to students in a caring manner. Stanford (1998) discovered that former teachers used pedagogical practices that encouraged their students to succeed despite negative attempts to hinder their success.

In direct relationship to the research that captures the significance of African American students' perceptions of their teachers and the behavior of these teachers is a relatively new body of literature that fills a void in research about teaching—the pedagogical practices of exemplary African American teachers. This body of research provides a lens through which the interplay of culture appreciation, caring, and teaching result in students' success.

Grant (1991) contended that there is a connection between the way teachers think and their life experiences. Foster (1997) published 20 African American teachers' views and experiences about the impact of socio-political forces on their teaching with hopes that these accounts will lead society to better understanding Black teachers experiences. In her previous works, Foster (1993, 1994a, 1994b) concluded that exemplary African American teachers possessed the ability to make the curriculum relevant to students' lives, possessed an understanding of the students' culture, and subscribed to a teaching philosophy that encompassed teaching the whole child. Ladson-Billings (1994) concluded that effective teaching for African American students is culturally relevant teaching. To practice culturally relevant teaching, teachers should possess positive self-concept and demand the best from their students, see themselves and students as contributing members to the community, foster teacher-student and student-student relationships, and adopt a critical view of knowledge and teach students how to do the same (Ladson-Billings, 1994). These studies focused on the views of African American students and teachers from urban areas, with an exception to Foster's (1997) compilation that described the life histories of urban and rural teachers.

Research studies that focus on African American teachers in rural areas include Foster's (1990) work where she examined the impact of racism as experienced in segregated and desegregated schools on the pedagogical practices of 16 African American teachers. The findings from this study indicated that experiencing segregation shaped how they taught African American students. These teachers reported that in addition to content knowledge, African American students needed skills to survive in a segregated society. Additionally, Walker's (1996) study revealed that African American teachers in segregated schools viewed education as an economical and political means to success. Similarly, Walker's (2000) study reported that African American teachers play a central role to providing students an education during school and outside of school.

Empirical research focusing on the instructional activities of African American teachers who taught school in rural schools during the 1940s until the late 1960s and students' perceptions of the effectiveness of these activities is limited. Such work that focused solely on Mississippi is almost absent from the literature. For decades, Mississippi's educational system has had the reputation of lagging behind those of other states. Although the Jim Crow period began in the late 1800s (Anderson, 1988), African Americans, including teachers, were still viewed as second-class citizens during the 1940s and beyond by the majority White society in Mississippi and other parts of the South. The separate and unequal education system for African Americans was intended to disenfranchise. However, African Americans were astute enough to leverage their limited educational resources and their strong commitment to attain a quality education that would be treasured by future generations. Gaining a deeper understanding of these treasured educational experiences may aid in enhancing the teaching practices used in the present public schools.

METHODS

This study employed qualitative methodology to explore the richness displayed in the participants' stories of their past educational experiences and to uncover the participants' intricate meaning of the world (Creswell, 1994). Current thinking is that the world consists of "multiple realities," that is, the world is not an objective object, but shaped by subjective views and interactions (Merriam, 1988,). Merriam's research allowed qualitative researchers to explore many of these realities through the lens of the participants. Narrative analysis, specifically the life history method was used to analyze the learning experiences and memories of teachers' behaviors valued by students who attended rural segregated schools in the South. Chase (as cited in Denzin & Lincoln, 2005) defined this qualitative research method as narratives that describe a significant period in a person's life. The stories of the participants in this study were examined to extrapolate the impact of their school experiences on their lives as professionals. Data were gathered using interviews which served as avenues for achieving purposeful information through focused interactive conversation (Lawler, 2002).

Purposive sampling techniques were used to select participants for this study (Stake, 2000). Face-to-face semi-structured interviews were conducted with five persons who attended elementary and secondary school in the rural South (Mississippi) from 1940–1969. Participants were selected based on the following criteria:

- Must be African American;
- Must have attended segregated elementary and secondary school in Mississippi between 1940 and 1969; and
- Must have pursued a career as an educator.

Eight persons were invited to participate in the study; however, five of these persons participated. Since there are no specific rules for sample size in qualitative research (Patton, 2002), the researcher concluded that the memories of the five participants would provide sufficient depth for the study.

Two one-hour interviews were conducted with each participant. The first interview was semi-structured. Semi-structured interviews allowed the researcher to ask all participants the same questions, yet allowed for the chance to probe areas of discussion introduced by participants. The interview questions focused on the following areas: Significant memories of elementary to high school years, perceptions of teachers' behaviors, and lessons learned that they still use. The focus areas of the interview questions were given to the participants in advance. As a result, many participants jogged their memories by writing down their responses. The second interview served as a follow-up that followed a semi-structured format and allowed for further investigation of themes.

PARTICIPANTS

The participants in this inquiry were students who attended rural segregated schools during the 1940s until the late 1960s and who later pursued careers as educators. Educators, teachers, and school leaders, help to shape the minds of countless numbers of students. The participants' minds, Booker T., Viola, Roscoe, Annie Mae, and Stella (all pseudonyms) were shaped by their teachers. A profile of each participant is provided.

Booker T.

Booker T. started first grade in 1949. His parents were sharecroppers who valued education. He attended a two-room school for the first eight years of his education. He received his first degree from an HBCU in the State of Mississippi. His graduate degrees, Master's and doctorate degrees are from a predominantly White university in the state. He taught chemistry at the high school level before becoming a high school principal. He led a successful career as a superintendent—twice being the first Black superintendent of two fairly large school districts in the state. After retirement from being a superintendent, he worked as the executive director for a large privately funded consulting organization. About four years later, he retired from this position and now works as an educational consultant for a state-based firm.

Viola

Viola began the first grade in 1955. She considered her parents to be affluent. She attended a school located in the town part of the county where she lived. She had money to purchase her lunch and snack at school instead of bringing them from home. She received her first degree from an HBCU in the State of Mississippi. Her graduate degrees, Master's, specialist, and doctorate, are from a predominantly White university in the state. She still lives in her home community. She taught English for more than 20 years at the high school level and later became the principal of the high school in the community where she grew up. After receiving the Ph.D. in educational leadership, she retired and now works as an educational consultant, part-time. She is also the mayor of her hometown.

Roscoe

Roscoe began the first grade in 1953. His parents owned a large farm. He attended a small community school with about 50 students, but later graduated from a high school with about 600 students. He received his associate degree from a predominantly Black junior college and his bachelor's degree from an HBCU in the State of Mississippi. His graduate degrees are from a university in Indiana (Master's) and a university in Minnesota (doctorate). He taught industrial arts in high school for about 10 years, served as a high school principal for about five years, and served as a tenured professor of industrial education for about 15 years. He is now retired and owns a thriving retail business. All of Roscoe's 16 siblings received a college education.

Annie Mae

Annie Mae began first grade in 1949. She describes her family as being poor. She attended a small community school. The word "Colored" was part of the school's name. Approximately 25 students attended this school. She received her bachelor's degree from an HBCU in the State of Mississippi. Her graduate degrees, master's, specialist, and doctorate, are from a predominantly White university. She taught elementary schools for 25 years in her hometown. After she retired, she became a full-time doctoral student. Six years later, she received her Ph.D. in curriculum and instruction. She now works as a curriculum consultant for her home school district.

Stella

Stella began first grade in 1953. Stella was reared in a single-parent home. She describes her family as being very poor. She attended the school in town. There were about 35 students in her graduating class. She received her associate degree from a community college that served predominantly Black students and her bachelor's and master's degrees from a predominantly White university. She worked for 20 years as a public relations director and taught business education at the community college, where she received her associate degree, for about 10 years. She left work because of a debilitating illness.

Information regarding each participant's education and professional career is found in Table 1.

Data Collection

Interviews were conducted with each participant. Since they were being asked to recollect memories from more than 50 years, time was allowed for them to reconstruct the memories of their elementary and high school years in their minds. Therefore, the interview questions were presented to them in advanced. This resulted in written responses and allowed the researcher to probe more deeply into the various questions during the first interview. The second interview was a follow-up and gave the participants the opportunity to review the interview transcripts for accuracy.

Table 1   Participant's Education and Career Profession

Participant's Education and Career Profession

Name	Year in 1st Grade	First Degree Institution Type	Highest Degree Institution Type	Career Profession
Booker T.	1949	B.S.	Ed.D.	Superintendent
		HBCU	PWI	
Viola	1955	B.S.	Ph.D.	High School Principal
		HBCU	PWI	
Roscoe	1953	A.S.	Ph.D.	College Professor
		PBI	PWI	
Annie Mae	1949	B.S.	Ph.D.	Elementary School Teacher
		HBCU	PWI	
Stella	1953	A.S.	M.S.	Community College Teacher
		PBI	PWI	

Note. B.S.–Bachelor of Science; A.S.–Associate of Science; M.S.–Master of Science; Ed.D.–Doctor of Education Degree; Ph.D.–Doctor of Philosophy Degree; HBCU–Historical Black College or University; PWI–Predominantly White Institution; PBI–Private Black Institution.

DATA ANALYSIS AND DISCUSSION

Interview transcripts were examined by each participant for accuracy. Data were organized based on research questions and interview questions. This study was bound by participants who attended schools in the same state during the same period of time.

Thematic analysis of the collected data was employed to identify recurring phrases and common themes that related to memories of schooling in the segregated South. Wholistic and selective reading thematic approaches were used to uncover significant themes. This was achieved by carefully reading and re-reading data from the interview transcripts in order to determine emerging and recurring themes and, at the same time, select statements from participants that helped to exemplify these themes (Van Manen, 2002). Hein and Austin (2001) posited that themes emerge from three sources: (a) the participant's meanings, (b) the investigator's meanings, and (c) the inter-subjective meanings from the participant and the investigator. Analysis of the data revealed three main categories of data themes: (a) significant experiences, (b) teachers' behaviors, (c) and applied learning. One theme dominated the participants' responses about significant experiences—desires to please the teacher. The themes for teacher behaviors were: Memories of caring teachers, memories of teachers as professionals, and memories of teachers as participants of the community. The theme for applied lessons was passing on the flame. These themes were reinforced with quotes from the collected data. The purpose of using quotations from participants, as explained by Van Manen (1990) allows the readers to be "in more direct contact with the world" as it was experienced and retrospectively described by participants (p. 9).

Desire to Please Teacher

In an attempt to uncover the impact of classroom/school experiences on student learning, the participants were asked to share significant memories of their elementary and high school years. Most of the participants remembered "achievement" days, county-wide song festivals, end-of-the-year programs, or other school-related competitions from elementary school. Recounting these activities evoked smiles on their faces and gladness in their voices. Viola, whose responses revealed a competitive spirit, rattled on about the activities of "achievement" days.

> We had sack races, egg races, and many other games. We had spelling bees. Classes competed against other classes.

In a similar fashion, Booker T., who attended a two-room, two-grade school with two teachers for students in first through eighth grade, had fond memories of the county-wide "song festivals." It was clear from the inflections in his voice that his desire to learn a song which he and most of his classmates could not pronounce the words and did not know the meaning was spurred by his desire to please his teacher. Also, he remembered the long hours his teacher must have spent preparing to teach the song, and her desire to provide students with cultural experiences by introducing them to songs that they may never sing again in their lives. This teacher, as he remembered, was committed to ensuring that her students learned more than the content of the curriculum handed to them by White school leaders. Seeing these commitments, Booker T. recalled, ignited his momentum to perform at his best.

Somewhat differently, however, Annie Mae focused her memories on her favorite teacher, "Teacher B." Teacher B, according to Annie Mae's description, was a renegade—she was not like the other teachers.

> Teacher B interacted with parents and the community. She planned fun activities, sleepovers, and field trips.

These activities seemed to have engaged students and introduced them to creative ways to have fun at school. Students appeared to have had a desire to win, at least for that day or for that activity. School and church, for most students, shared the central focus of their lives, and after school was spent working the fields or helping around the house. Furthermore, these activities ignited the desire to prove themselves to their teachers—to make their teachers proud. Teachers had the desire to expose students to experiences that would enrich their awareness of their culture and mainstreamed cultures—to expose them to the real world.

Two participants did not recollect a specific event, but responses signified the importance placed on academic performance and pleasing their teachers. Roscoe, who revealed that he benefited from having older siblings and family in the school system, responded, "*I consider teacher enthusiasm and the inculcation of the "can do" attitude in students as very significant. ...*" Roscoe shared that it was his teacher's instilling this "can do" attitude in him that helped him develop into a confident student. His teacher gave him confidence in his "ability to learn and to do quality work." This confidence allowed him to achieve a doctoral degree. He credits his teacher for his love of reading and his development of a high quality vocabulary.

Stella, who described her school and community as being "a close-knit family atmosphere," recounted a significant experience in this manner.

> Attending a segregated school in a small, rural community served as another arm of the extended family environment which enabled many children of my generation to thrive and go on to be successful despite the odds.

School experiences taught students to be disciplined and responsible. Viola recollected how elementary school students were expected to conduct themselves in an adult-like manner. They were not guided from class to lunch or from lunch to activity period by the teacher. "We played on the play ground. I do not recall teachers having to take us to lunch. We went to the cafeteria, which was a building away from the school, by ourselves. " Because teachers had instilled in them responsible behaviors, they made a great effort not to disappoint their teachers.

In an attempt to uncover the behaviors—how teachers taught, how they interacted with students inside and outside the classroom—participants were asked to describe their memories of their teachers' behaviors that impacted their academic and career success. Their responses yielded three themes—memories of teachers caring, memories of teachers as professionals, and memories of teachers as participants of the community.

Memories of teachers caring. African American teachers during this era had to face many challenges brought on by socio-political factors. In addition to teaching in substandard buildings and using second-hand school books, they were confronted with issues of racism. Booker T., who had the same teacher for the first eight grades of his schooling, spoke passionately about his teacher: "Despite challenging circumstances, Mrs. G. came to teach at School. And teach she did!"

These circumstances of time did not interfere with teachers doing their job; they were motivated to work harder to ensure that their students learned so their lives would not be hampered by similar circumstances. Caring was conveyed by the teacher's acceptance of all students and her insistence of students doing their very best. In addition to teaching the required content, Booker T. noted, "She taught respect, responsibility, and most of all she taught children."

Viola, who pointed out that when she was in the fifth grade a new "brick" school was built, and this was the "first school I had attended that had indoor facilities," also recounted memories of her teachers demonstrating care for their students. Her memories of caring teachers were reflected in her teachers' attitude about what was to go on in the classroom, "When we were in the classroom, we had class. " Her teachers were constantly communicating to students the importance of learning. Care was demonstrated to the students by ensuring that students got the best education possible for them. "The teachers were serious about teaching and about us learning."

Roscoe, who came from a huge family and had many extended family members as teachers, equated the caring behaviors of his teachers to parental care and concern.

> Teachers were nurturers and guides. Just as our parents, they expected good personal grooming, manners, your best effort, respect, and personal responsibility.

He hinted to the fact that because his teachers knew his parents and because some of his teachers were distant relatives, he worked harder to perform well because he wanted them to make good reports to his parents. These good reports not only made him look good, but had a good reflection on his parents and his "well-educated" family.

Annie Mae, who recalled vividly the scarcity of educational materials in her schools, described her teachers' behaviors in the following manner. "Teacher B knew how to motivate students to work hard." Particularly, this teacher always encouraged students to do their best. Also, she thought her teachers cared because they made frequent reports to her parents about her performance and behavior at school.

Stella, who viewed teaching as the ideal profession described her teachers as very effective.

Teachers were nurturing, resourceful, and versatile. They were caring, hardworking professionals who were able to be highly effective educators with very limited and/or substandard resources. In those days, "separate but equal" generally translated as a new school facility (separate) and second-hand book and equipment which were cast-offs from the White schools (unequal).

Through their teachers' behaviors, they knew that the teachers expected only their best performance. Booker T. recalled "Mrs. G. insisted on the very best" and Roscoe remembered "I always felt that my teachers expected me to do well. ..." One way the teachers demonstrated that they cared about the students was by informing the parents of their children's progress in school. The dominance of this theme from the data is consistent with conclusion from Stanford's (1998) study in which she found that teachers were interested in more than students' cognitive abilities. They were concerned about students' "social and emotional growth" as well. The works of Ladson-Billings (1994), Foster (1997), Walker (1996), and Savage (2001) identified caring as a visible characteristic of African American teachers who taught in segregated schools.

Memories of professionalism. Teachers' behaviors also sent messages to students about how they viewed their jobs as teachers. Annie Mae recalled that her teacher's behavior sent a message that they were serious about their job "... but their demeanor was one of professionalism . ...." She also noted that the job of teaching was distinguishable from other jobs in the community, "Teachers were professionals. ... The majority of the community people were farmers."
Stella, who wanted to emulate two of her teachers, expressed

Teachers were the elite of Black society due to their level of educational attainment and higher standard of living compared to other Blacks in the community. As such, they were generally the only professional role models that Black students had.

Professionalism was communicated in the manner teachers performed their teaching responsibilities which was to ensure that students learned. While at school, teachers taught, and as Viola remembered, teachers were about the business of teaching, "there was no time for goofing-off in class." A couple of the participants noted, " Teachers were strict," "teachers were firm" which hinted to classroom management style. Additionally, Stella equated professionalism to the way her teacher dressed and presented themselves in public. Also, professionalism was communicated through their level of education. Roscoe remembered, "Our county employed many teachers from   College who were not only impressive with their educational experiences. ..." From the participants' memories, professionalism was visible from the teachers' presentation of themselves—orally and visually, and from their relationships with their students and their students' parents. Teachers were perceived by everyone as upstanding citizens.
Memories of teachers as participants in the community. Also, these students' memories provided a glimpse into the teachers' lives outside of school. For most, there was a powerful

relationship between the school and the larger community. In Viola's community, when "end-of-the-year programs" and "field days" were held, the parents brought the food and everybody in the community attended. When students went to church on Sunday, they saw their teachers. Roscoe remarks "… they were considered a normal part of the community." He also remembered that learning extended from the school into the home into the church into the doctor's and dentists' offices. The entire community wanted to see how much children were learning in school. Annie Mae remembered, "My elementary teachers resided in the same community as students." Additionally, Stella thought it was important to point out that

> Because the teachers knew their students' families, and/or attended the same churches, they had a relationship with the students both inside and outside of the classroom. This provided unusual insight into the strengths, weaknesses and character of their students and the opportunity to relate to them on many levels.

The teachers' presence and involvement in the community gave the students and their parents a sense of assurance of teachers' competence to do their job and of their interest in providing children with a quality education. Because teachers lived in the school community, they know their students' parents and sometimes grandparents. This shared relationship, perhaps, contributed to their responsibility not only for their students' academic development, but for their social and moral development as well.

Passing on the flame. During the analysis of the data, the responses to a particular interview question seemed to contribute greatly to this study. Participants were asked to tell about a specific school encounter with their teacher that replays often in their minds that they use to push others to achieve. Booker T.'s teachers taught him to persevere.

> I can say without any hesitation that she gave me my start on the path to high achievement. Throughout my years in Mrs. G's classroom, I learned that your best may not always result in your winning in the short term. However, if you persevere, you will ultimately succeed.

This is a lesson that has traveled with him even until this day. Not only did he share this discovery with students when he taught science classes, but he shared it with teachers and principals as well.

Viola's response to this question, although quite lengthy, displayed her desire to demonstrate her smarts to her teacher.

> One of my memorable moments was in my 7th grade English class … the English teacher, asked a question from our home work assignment. She wanted to know the subject of the sentence, "Stop talking." Everyone she asked gave the wrong answer. I raised my

hand to answer, and she said [Viola] take your hand down. I do not want you to answer because you want to answer everything. Finally she had to ask me. I answered, "You". She then wanted to know, why did [Viola] I say the answer is you when the word, "you," is not in the sentence. No one answered. I raised my hand. She said okay [Viola], why. I replied because it is understood ... I had to tell where I had read it in the book. Everyone else had to read it aloud in class.

Thinking back, Viola thought that this incident helped to validate her need to know that she could do well and to prove her competence to her teachers. She recalled sharing this experience to one of her committee members during her doctoral studies.

Roscoe's, Annie Mae's, and Stella's responses, demonstrates deep reflections about their teachers and the practicality of their teachers' behaviors. Roscoe expressed,

In high school, my cognitive ability far exceeded my applied ability. In my mechanical drawing class Mr. L. M. noticed that I could make an A on any written test he gave but struggled with drawing figures, getting angles precise and proper lettering. I was impressed that he did not fuss, but made special notes on my papers ... encouraged me after class. His encouragement, and the fact that he did not hold me up before the class, boosted my confidence and my drawing and lettering, and was a major reason I decided to major in industrial arts in college.

From this experience Roscoe not only learned how to be patient with his students, but he also learned to be a patient parent.

I used a similar tactic with our oldest son when he was a piano student. Instead of fussing, I would get on my knees beside the piano and gently talk to him, clap rhythms, and at the proper moment, fix him a snack. He and I developed the saying that 'the budding pianist needs a refreshing snack.'

Annie Mae's response centered on her favorite and most influential teacher.

Teacher B changed my life. She recognized that I had great academic potential. She recognized that I could compete with older students, therefore her high expectations and belief in me motivated me to strive for excellence in the classroom. Before the semester had ended, she promoted me to another grade.

Annie Mae has used this story to encourage struggling students to "always strive to do their best, and not allow negative circumstances to hold them back. "

Stella told of two such experiences that have impacted her life. One helped to shape her sense of self—specifically how she dressed.

There were two teachers that I admired and wanted to emulate: My 5th grade teacher and Home Economics teacher … both were very attractive, professional, and fashionably dressed women who symbolized the kind of woman I wanted to be.

Stella explained how some of her community college students said they admired her and wanted to emulate her when they got jobs. The other experience impacted her life to a greater degree.

My principal was a short, dumpy, bald-headed man with one leg shorter than the other. His shoes would creak when he walked down the hall so much so that you always knew he was coming before you actually saw him. He was both feared and revered. Feared due to his liberal use of the strap; and revered because of his brilliance, intelligence, and versatility. In addition to being the principal, he taught literature, directed the award-winning choir, and taught band. I credit him with instilling in me a love of music, reading, and the arts.

As a result of her principal's and teacher's influences, Stella passed on the love for the arts to her students.

The reflections of students who attended segregated school in Mississippi during the 1940s–1960s were dominated by memories that taught them to respect their teachers. In respecting their teachers, these students were obedient and responsible, and as a result, they participated in school events and performed to the best of their abilities. Additionally, because school events were community events, students' preparedness or performance was sometimes viewed as an indication of how hard the teacher worked. Some participants recalled specific events while others recalled a more general impression of their memories.

When participants shared their memories of teachers' behaviors that impacted their academic and career successes, their thoughts elicited memories of teachers being caring, professional, and involved individuals. The act of caring was often demonstrated through classroom interactions, teachers' classroom persona, and the teachers' interaction with students' parents. The way teachers dressed and managed their classrooms were visible signs of professionalism. Professionalism was also evident in their educational preparation and the community's perception of them.

There is a body of literature that posits teachers teach the way they are taught—this thought perhaps describes the impact of these participants' teachers on their lives (Lortie, 1975; "Teachers Teach," 1970). Even more importantly, if this is valid, these participants who taught school for a significant portion of their career have displayed the same type of behaviors in their classrooms thereby transmitting the same sentiments to their students through the similar behaviors.

Finally, the descriptions of the memories that replay in their minds and those that they have used for some purpose in their lives, are prime examples of how powerful and long-lasting the education was that took place in those small, dilapidated buildings in the rural segregated South—the Black segregated schools.

CONCLUSIONS

The purpose of this study was to uncover the types of learning experiences and teachers' behaviors that the students who attended southern rural segregated schools during the 1940s through the 1960s valued, and in their opinion, contributed to their academic achievement and career success. In order to make sense of the data, it is necessary to understand the sociopolitical and economical factors that affected this time period. The five participants who shared their life stories about their early school experiences were Black, lived in Mississippi, were children of sharecroppers and farmers, and started elementary school as early as 1949. This period in Mississippi history is referred to as the Jim Crow era—Blacks had few if any rights and were considered second-class citizens. Despite the severe societal injustices, these participants' teachers achieved an education and attained jobs as teachers in Black schools. Understanding this, these teachers took into their classrooms a life-time of struggles, hard work, dreams, and hopes for change that shaped their perspectives about teaching and learning. Their awareness of the harshness and inhumane-ness of a society that the students would be exposed to because of their race was displayed in the classroom through fortifying teaching behaviors. It was the responsibility of the teachers, with assistance from the parents and the church, to educate these students—to provide them with the brain power ("respect, responsibility, to read constantly and to develop a high quality vocabulary") to combat the injustices of society. These teachers, as described by the participants, were firm, strict disciplinarians, role models who taught students respect, responsibility, perseverance, and the importance of learning.

The findings from this study contribute to the national dialogue about teachers in the rural segregated South in the following ways. First, the aforementioned behavioral characteristics of these educators communicated to the students that their teachers cared about them. Although this finding is consistent with the previous research of Walker (2000), Foster (1991, 1997), Howard (2002), Stanford (1997, 1998), Ladson-Billings (1994), and Walker and Tompkins it suggests that certain aspects of teaching caring behaviors are, or can be, transmitted with time. The participants' stories showed examples of how teachers caring behaviors were not only visible at school, but also present in the larger community. Equally important, the findings of this study suggest that the caring behaviors of these teachers were so powerfully etched that it continues to impact the participants' lives.

Another significant contribution to the national dialogue is the demonstrated importance of teacher approval. Teacher approval sparked students' interest and propelled them to participate when they did not want to or when they did not understand the purpose of their learning. These participants' stories suggest and they reported that their experiences with these teachers helped to shape their lives and the lives of their children and students. Moreover, these findings echo research surrounding the use of teacher approval and its impact on students' academic performance through their school experiences. Also, these students' perceptions of their teachers' opinions and expectations about their performance were internalized and accompanied them throughout their lives.

Finally, this study fills a gap in the literature about schooling in the segregated South by unlocking the memories of students who attended schools in Mississippi during the Jim Crow era. Hearing their voices can only add depth to the history of education.

REFERENCES

Anderson, J. (1988). *The education of Blacks in the South*, 1860–1935. Chapel Hill: University of North Carolina Press.

Ashmore, H. S. (1954). *The Negro and the schools.* Chapel Hill: University of North Carolina Press.

Bullock, H. (1967). *A history of Negro education in the South from 1619 to the present.* Cambridge: Harvard University Press.

Chase, S. E. (2005). Narrative inquiry: Multiple lenses, approaches, voices. In N. K. Denzin & Y. S. Lincoln (Eds.), *The Sage handbook of qualitative research*, 3rd ed. (pp. 651–679). Thousand Oaks, CA: Sage.

Clift, V., Anderson, A., & Hullfish, H. (Eds.). (1962). *Negro education in America: Its adequacy, problems, and needs.* New York: Harper & Brothers.

Creswell, J. W. (1994). *Research design: Qualitative & quantitative approaches.* Thousand Oaks, CA: Sage.

Fairclough, A. (2004). The costs of *Brown*: Black teachers and school integration. *The Journal of American History*, 91, 43–55.

Foster, M. (1990). The politics of race: Through the eyes of African American teachers. *Journal of Education*, 172, 123–141.

Foster, M. (1991). Constancy, connectedness, and constraints in the lives of African American women teachers. *National Association of Women's Studies Journal*, 3, 70–97.

Foster, M. (1993). Educating for competence in community and culture: Exploring exemplary African American teachers. *Urban Education*, 27, 370–394.

Foster, M. (1994a). Education for competence in community and culture. In M. J. Shujaa (Ed.) *Too much schooling, too little education: A paradox of Black life in White societies* (pp. 221–244). Trenton, NJ: Africa World Press.

Foster, M. (1994b). Effective Black teachers: A literature review. In E. R. Hollins, J. E. King, & W. C. Hayman (Eds.), *Teaching diverse populations* (pp. 225–241). Albany: State University of New York Press.

Foster, M. (1997). *Black teachers on teaching.* New York: The New Press.

Fultz, M. (1995a). Teacher training and African American education in the South, 1900–1940. *The Journal of Negro Education*, 64, 196–210.

Fultz, M. (1995b). African American teachers in the South, 1890–1940: Powerless and the ironies of expectations and protest. *History of Education Quarterly*, 35, 401–422.

Grant, C. A. (1991). Culture and teaching: What do teachers need to know? In M. M. Kennedy (Ed.), *Teaching academic subjects to diverse learners* (pp. 237–256). New York: Teachers College Press.

Hein, S. F., & Austin, W. J. (2001). Empirical and hermeneutic approaches to phenomenological research in psychology: A comparison. *Psychological Methods*, 6, 3–17.

Howard, T. C. (2002). Hearing footsteps in the dark: African American students' descriptions of effective teachers. *Journal of Education for Students Placed At Risk*, 7, 425–444.

Johnson, C. (1941). *Growing up in the Black belt: Negro youth in the rural South.* Washington, DC: American Council on Education.

Ladson-Billings, G. (1994). *The dreamkeepers: Successful teachers of African American children.* San Francisco: Jossey-Bass.

Lawler, S. (2002). Narrative in social research. In T. May (Ed.), *Qualitative research in education* (pp. 242–258). Thousand Oak: CA: Sage.

Lortie, D. (1975). *Schoolteacher: A sociological study.* Chicago: University of Chicago Press.

Merriam, S. B. (1988). *Case study research in education: A qualitative approach.* San Francisco: Jossey-Bass.

Patton, M. Q. (2002). *Qualitative research & evaluation methods*, 3rd edition. Thousand Oaks: Sage.

Savage, C. J. (2001). "Because we did more with less": The agency of African American teachers in Franklin, Tennessee: 1890–1967. *Peabody Journal of Education*, 76, 170–203.

Riley, K. L. (1998). *Teacher education in Southern Negro school: The summer of 1915.* Retrieved from http://www.psy.kuleuven.ac.be/ische/abstracts/

Stake, R. (2000). Case studies. In N. K. Denzin & Y. S. Lincoln (Eds.), *Handbook of qualitative research*, (2nd. ed., pp. 435–454). Thousand Oak, CA: Sage.

Stanford, G. C. (1997). Successful pedagogy in urban schools: Perspectives of four African American teachers. *Journal of Education for Students Placed At Risk*, 2, 107–119.

Stanford, G. C. (1998). African-American teachers' knowledge of teaching: Understanding the influence of their remembered teaches. *The Urban Review*, 30, 229–243. Teachers teach as they are taught. (1970). *Change*, 2, 18–19.

Van Manen, M. (1990). *Researching lived experiences.* New York: State University of New York Press.

Van Manen, M. (2002). *Phenomenology online: Describing experiences.* Retrieved from http://www.phenomenologyonline.com.

Walker, V. S. (1996). *Their highest potential.* Chapel Hill: North Carolina Press.

Walker, V. S. (2000). Valued segregated schools for African American children in the South, 1935–1969: A review of common themes and characteristics. *Review of Educational Research*, 70, 253–285.

Walker, V. S., & Tompkins R. H. (2004). Caring in the past: The case of a southern segregated African American school. In V. S. Walker, & J. R. Snarey (Eds.), *Race-ing Moral Formation: African American Perspectives on Care and Justice* (pp. 77–92), New York: Teachers College Press.

Discussion Questions:

1. Did you examine the footnotes of the authors yet? What are the strengths of the sources each author used? What are the weaknesses of the sources each author used? For example, is the source the story or experience of just one person, or is it the result of empirical (scientific

research) studies? Is the story of one person's experience as valid as information gained from scientific research?

2. What was the bias or biases of each author? Part of the bias of each author can be found within his or her writings. Also, researching the author can help one understand the biases of the author. What else has the author published? Is there a theme within the topics of the author's writings? Does the author tend to examine all topics from one perspective? For example, in the Bowles and Gintis article, do the authors tend to argue for the benefits of schooling in a capitalistic society, or do they emphasize the weaknesses of education in democratic society?

3. Thus far, I have focused on identifying the bias of an author, as well as examining the quality of sources used as evidence. A third step in examining a scholarly article is looking at the organization of the argument—every piece of scholarship is ultimately an argument. For example, in the Coats piece, the author uses in the title the words "segregated South," not "African American school, 1870–1950." The word "segregated" suggests the initial research question. The argument is shaped by the evidence discovered while researching the article, then organized in such a way as to make a point. In the Edwards piece, the title of the article strongly suggests that the author will put forth the argument that Southern history is U.S. history, thus giving Southern history more significance. Did each of the authors convince you of their argument? How did they persuade you, or why might they have not persuaded you? Did your own biases filter what you accepted as truth or rejected?

ACTIVITIES

1. Compare and contrast the history presented in Chapter One with the histories presented in this chapter. Examine the arguments presented, the evidence utilized to support their position, and the bias of each author. What do you know as a result of this examination?

2. Below is a list of professional journals that are likely to publish educational history articles. Examine each site to determine the bias of the editorial board. For example, on the home page of the History of Education journal site, they list their "Aims & Scope." What does this list suggest regarding the bias of this journal? Also on the home page are the phrases "peer-reviewed journal" and "based on initial editor screening." This means that editorial board will first determine if the article meets the standards of the journal; if so, the article will be sent to experts in the field of educational history (professors) to evaluate and determine if the article is worthy of publication. Who is on the editorial board? Does the website identify the members of the editorial board? Does the journal provide biographies of members of the editorial board? What is the location in which the journal is published? Is it a university or another location? What other sources might you use to further evaluate the validity of the journal?

ONLINE RESOURCES

1. History of Education   http://www.tandf.co.uk/journals/titles/0046760X.asp
2. History of Education Quarterly   http://www.wiley.com/bw/journal.asp?ref=0018-2680
3. The History Teacher   http://www.thehistoryteacher.org/
4. American Educational History Journal   http://www.edhistorians.org/aehj/aehj.html
5. Paedagogica Historica   http://www.tandf.co.uk/journals/titles/00309230.asp
6. History of Education Review   http://www.emeraldinsight.com/products/journals/journals.htm?id=her
7. History of Education Review Journal   http://www.anzhes.com/journal/journal.shtml
8. Journal of Philosophy and History of Education   http://www.journalofphilosophyandhistoryofeducation.com/
9. The Journal of American History   http://www.journalofphilosophyandhistoryofeducation.com/
10. Journal of Social History   http://muse.jhu.edu/journals/jsh/summary/v042/42.2.lassonde.html

CHAPTER THREE
EDUCATIONAL CASE LAW: AN OVERVIEW

A re teachers permitted to talk about their own religion in their place of worship with one of their students? Do teachers have freedom of speech, as protected by the First Amendment, in the classroom? Is a student in an art class permitted to paint the Ten Commandments? If so, can that painting be displayed by the school with other art pieces by students? Are the prayers before sporting events legal? Is it legal to sing *Rudolph the Red-Nosed Reindeer* in public school? Is it consistent with the U.S. Constitution to assign students to a school based on race? If a school has only one student with a first language other than English, is that school required to hire an ESL teacher?

Do not assume that if something occurred in your school that it was legal; also do not assume that if something did not occur in your school that it was illegal. School funding, or lack thereof, and the threat of a lawsuit can influence the actions of school personnel, regardless of actual laws. If a school system is sued, regardless of the strength of the suit, the district must still hire a lawyer to deal with the court process. Thus, the simple threat of a lawsuit has power in schools. The power of the threat, however, can be neutralized; the attempt at intimidation can be countered; an increase in the perception of teachers as professionals can occur; and improved community relations can transpire if teachers and administrators understand educational law.

WHAT IS EDUCATIONAL LAW?

Educational law can be broken down into constitutional rights, case law, and federal and state legislation. This chapter will deal with the first two categories; federal and state legislation will be addressed in Chapter Five. The U.S. Constitution defines rights for all Americans; case laws further define how those rights exist in a school. Another way to organize educational laws are constitutional rights, case laws that further define constitutional rights, and laws of educational access. These last two categories define who is permitted through the schoolhouse door (educational access) and what is done to guarantee access to instruction once inside the classroom.

Case law—law determined, defined, or refined by the courts—begins at the local level. Anyone can initiate a case law. It begins with an individual or group of individuals suing someone or some institution. For example, in the famous *Brown v. Board of Education* case, a father tried to enroll his daughter in a local school district, so that she would not be required to walk across a dangerous railroad crossing. When his daughter was denied admittance to the all-white school, he sued the district. The official name of the suit was *Brown v. Topeka Board of Education*. Eventually the NAACP took on the case and joined it with five other similar cases in which black parents were suing their local school district for the right of their children to attend the local all-white public school.[1]

Whenever a case makes its way to the Supreme Court, it must snake its way through all the lower courts at the state and federal levels first. This occurs when the side that did not get the ruling they wished appeals the decision of the lower court. The Supreme Courts at the federal and state levels can choose to listen to a case appealed to them or deny hearing the case. The cases they choose to hear are ones that pertain to their own constitution. For example, the Ohio Supreme Court only hears cases tied to the Ohio Constitution; the U.S. Supreme Court only hears cases tied to the Constitution of the United States. For the *Brown v. Board* case, the U.S. Supreme Court chose to hear the case, and their decision became national law. In the case mentioned above regarding NCLB, the Supreme Court refused to hear the case. In doing so, they affirmed or approved the lower court's decision.

U.S. Constitutional Law and Schools

The two amendments to the U.S. Constitution that most often come into play in case laws involving schools are the First and Fourteenth. The First Amendment to the U.S. Constitution states[2]:

> Congress shall make no law respecting an establishment of religion, or prohibiting the free exercise thereof; or abridging the freedom of speech, or of the press; or the right of the people peaceably to assemble, and to petition the government for a redress of grievances.

Notice that nowhere in this amendment are the words "teachers" or "schools"; furthermore, it regulates Congress. Also observe that the words "separation of church and state" are not

---

1   U.S. Courts, Educational Resources, "History of Brown vs. Board of Education" retrieved July 28, 2011, from http://www.uscourts.gov/EducationalResources/ConstitutionResources/LegalLandmarks/HistoryOfBrownVBoardOfEducation.aspx

2   Cornell University Law School, Legal Information Institute, retrieved July 28, 2011, from http://topics.law.cornell.edu/constitution/billofrights#amendmenti

mentioned. Finally, the word "respecting" is quite noteworthy. Congress shall not *respect* any one religion. Nonetheless, most political speeches ended with the words, "God Bless America." Congress begins each session with a prayer by the chaplain of the body who is paid with tax dollars. Our money has the words, "In God We Trust." In our courts and when lawmakers are sworn into office, they do so by putting their hand on a religious text; the Bible is the norm. Every year, a large tree is chopped down and taken to Washington, D.C., for the official lighting of the national Christmas tree. All of these are acts of Congress respecting religion. Or are they? Even more important for this discussion: Are similar acts permitted in schools?

Also note that in the First Amendment, the Congress shall not abridge or limit freedom of speech, press, or peaceful assembly. This half of the amendment is much more closely followed by members of Congress and the federal government in general. One of the most recent cases demonstrating this involves the Westboro Baptist Church, who protests the funerals of soldiers who have died in battle.[3] Albert Synder, the father of a fallen soldier, sued the church when they protested at his son's funeral. In a lower court ruling, Synder was awarded $5 million by a jury; however, the U.S. Supreme Court chose to hear the case and ruled in favor of the church. Chief Justice Roberts wrote in the majority decision, "As a nation we have chosen a different course—to protect even hurtful speech on public issues to ensure that we do not stifle public debate."[4] In another case, which reversed federal finance laws, the U.S. Supreme Court granted corporations and unions the right to contribute to political campaigns. Justice Kennedy, writing the majority decision, stated, "There is no basis for the proposition that, in the political speech context, the government may impose restrictions on certain disfavored speakers." He continued, "The government may regulate corporate speech through disclaimer and disclosure requirements, but it may not suppress that speech altogether." Thus, for individuals, corporations, and unions, freedom of speech is extensively defended. Are these same rights extended to teachers and students? This and questions regarding freedom of religion in schools will be discussed in later sections of this chapter.

Three components of the Fourteenth Amendment to the U.S. Constitution that most apply to schools are all found in the first section:

> All persons born or naturalized in the United States, and subject to the jurisdiction thereof, are citizens of the United States and of the state wherein they reside. No state shall make or enforce any law, which shall abridge the privileges or immunities of citizens of the United States; nor shall any state deprive any person of life, liberty, or property, without due process of law; nor deny to any person within its jurisdiction the equal protection of the laws.[5]

---

3 Warren Richey, *Christian Science Monitor*, retrieved July 28, 2011, from http://www.csmonitor.com/USA/Justice/2011/0302/Supreme-Court-hurtful-speech-of-Westboro-Baptist-Church-is-protected
4 Ibid.
5 Cornell University Law School, Legal Information Institute, retrieved July 28, 2011, from http://topics.law.cornell.edu/constitution/billofrights

The first key point in the above section is the statement that "No state shall make or enforce any law …" which, to paraphrase, means that no state may make a law which contradicts the U.S. Constitution. The second key piece is "No state shall … abridge the privileges or immunities of citizens." In others words, states may not grant services to one population in the state and restrict others in the state from receiving those same services. Nor may a state make a law that only applies to one subpopulation of the state. The third key piece is the phrase, "equal protection of the laws." This phrase in particular has played a key role in cases involving religion in schools.

RELIGION AND SCHOOLS

To understand laws pertaining to religion in schools, a critical element is understanding the difference between the Establishment Clause, "Congress shall make no law respecting an establishment of religion,"[6] and the Free Exercise Clause, "or prohibiting the free exercise thereof."[7] The Establishment Clause restricts the government from imposing a religion on citizens; the Free Exercise Clause restricts government officials from limiting or hindering the practice of religion by citizens.

The interaction of the First and Fourteenth Amendments is very evident in laws regarding religion and schooling. The First Amendment states that "Congress shall make no law respecting the establishment of religion," which means that our laws cannot give priority to one religion over the next. However, in schools it means much more than that. The Fourteenth Amendment articulates that states cannot make laws that contradict federal mandates. In other words, a state may not make laws that skirt around the U.S. Constitution, and that has especially played a role in school case laws.

In 1946 a taxpayer by the name of Everson sued the board of education of Ewing Township because tax dollars were being used to reimburse parents of private Catholic school students for the cost of transportation to the school.[8] Everson's argument was that, by New Jersey having a policy that allowed this, the state was violating the U.S. Constitution. The case made its way to the U.S. Supreme Court, which ruled in a 5-4 decision that the state statue was permissible.[9]

The Everson decision is significant for three reasons. First, the vote is commonly referred to as a split vote, one in which the justices were divided in their decision and the final decision was won by only one vote. Justice Rutledge, in the dissent, wrote somewhat prophetically:

> Public money devoted to payment of religious costs, educational or other, brings the
> quest for more. It brings too the struggle of sect against sect for the larger share or for

---

6 Ibid.
7 Ibid.
8 Douglas O. Linder, "Exploring Constitutional Law." Cornell University Law School, Legal Information Institute. retrieved July 28, 2011. from http://law2.umkc.edu/faculty/projects/ftrials/conlaw/everson.html
9 Ibid.

any. Here one by numbers alone will benefit most, there another. That is precisely the history of societies which have had an established religion and dissident groups. It is the very thing Jefferson and Madison experienced and sought to guard against, whether in its blunt or in its more screened forms. The end of such strife cannot be other than to destroy the cherished liberty. The dominating group will achieve the dominant benefit; or all will embroil the state in their dissensions. ...[10]

Today, Evangelical Christians play a central role in politics at the national level. In regard to schools, religious schools can now receive federal money via vouchers, a practice that will be explained in Chapter Five concerning No Child Left Behind.

The second reason why the Everson decision was important is that, in the majority decision, Justice Black equated the right to safe passage to school to that of other public services:

Moreover, state-paid policemen, detailed to protect children going to and from church schools from the very real hazards of traffic, would serve much the same purpose and accomplish much the same result as state provisions intended to guarantee free transportation of a kind which the state deems to be best for the school children's welfare. And parents might refuse to risk their children to the serious danger of traffic accidents going to and from parochial schools, the approaches to which were not protected by policemen. Similarly, parents might be reluctant to permit their children to attend schools which the state had cut off from such general government services as ordinary police and fire protection, connections for sewage disposal, public highways and sidewalks. Of course, cutting off church schools from these services, so separate and so indisputably marked off from the religious function, would make it far more difficult for the schools to operate. But such is obviously not the purpose of the First Amendment. That Amendment requires the state to be a neutral in its relations with groups of religious believers and non-believers; it does not require the state to be their adversary. State power is no more to be used so as to handicap religions than it is to favor them.[11]

Does this suggest that schooling in our nation is a right? According to Justice Black, schooling is an obligation:

This Court has said that parents may, in the discharge of their duty under state compulsory education laws, send their children to a religious rather than a public school if the school meets the secular educational requirements which the state has power to impose. It appears that these parochial schools meet New Jersey's requirements. The State contributes no money to the schools. It does not support them. Its legislation, as

---

10 Ibid.
11 Ibid.

applied, does no more than provide a general program to help parents get their children, regardless of their religion, safely and expeditiously to and from accredited schools.[12]

Thus, the state has an obligation to make sure that children arrive safely to a school, regardless if it is a religiously oriented school or a public school.

A final key piece of the Everson decision is reference to it in cases that followed regarding religion and schools. Of note, the dissenting view, the votes that opposed the ruling of the court, were cited in cases that followed. In other words, even those views of the justices who oppose the ruling of the court become part of the case law record. This can be seen in the *Abington v. Schempp* case regarding Bible reading in schools,[13] but first it is necessary to gain an understanding of *Engel v. Vitale*.

In 1962 parents in Union Free School District sued the school over use of the Regents Prayer. The State Board of Regents for New York had written a prayer, commonly known as the Regents Prayer as part of their "Statement on Moral and Spiritual Education in Schools."[14] This lawsuit, which found its way to the U.S. Supreme Court. became known as *Engel v. Vitale*.[15] Those opposed to the recitation of the prayer in school were opposed to the idea that government officials wrote the prayer, thereby violating the Establishment Clause of the First Amendment. In contrast, the respondents argued that the prayers did not violate the First Amendment because it was "nondenominational" in content.

Representing the majority decision, Justice Black wrote that the Regents Prayers did violate the Establishment Clause, since government officials wrote the prayer:

> When the power, prestige and financial support of government is placed behind a particular religious belief, the indirect coercive pressure upon religious minorities to conform to the prevailing officially approved religion is plain. But the purposes underlying the Establishment Clause go much further than that. Its first and most immediate purpose rested on the belief that a union of government and religion tends to destroy government and to degrade religion. The history of governmentally established religion, both in England and in this country, showed that whenever government had allied itself with one particular form of religion, the inevitable result had been that it had incurred the hatred, disrespect and even contempt of those who held contrary beliefs.[16]

In other words, the Regents Prayer not only violated the Establishment Clause, but also, in doing so, it tainted religion in general. Justice Black went further to explain the underlying

---

12   Ibid.
13   FindLaw, U.S. Supreme Court, *Abington School Dist. v. Schempp*, 374 U.S. 203 (1963), retrieved July 28, 2011, from http://caselaw.lp.findlaw.com/scripts/getcase.pl?court=us&vol=374&invol=203
14   FindLaw, U.S. Supreme Court, *Engel v. Vitale*, 370 U.S., 370 U.S. 421 (1962), retrieved July 28, 2011, from http://caselaw.lp.findlaw.com/cgi-bin/getcase.pl?court=us&vol=370&invol=421
15   Ibid.
16   Ibid.

purpose of the Establishment Clause, "religion is too personal, too sacred, too holy, to permit its 'unhallowed perversion'[17] by a civil magistrate."[18] Later in his ruling, Justice Black rejected the respondents' claim that to prohibit state laws from respecting an establishment of religious services in public schools is hostile toward religion:

> Nothing, of course, could be more wrong. ... And there were men of this same faith in the [370 U.S. 421, 435]   power of prayer who led the fight for adoption of our Constitution and also for our Bill of Rights with the very guarantees of religious free-dom that forbid the sort of governmental activity which New York has attempted here. These men knew that the First Amendment, which tried to put an end to governmental control of religion and of prayer, was not written to destroy either. They knew rather that it was written to quiet well-justified fears which nearly all of them felt arising out of an awareness that governments of the past had shackled men's tongues to make them speak only the religious thoughts that government wanted them to speak and to pray only to the God that government wanted them to pray to. It is neither sacrilegious nor antireligious to say that each separate government in this country should stay out of the business of writing or sanctioning official prayers and leave that purely religious function to the people themselves and to those the people choose to look to for religious guidance.[19]

In other words, the First Amendment actually protects religion from government interven-tion. Thus, separating church and state in school is for the purpose of protecting the rights of citizens, as well as individual religions.

Prior to 1963, schoolchildren in Pennsylvania were required to read ten Bible verses and recite the Lord's Prayer to begin the school day. The Schempp family sued the Abington School district, claiming that their rights were being violated under the Fourteenth Amendment.[20] In other words, their claim was that they were not afforded equal protection of laws by the Pennsylvania statute. The case ended up before the U.S. Supreme Court, which ruled in favor of the Schempp family.

Citing the dissenting decision in the Everson decision, Justice Clark wrote:

> "The [First] Amendment's purpose was not to strike merely at the official establishment of a single sect, creed or religion, outlawing only a formal relation such as had prevailed in England and some of the colonies. Necessarily it was to uproot all such relationships. But the object was broader than separating church and state in this narrow sense. It was

---

17   Memorial and Remonstrance against Religious Assessments, II Writings of Madison, at 187, as cited in ENGEL v. VITALE, 370 U.S. 421 (1962), retrieved on July 19, 2011, from http://caselaw.lp.findlaw.com/cgibin/getcase. pl?court=us&vol=370&invol=421
18   Ibid.
19   Ibid.
20   FindLaw, U.S. Supreme Court, *Abington School Dist. v. Schempp*, 374 U.S. 203 (1963), retrieved July 28, 2011, from http://caselaw.lp.findlaw.com/scripts/getcase.pl?court=us&vol=374&invol=203

to create a complete and permanent separation of the spheres of religious activity and civil authority by comprehensively forbidding every form of public aid or support for religion." Id., at 31–32.[21]

The Court's majority decision also clarified when religion should be permitted in schools, for secular reasons only:

That is to say that to withstand the strictures of the Establishment Clause there must be a secular legislative purpose and a primary effect that neither advances nor inhibits religion … It is insisted that unless these religious exercises are permitted a "religion of secularism" is established in the schools. We agree of course that the State may not establish a "religion of secularism" in the sense of affirmatively opposing or showing hostility to religion, thus "preferring those who believe in no religion over those who do believe." Zorach v. Clauson, supra, at 314. We do not agree, however, that this decision in any sense has that effect. In addition, it might well be said that one's education is not complete without a study of comparative religion or the history of religion and its relationship to the advancement of civilization. It certainly may be said that the Bible is worthy of study for its literary and historic qualities. Nothing we have said here indicates that such study of the Bible or of religion, when presented objectively as part of a secular program of education, may not be effected consistently with the First Amendment.[22]

In 1969 Rhode Island passed the Salary Supplement Act, which paid teachers in private schools a 15 percent salary supplement for education that was secular in nature.[23] In 1968 Pennsylvania passed Nonpublic Elementary and Secondary Act authorizing "the state Superintendent of Public Instruction to 'purchase' certain 'secular educational services' from nonpublic schools, directly reimbursing those schools solely for teachers' salaries, textbooks, and instructional materials."[24] The U.S. Supreme Court. in a case known as Lemon v. Kurtzman. found that both statutes led to "excessive entanglement" of church and state:

(a) The entanglement in the Rhode Island program arises because of the religious activity and purpose of the church-affiliated schools, especially with respect to children of impressionable age in the primary grades, and the dangers that a teacher under religious control and discipline poses to the separation of religious from purely secular aspects of elementary education in such schools. These factors require continuing state surveillance to ensure that the statutory restrictions are obeyed and the First Amendment otherwise

---

21   Ibid.

22   Ibid.

23   FindLaw, U.S. Supreme Court, Lemon v. Kurtzman, 403, U.S. 602 (1971), retrieved July 28, 2011, from http://caselaw.lp.findlaw.com/cgi-bin/getcase.pl?court=us&vol=403&invol=602

24   Ibid.

respected. Furthermore, under the Act the government must inspect school records to determine what part of the expenditures is attributable to secular education as opposed to religious activity, in the event a nonpublic school's expenditures per pupil exceed the comparable figures for public schools. Pp. 615–620.[25]

(b) The entanglement in the Pennsylvania program also arises from the restrictions and surveillance necessary to ensure that teachers play a strictly nonideological role and the state supervision of nonpublic school accounting procedures required to establish the cost of secular as distinguished from religious education. In addition, the Pennsylvania statute has the further defect of providing continuing financial aid directly to the church-related schools. Historically governmental control and surveillance measures tend to follow cash grant programs, and here the government's post-audit power to inspect the financial records of church-related schools creates an intimate and continuing relationship between church and state. Pp. 620–622.[26]

The ruling of the court also provided teachers with a guide for their professional actions regarding issues of religion in schools. This became commonly known as the Lemon Test,[27] and as written in the majority decision by Justice Burger, states:

First, the statute must have a secular legislative purpose; second, its principal or primary effect must be one that neither advances nor inhibits religion; finally, the statute must not foster an excessive government entanglement with religion.[28]

To paraphrase, for teachers it reads as follows:

1. Religion in schools must only be for secular educational purposes.
2. Religion in schools should not advance or inhibit religion.
3. No excessive entanglement with religion should exist in the activities of a school.

So, can students sing *Rudolph the Red Nosed Reindeer* in schools? Does it have a secular purpose? Yes, the Christmas holiday is the only national holiday that coincides with a religious holiday and thus is both secular and religious. Does it promote or inhibit religion? No, unless a religion exists regarding snowmen. Does it lead to excessive entanglement of religion and schools? No, it has no church affiliation. In contrast, the song *Away in a Manger* violates all three prongs of the Lemon Test.

What about Christian student groups in schools? The key is who initiates and who advises the group. If the school permits students to form groups around similar interests, prohibiting the

---

25   Ibid.
26   Ibid.
27   Earley v. DiCenso and Robinson v. Di Censo, We the People, Religious Freedom Page, retrieved July 28, 2011, from http://religiousfreedom.lib.virginia.edu/court/lemo_v_kurt.html
28   Ibid.

formation of a Christian group would be a violation of the second prong of the Lemon Test in that it would inhibit religion. If teachers were to decide that the school should have a Christian student group, that too would violate the second prong of the Lemon Test, because it would be the school promoting religion. If students organize the group, can a teacher serve as the adviser? Yes, but only in a limited capacity. Leading the group in prayer, organizing events, doing anything proactive would be viewed as promoting religion. Thus, the adviser teacher's role would be limited to advising the group regarding school policies or possibly unlocking a door for the group's meeting.

FREEDOM OF SPEECH AND SCHOOLS

In December 1965, the Tinker children, John and Mary Beth, wore black armbands to their school in Des Moines, Iowa, in protest of the Vietnam War.[29] They were sent home from school and told not to return wearing the armbands. The Tinker family sued the school district, and the case traveled through the courts until finding itself before the U.S. Supreme Court. The court found in favor of the children. Justice Fortas, writing for the majority, stated, "It can hardly be argued that either students or teachers shed their constitutional rights to freedom of speech or expression at the schoolhouse gate."[30] In doing so, the Supreme Court extended to teachers and students freedom of speech in schools.

In May of 1983, Robert Reynolds, the principal of Hazelwood School District in St. Louis County, Missouri, rejected two stories students wrote for the school newspaper—one regarding teenage pregnancy and the other about divorced parents.[31] The students involved in writing these pieces sued the school. The case made its way to the U.S. Supreme Court, and the Court found in favor of the school district. However, in doing so, they also clarified further freedom of speech in schools. Writing for the majority, Justice White stated, "We hold that educators do not offend the First Amendment by exercising editorial control over the style and content of student speech in school-sponsored expressive activities so long as their actions are reasonably related to legitimate pedagogical concerns."[32] In other words, schools may limit freedom of speech for educational purposes.

On April 26, 1983, Matthew Fraser delivered a speech in a school assembly regarding student elections and "referred to his candidate in terms of an elaborate, graphic, and explicit sexual

---

29　Thomas L. Tedford and Dale A. Herbeck, *Freedom of Speech in the United States*, 6th ed. State College, PA: Strata Publishing, Inc., 2009, retrieved July 28, 2011, from http://www.bc.edu/bc_org/avp/cas/comm/free_speech/tinker.html

30　Ibid.

31　Thomas L. Tedford and Dale A. Herbeck, *Freedom of Speech in the United States,* 6th ed. State College, PA: Strata Publishing, Inc., 2009, retrieved July 28, 2011, from http://www.bc.edu/bc_org/avp/cas/comm/free_speech/hazelwood.html

32　Ibid.

metaphor."[33] For doing so, he was given a three-day suspension. He sued his school district, Bethel High School in Pierce County, Washington, and the case made it way to the U.S. Supreme Court. The Court found in favor of the school district. Writing for the majority, Justice Burger stated:

> Surely it is a highly appropriate function of public school education to prohibit the use of vulgar and offensive terms in public discourse. Indeed, the "fundamental values necessary to the maintenance of a democratic political system" disfavor the use of terms of debate highly offensive or highly threatening to others. Nothing in the Constitution prohibits the states from insisting that certain modes of expression are inappropriate and subject to sanctions. The inculcation of these values is truly the "work of the schools." The determination of what manner of speech in the classroom or in school assembly is inappropriate properly rests with the school board ... Accordingly, it was perfectly appropriate for the school to disassociate itself to make the point to the pupils that vulgar speech and lewd conduct is wholly inconsistent with the "fundamental values" of public school education.[34]

Thus, vulgar and lewd speech in schools, which conflicts with the "fundamental values" of public schooling, is not protected. It is up to the discretion of school officials to determine what is vulgar and lewd, the "fundamental values of the school," and what violates those values. Of interest, in both the Bethel and Hazelwood decisions, the justices mentioned the role of schools in establishing values for children. In the Hazelwood decision, the phrase "high standards" was part of the wording in the majority decision; in the Bethel decision, the phrase "schools must teach by example the shared values of a civilized social order," was included in the majority decision.[35] These statements are curious in a democratic society that often disagrees on common values.

Even more perplexing is the decision in the *Mayer v. Monroe County School Corporation* case.[36] Deborah Mayer was a first-year teacher who chose to use *TIME for Kids* in a current events discussion of the impending war in Iraq. The article mentioned a peace march against the war in Washington, D.C. When asked by her students if she had ever participated in a protest, Mayer replied that she drove past a demonstration in which one of the signs stated, "Honk for Peace." She told her class that she did honk her horn and that she thought peaceful solutions should be sought before going to war. She also gave the example of conflict resolution programs that they used in the school to avoid fights on the playground. Parents complained about Mayer's mention of peace in the classroom, and the principal of the school notified Mayer that she was not

---

33   Douglas O. Linder, "Exploring Constitutional Law." Cornell University Law School, Legal Information Institute, retrieved July 28, 2011, from http://law2.umkc.edu/faculty/projects/ftrials/firstamendment/bethel.html
34   Ibid.
35   Ibid.
36   Mark Walsh, "Teacher's Free Speech Case Denied," Edweek, retrieved July 31, 2011, from http://www.edweek.org/tm/news/profession/2007/10/05/ew_freespeech_web.h19.html

to discuss peace in her classroom. He also cancelled the traditional Peace Month at the school. At the end of that school year, Mayer's contract was not renewed.[37]

Mayer sued the school district, and the case made its way to the Seventh District Federal Court, which ruled in favor of the school district. Writing for the majority, Chief Judge Eastbrook stated:

> Mayer was told that she could teach the controversy about policy toward Iraq, drawing out arguments from all perspectives, as long as she kept her opinions to herself. The Constitution does not entitle teachers to present personal views to captive audiences against the instructions of elected officials … This is so in part because the school system does not "regulate" teachers' speech as much as it hires that speech. Expression is a teacher's stock in trade, the commodity she sells to her employer in exchange for a salary … Children who attend school because they must ought not be subject to teachers' idiosyncratic perspectives. Majority rule about what subjects and viewpoints will be expressed in the classroom has the potential to turn into indoctrination; elected school boards are tempted to support majority positions about religious or patriotic subjects especially. But if indoctrination is likely, the power should be reposed … in someone the people can vote out of office, rather than tenured teachers. At least the board's views can be debated openly, and the people may choose to elect persons committed to neutrality on contentious issues. That is the path Monroe County has chosen; Mayer was told that she could teach the controversy about policy toward Iraq, drawing out arguments from all perspectives, as long as she kept her opinions to herself. The Constitution does not entitle teachers to present personal views to captive audiences against the instructions of elected officials.[38]

The Seventh Circuit Court in effect declared that teachers, who are hired for their professional knowledge and skills, do not have freedom of speech in classrooms. Instead, elected officials, who may or may not have classroom experience, should and may regulate the speech of teachers for the simple fact that they can be voted out of office. Mayer appealed this decision to the U.S. Supreme Court, which refused to hear the case; in effect affirming the decision of the lower court.

How is it possible that, on one hand, educators are expected to regulate the speech of students by commonly understood shared national values, but on the other hand, cannot be trusted with freedom of speech in the classroom? Both seemingly contradictory positions are supported by U.S. Supreme Court decisions, or lack thereof. The explanation for this is that, although Supreme Court justices have lifelong appointments, they do eventually leave office. Each retirement from the Court has the potential to change the ideological position of the Court. Though Court decisions are based on precedents (previous courts' decisions) and the law (U.S. Constitution and

---

37   Ibid.
38   Whitted, Cleary, and Takiff, LLC, 2008, retrieved July 31, 2011. from http://www.wct-law.com/CM/Custom/ Mayer%20v%20Monroe%20County%20Community%20School%20Corporation.pdf

federal acts), justices, like everyone else, are human, and therefore biased. They too view facts through the lenses of their ideological perspectives.

EQUALITY OF ACCESS

Laws that fall under the category of equality of access determine who may enter a school and to what degree they can actively participate in all school functions. The two laws that exemplify this concept are *Brown v. Board of Education* and *Lau v. Nichols*.

Brown v. Board of Education of Topeka, Kansas, was actually a combination of cases from Kansas, South Carolina, Virginia, and Delaware.[39] At issue was whether or not requiring students to attend separate schools based on race was a violation of "equal protection under the law" portion of the Fourteenth Amendment. Chief Justice Warren wrote the unanimous ruling of the Court:

> We conclude that in the field of public education the doctrine of "separate but equal" has no place. Separate educational facilities are inherently unequal. Therefore, we hold that the plaintiffs and others similarly situated for whom the actions have been brought are, by reason of the segregation complained of, deprived of the equal protection of the laws guaranteed by the Fourteenth Amendment.[40]

The *Brown* decision was truly monumental; however, the aftermath is a lesson in how state and local governments, school districts, and even later, U.S. Supreme Court bodies work toward avoiding or twisting laws to which they disagree. Following the *Brown* decision, many Southern states' legislatures imposed laws that penalized anyone involved in the desegregation of schools.[41] In some communities, schools were closed to avoid desegregation and in other communities, parents of white children were given vouchers to send their children to private schools.[42] States and local communities were able to impede the ruling of *Brown v. Board* because of wording in the second case, *Brown v. Board II*, which stated that schools must segregate with "all deliberate speed."[43]

39   FindLaw, Brown v. Board of Education, 347 U.S. 483(1954), retrieved July 31, 2011, from http://caselaw.lp.findlaw.com/scripts/getcase.pl?court=us&vol=347&invol=483
40   Ibid.
41   Timeline of Events Leading to Brown v. Board of Education Decision, 1954, retrieved July 31, 2011, from http://www.archives.gov/education/lessons/brown-v-board/timeline.html
42   Ibid.
43   Ibid.

Much of the anger regarding the *Brown* decision came to a head in Little Rock Arkansas, when nine black students attempted to enroll in the local high school. The following photo exemplifies the bravery of these students, who became known as the Little Rock Nine.[44]

45

In the picture, notice the soldier in the upper-left-hand corner. He was not there to protect this child as she attempted to get to the school. Rather, he was there to keep her out of the school. The *Brown* decision was in 1955, but the school board of Little Rock, Arkansas, decided to initiate a gradual implementation. In 1957 they started by permitting black students to enroll in the high school. Upon hearing of this decision, white citizens formed the Capital Citizens Council and the Mothers' League of Central High School.[46] In August 1957, the Mothers' League attempted to get an injunction in opposition to desegregation "on the grounds that integration could lead to violence."[47] On September 4, 1957, Governor Orval Faubus ordered the National Guard to surround the school to prevent the black students from entering.[48]

The photo above is of Elizabeth Eckford, one of the Little Rock Nine. The night before the students were to first attend the high school, the local NAACP became aware of death threats against the students, as well as the planned protest. As a result, they called each of the students to notify them to meet at the house of Daisy Bates, the president of the local branch of the NAACP.[49] Unfortunately, Eckford's family could not afford a telephone, so Elizabeth did not receive the notification. The next day she faced the mob alone; when she came to the sidewalk

---

44   History of Little Rock Schools Desegregation, retrieved July 31, 2011, from http://www.centralhigh57.org/1957-58.htm

45   "Troops Block Negro Students at School," Library of Congress, retrieved July 31, 2011, from http://www.loc.gov/pictures/item/00649675/

46   History of Little Rock Schools Desegregation, retrieved July 31, 2011, from http://www.centralhigh57.org/1957-58.htm

47   Ibid.

48   Little Rock Central National Historic Site, History of Little Rock Schools Desegregation, retrieved July 31, 2011, from http://www.centralhigh57.org/1957-58.htm http://www.nps.gov/nr/travel/civilrights/ar1.htm

49   Daisy Bates, *The Long Shadow of Little Rock*. New York: D. McKay, 1962.

leading to the school, a National Guardsman prevented her from passing. Eventually, she found a bus bench and sat down because fear overcame her ability to walk. According to Bates, if not for a *New York Times* reporter who sat next to her and put her arm around Eckford, Elizabeth would have likely been lynched.[50]

The result of Eckford's bravery, as well as many others, is sadly almost nonexistent today. Whites continue, for the most part, to go to school with other white children; ethnic minority children continue to go to school with other ethnic minority children.[51] Many reasons exist for the resegregation of our schools; however, recent court decisions suggest that there has been a reversal of beliefs regarding desegregation. Whereas prior to *Brown v. Board*, school districts had policies to separate children by race; now it is the actions of the courts themselves that lead to separation of the races.

Beginning in the 1980s[52], "courts turned against desegregation plans—denying new petitions to desegregate schools, ending previous court imposed plans and even striking down voluntary plans created by local school districts."[53] In *Board of Education of Oklahoma City v. Dowell*, the Supreme Court ruled that "federal supervision of local school systems always having been intended as a temporary measure to remedy past discrimination."[54] In addition, " to allow the injunction to be dissolved, the District Court, on remand, should address itself to whether the Board had complied in good faith with the desegregation decree since it was entered, and whether, in light of every facet of school operations, the vestiges of past de jure segregation had been eliminated to the extent practicable."[55] In other words, as long as a school in the past demonstrated an effort to desegregate the school, they are no longer obligated to do so.

Writing for the majority in *Missouri v. Jenkins*, , Chief Justice Rehnquist wrote:

> This Court should never approve a State's efforts to deny students, because of their race, an equal opportunity for an education. But the federal courts also should avoid using racial equality as a pretext for solving social problems that do not violate the Constitution … We must forever put aside the [MISSOURI v. JENKINS, ___ U.S. ___ (1995) , 27] notion that simply because a school district today is black, it must be educationally inferior.[56]

---

50   Ibid.

51   Amanda Paulson, "Resegregation of Schools Deepening," *Christian Science Monitor*, retrieved July 31, 2011, from http://www.csmonitor.com/USA/Society/2008/0125/p01s01-ussc.html

52   Erwin Chemerinsky, "The Segregation and Resegregation of American Public Education: The Court's Role," retrieved July 31, 2011, from http://scholarship.law.duke.edu/cgi/viewcontent.cgi?article=1712&context=faculty_scholarship&sei-redir=1#search=%22resegregation%20court%22

53   Gary Orfile and Chungmei Lee, "Brown at 50: King's Dream or Plessy's Nightmare?" Civil Rights Project at Hartville University, retrieved July 31, 2011, from http://www.civilrights.org/education/resegregation/

54   FindLaw, Board of Ed. of Oklahoma City v. Dowell, 498 U.S. 237 (1991), retrieved July 31, 2011, v. Di Censohe cite.from here on out. from http://caselaw.lp.findlaw.com/scripts/getcase.pl?court=us&vol=498&invol=237,

55   Ibid.

56   FindLaw, Missouri v. Jenkins, 495, U.S. 33, 1990, retrieved July 31, 2011, from http://www.law.cornell.edu/supct/html/historics/USSC_CR_0495_0033_ZS.html

This last statement completely reversed *Brown v. Board*, which concluded that separate schools for blacks and whites was inherently unequal. Rehnquist continued:

> Even if segregation were present, we must remember that a deserving end does not justify all possible means. The desire to reform a school district, or any other institution, cannot so captivate the Judiciary that it forgets its constitutionally mandated role. Usurpation of the traditionally local control over education not only takes the judiciary beyond its proper sphere, it also deprives the States and their elected officials of their constitutional powers. At some point, we must recognize that the judiciary is not omniscient, and that all problems do not require a remedy of constitutional proportions.[57]

Thus, local control of schools trumps court decisions in that it deprives elected officials of their power. The concepts of "court restraint" and "local control" are somewhat arbitrarily applied to schooling in the United States. But in regard to desegregation of schools, the U.S. Supreme Court concluded that local control of schools and court restraint are more important than desegregation. Since this ruling, local courts, as well as school districts, have dismantled desegregation policies that led to a resegregation of schools.[58]

Erwin Chemerinsky, an expert in constitutional law and civil rights, writes[59]

> People can devise rationalizations to make this desegregation failure seem acceptable: that courts could not really succeed; that desegregation does not matter; that parents of minority students do not really care about desegregation. But none of these rationalizations are true. Brown v. Board of Education stated the truth: separate schools can never be equal. Tragically today America has schools that are increasingly separate and unequal.[60]

In a complete reversal of the spirit of the *Brown v. Board* decision, the U.S. Supreme Court denied Seattle schools' attempts for racial balance in the schools because "the Seattle schools were never segregated by law nor subject to court-ordered desegregation."[61] Writing for the majority ruling, Chief Justice Roberts wrote, "The school districts have not carried their heavy burden of showing that the interest they seek to achieve justifies the extreme means they have chosen—discriminating among individual students based on race by relying upon racial classifications in making school assignments."[62] Furthermore, according to Chief Justice Roberts:

---

57   Ibid.
58   Chemerinsky, ibid.
59   Faculty pages, School of Law, University of California at Irvine, retrieved July 31, 2011, from http://www.law.uci.edu/faculty/page1_e_chemerinsky.html
60   Chemerinsky, i p. 1622.
61   Cornell University Legal Information Institute, Parent Involved in Community Schools v. Seattle School District No. 1 et al., retrieved July 31, 2011, from http://www.law.cornell.edu/supct/html/05-908.ZS.html
62   Ibid.

The Court need not resolve the parties' dispute over whether racial diversity in schools has a marked impact on test scores and other objective yardsticks or achieves intangible socialization benefits because it is clear that the racial classifications at issue are not narrowly tailored to the asserted goal. In design and operation, the plans are directed only to racial balance, an objective this Court has repeatedly condemned as illegitimate. They are tied to each district's specific racial demographics, rather than to any pedagogic concept of the level of diversity needed to obtain the asserted educational benefits.[63]

Justice Roberts even used the *Brown* decision to justify the court's reversal of that decision:

In *Brown* v. *Board of Education*, 347 U. S. 483 , the Court held that segregation deprived black children of equal educational opportunities regardless of whether school facilities and other tangible factors were equal, because the classification and separation themselves denoted inferiority. *Id.,* at 493–494. It was not the inequality of the facilities but the fact of legally separating children based on race on which the Court relied to find a constitutional violation in that case. *Id.,* at 494. The districts here invoke the ultimate goal of those who filed *Brown* and subsequent cases to support their argument, but the argument of the plaintiff in *Brown* was that the Equal Protection Clause "prevents states from according differential treatment to American children on the basis of their color or race," and that view prevailed—this Court ruled in its remedial opinion that *Brown* required school districts "to achieve a system of determining admission to the public schools *on a nonracial basis.*" *Brown* v. *Board of Education*, 349 U. S. 294 (emphasis added). Pp. 28–41.[64]

In other words, 52 years after the *Brown v. Board* decision, the U.S. Supreme Court ruled that efforts by a school to achieve racial balance in its school buildings was unconstitutional, if they used race as a means of assigning children to various school buildings. Not only did they declare that doing so was unconstitutional, they added that doing so was a violation of the case law with the intent to end segregation in schools.

Another struggle for ethnic equality in schools has involved the issue of bilingual education. The first prohibition of a language other than English began in 1879 with the enforcement of Americanization policies against Native American children, who were prohibited from speaking their language or practicing their culture and religion.[65] In contrast, in 1839 Ohio passed the first bilingual education act, allowing parents of German descent to request German-English

---

63 Ibid.
64 Ibid.
65 Public Broadcast Services, School: The Story of American Schools, retrieved July 31, 2011, from http://www.pbs. org/kcet/publicschool/roots_in_history/bilingual_timeline2.html

instruction.[66] By 1900, 600,000 elementary students were receiving part of their instruction in German.[67] Thus, it could be easily argued that the bilingual education issue was directly tied to ethnicity.

The connection between speaking English and nationalism was seen in the acceptance of states to this nation. Only those with a sufficient population of English-speaking settlers were granted statehood, which is why California was granted statehood in 1850, but New Mexico and Arizona were not granted statehood until 1912.[68] The Treaty of Guadalupe Hidalgo, following the Spanish American War, gave citizenship to those Mexicans living in the region Mexico handed over to the United States as part of the peace treaty, but the right of statehood was delayed until a significant portion of those citizens spoke English.[69] In 1910 the U.S. Congress passed an act to "enable" the two territories to become states; one of the two prongs of this act was that English only would be taught in schools.[70]

As discussed in Chapter One, following World War I, a fear of anything foreign spread across the United States. A key target of that fear was any language other than English. As a result, states enacted laws, which required English-only instruction and targeted elementary schools in particular, which were not to teach foreign languages.[71] The traces of these policies continue in schools today, though the laws have been revoked for the most part. Teaching foreign languages often begins in the middle school or high school level.

In 1971, 16 years after the passage of *Brown v. Board*, the San Francisco school system integrated.[72] For students of Chinese descent, this was particularly significant, because they were previously banned from the public school system. At this time the California Education Code stated "English shall be the basic language of instruction in all schools,"[73] which helped schools determine when and if bilingual instruction was permitted.[74]

> That section permits a school district to determine "when and under what circumstances instruction may be given bilingually." That section also states as "the policy of the state" to insure "the mastery of English by all pupils in the schools." And bilingual instruction

---

66 Ibid.

67 Ibid.

68 David Nieto, "History of Bilingual Education in the United States," Perspective on Urban Education, University of Pennsylvania, Graduate School of Education, 2009, retrieved July 31, 2011, from http://www.urbanedjournal.org/Vol.%206%20Immigration%20Issues%20in%20Urban%20Schools/61-72--Nieto.pdf and "Language Rights and New Mexico Statehood," U.S Commission on Human Rights, retrieved July 31, 2011, from http://www.ped.state.nm.us/BilingualMulticultural/dl09/Language%20Rights%20and%20New%20Mexico%20Statehood.pdf

69 Ibid.

70 Ibid.

71 History of Bilingual Education, Rethinking Schools, retrieved July 31, 2011, from http://www.rethinkingschools.org/restrict.asp?path=archive/12_03/langhst.shtml

72 FindLaw, Lau v. Nichols, 414, U.S. 563 (1974), retrieved July 31, 2011, from http://caselaw.lp.findlaw.com/scripts/getcase.pl?court=us&vol=414&invol=563

73 Ibid.

74 Ibid.

is authorized "to the extent that it does not interfere with the systematic, sequential, and regular instruction of all pupils in the English language."[75]

In the San Francisco school system, of the 2,856 students who spoke Chinese, 1,800 were not given supplemental instruction in English.[76]

A group of Chinese parents in the San Francisco school district sued the school under the Fourteenth Amendment, seeking relief. The parents did not specify how they wanted assistance, only that they wanted some form of assistance for their children. The U.S. Supreme Court ruled that the San Francisco school system was in violation of the Civil Rights Act of 1968.[77] Writing for the majority, Justice Douglas stated:

> Under these state-imposed standards there is no equality of treatment merely by providing students with the same facilities, textbooks, teachers, and curriculum; for students who do not understand English are effectively foreclosed from any meaningful education.
>
> Basic English skills are at the very core of what these public schools teach. Imposition of a requirement that, before a child can effectively participate in the educational program, he must already have acquired those basic skills is to make a mockery of public education. We know that those who do not understand English are certain to find their classroom experiences wholly incomprehensible and in no way meaningful.[78]

Citing regulations established by the Department of Health, Education and Welfare, Justice Douglas added:

> "[s]chool systems are responsible for assuring that students of a particular race, color, or national origin are not denied the [414 U.S. 563, 567] opportunity to obtain the education generally obtained by other students in the system." ... "to rectify the language deficiency in order to open" the instruction to students who had "linguistic deficiencies ..."[79]

Justice Douglas continued:

> It seems obvious that the Chinese-speaking minority receive fewer benefits than the English-speaking majority from respondents' school system which denies them a

---

75 Ibid.
76 Ibid.
77 Ibid.
78 Ibid.
79 Ibid.

meaningful opportunity to participate in the educational program—all earmarks of the discrimination banned by the regulations.[80]

Though the *Lau* decision clearly found in favor of the parents and against the school, it did not define any specific remedies. That same year, 1974, another case, *Castaneda v. Pickard*,[81] made its way to the Fifth Circuit Court, which further defined how the requirement of bilingual education should be implemented. In this case, Mexican American parents claimed that the Texas Independent School District was ability-grouping children based on race and ethnicity, failing to promote teachers based on race and ethnicity, and were inadequately providing bilingual education services. The ruling of the Fifth Circuit Court resulted in three bilingual education requirements:

> … when implementing programs to help language minority students overcome language barriers: The program (1) must be based on sound educational theory, (2) must have sufficient resources and personnel, and (3) must prove to be effective in teaching students English …[82]

Support for bilingual education that leads to the acquisition of English speaking, reading, and writing skills has been consistently supported by the courts since the *Lau v. Nichols* decisions. The same is not true, however, in regard to state and federal policies. As will be discussed in Chapter Five, the report "A Nation at Risk" played a key role in re-emphasizing English-only instruction in our schools, beginning with the Reagan administration. The English-only movement has found its way to state-level government mandates.

For both the issue of desegregation and the issue of bilingual education geared toward the acquisition of the English language, a central concern for schools is funding. With desegregation, the court not only alleviated this burden on school budgets, but also restricted any activities that could lead to desegregation. No such relief has occurred regarding bilingual education. What explains this contradiction? According to Chemerinsky, "The answer is obvious: its decisions result from a conservative ideology of the majority of Justices who sat on the cases when the cases were heard."[83]

---

80 Ibid.
81 Ken Romeo, Stanford University, United States Court of Appeals, Fifth Circuit. Unit A., 648 F. 2d 989, 1981 U.S. App. Lexis 12063, June 23, 1981, retrieved July 31, 2011, from http://www.stanford.edu/~kenro/LAU/IAPolicy/IA1bCastanedaFullText.htm
82 Nieto, p. 64.
83 Chemerinsky, p. 1620.

CONCLUSIONS

Law, much like history, is perceived via one's worldview. Such is true for the teacher who reads a law, as well as justices who sit on the U.S. Supreme Court. However, whereas justices can directly change the law, teachers have no such power. Teachers have power politically, but it is in their collective voices (a point which will be discussed further in later chapters). Teachers, especially given the *Mayer* decision, have much less individual power. Thus, it is important for teachers to know the laws which govern schooling in their state and nationally.

In this chapter, I did not discuss every case law involving schools. I was selective in choosing those I viewed as most important; that selection was governed by my biases. Being aware of my biases is one of the primary reasons that I included so many quotes in this chapter, specifically quotes taken directly from court rulings. However, I was, of course, selective in which quotes I chose to include, and that too was governed by my biases. As a result, I caution you to remember that this chapter is simply an introduction to educational case law, and preservice teachers should not stop their reading of educational laws with this or the next chapter.

Furthermore, what is legal today may very well be illegal five, ten, or 50 years from now. The story of the *Brown v. Board* decision and its aftermath exemplifies the fluidity of laws, as well as how they can be twisted to mean the complete opposite of what was intended. The Founding Fathers' thoughts regarding the U.S. Constitution are often cited by politicians and pundits to justify their ideological interpretation of a current issue. Either intentionally or via pure ignorance, references to what the Founding Fathers intended is often quite different than what history or laws tells us. Thus, it is critical that, as citizens of this nation, we are vigilant regarding what is professed by politicians and pundits alike, and that instead, we educate ourselves on these topics. For teachers this is particularly true; their students—as well as their employment—depend on it.

DISCUSSION QUESTIONS

1. As an undergraduate student I tended to skip all indented paragraphs when reading. Not until graduate school did I realize the importance of indented paragraphs. How does this chapter read without the indented paragraphs verses how it reads with them? Do the indented paragraphs strengthen the chapter or weaken it? How so?

2. In the conclusion, I stated that the quotes I chose to use from actual court cases were because of my acknowledgement of my own biases. They also serve the purpose of giving credibility to what I wrote. Nonetheless, they do not negate my biases. What are my biases when it comes to educational laws? If you and your class would like to check if you are correct regarding my bias, please feel free to contact me at dlclark@kent.edu. Please put "student from (your college)" or I might accidently delete your e-mail as spam.

3. What about the evidence I used to support my bias? Did my sources strengthen my arguments? Should I have used other sources? For example, with the discussion of the *Brown*

decision, I relied on the writings of a constitutional and civil rights expert, much more so than any other section. Should I have included the writings of legal experts more?

4. Using the Lemon Test, discuss if each of the following school activities are constitutional:
    a. Prayers at sporting events
    b. Prayers at graduation ceremonies
    c. See You at the Pole activities
    d. Restricting gay or lesbian couples at school dances
    e. Christmas concerts
    f. Classroom Christmas parties
    g. The Pledge of Allegiance
    h. Moments of silence in schools

5. How might teachers balance the claim by the *Bethel* decision that they must teach the values of our nation with the *Mayer* decision, in which teachers must not give their opinion regarding values? For example, if a school district has a chapter of the KKK, and a student asks a teacher his or her opinion of that organization, how might the teacher explain the values of our nation regarding the topic of diversity without discussing his or her opinion? Should he or she maintain a neutral stance, and in doing so give credence to the values of the KKK and other hate groups? Is doing so a promotion of our democratic values, or is it hate speech?

6. Should schools and our nation take another attempt at desegregation? What would be required this time, to accomplish that goal?

ACTIVITIES

1. Using the online resources in the following section, identify what you believe are the five most important events or educational case laws in the history of education in the United States. At least three items on your list should be items I did not discuss. What does your choice say regarding your bias of the educational laws?

2. In 1995 U.S. secretary of education Riley brought together many organizations interested in the topic of religion in schools to write a joint statement regarding their interpretation of case laws regarding religion in schools. That document can be located by clicking on the first link below under "Online Resources." Return to the answers you gave for discussion question 4 and compare and contrast your answers to that of the document published by the U.S. Department of Education.

ONLINE RESOURCES

1. Religion In The Public Schools: A Joint Statement of Current Law   http://www.aclu.org/religion-belief/joint-statement-current-law-religion-public-schools

2. <u>Findlaw: Education Law Center</u>   http://education.findlaw.com/
3. <u>Legal Information Institute of Cornell University Law School</u>   http://topics.law.cornell.edu/wex/
4. <u>United States Courts</u>   http://www.uscourts.gov/Home.aspx
5. <u>United States Constitution, Bill of Rights</u>   http://topics.law.cornell.edu/constitution/billofrights

Chapter Four
Educational Law Scholarship

Why Do I Need to Know This?

Legal proceedings and scholarship depend on precedents, educational scholarship, but not necessarily practice—it depends on the literature. In other words, in court cases and legal proceedings, lawyers cite previous case law, which is the scholarship of their profession. Teachers do not do the same with their pedagogy. This disconnect is one of the reasons why teachers are not viewed as professionals—because the scholarship and practice of a professional is directly connected. If teachers are to ever be respected as professionals, they must begin tying their practice to scholarship. The arena of educational law is one place to start such a habit.

As indicated in the previous chapter, reading one chapter in a textbook is not where teachers should stop in understanding educational law. Multiple sources exist in explaining educational law. *Edweek*,[1] an online and hardcopy newspaper that focuses on issues in education, is an excellent source for keeping up to date on what is new in educational law. *NEA Today*[2] and *American Teacher*,[3] publications of the two largest teachers' unions, are a means for learning about new topics directly tied to teachers' rights. Special interest groups such as Stop Bullying Now![4] can keep one abreast of current trends regarding specific issues in education.

With union and special interest group publications, it is easy to identify bias. A teachers' union publication is not going to publish an anti-union article; a special interest group that wants to end bullying is not going to publish an article that defends teachers who ignore bullying behavior. With a publication such as *Edweek*, identifying the bias of an article or publication is much more difficult. The same is true with scholarship articles. This chapter provides examples of scholarly articles on educational law. Among the online resources, at the end of this chapter, are links to other publications such as *Edweek*.

---

1   Retrieved July 31, 2011, from http://www.edweek.org/ew/index.html
2   Retrieved July 31, 2011, from http://www.nea.org/home/1814.htm
3   Retrieved July 31, 2011, from http://www.aft.org/newspubs/periodicals/ae/issues.cfm
4   Retrieved July 31, 2011, from http://www.stopbullyingnow.com/

A tendency exists to say, "Well, that's the law." Hopefully, reading the previous chapter helped you move away from that tendency. The law is the law, but what is legal today may be illegal tomorrow, and what is illegal now may become legal. The job of a teacher as far as educational law is to keep abreast of what is going on in the courts regarding educational law, developing an understanding of legal trends, such as the biases associated with rulings, as well as having a clear picture of the biases of the publication they utilize to keep abreast of educational laws.

WHAT IS EDUCATIONAL LAW SCHOLARSHIP?

Scholarship in educational law originates from two primary sources: educators and lawyers. The generic question guiding educators' scholarship is, "What does this (a new law) mean for educators?" The generic question guiding lawyers' scholarship is, "What does this mean for the legal system?" In law, the concept of *precedent* plays a key role in guiding judicial decisions. A motion in court is when a lawyer asks the judge of a trial to make a legal decision regarding a proceeding. Is a lawyer permitted to introduce a specific type of evidence in court? Is a specific individual permitted to testify in court? When a person testifies, what questions are permitted? A motion cannot be won in court without citing previous court cases. The citing of a previous court case is what is meant by *precedent*.

 In education, the issue is not precedent, it is literature. Not literature like Shakespeare, rather theories and research on the topic of the article. What have other scholars said about a given topic? Who were the scholars who wrote on the topic? Were they well-known or well-respected scholars, or someone no one has heard of previously? What has other research indicated about a specific topic? Was the research quantitative (using the scientific method) or qualitative (other research methods, such as ethnography, used by anthropologists to study a culture)? Thus, a common piece in all educational scholarship is the literature review which identifies where the current article belongs in the tradition of scholarship on a particular topic.

 The generic principles of law and educational scholarship do not eliminate bias. The bias of education and legal scholars can often be found in their specialization area. In Chapter Three, I cited a lawyer by the name of Chemerinsky who specializes in civil rights and constitutional law. Thus, he views all legal proceedings through the lens of civil rights, which strongly suggests equal rights based on demographics (race, gender, social class, etc.) are tied to his bias. In the articles that follow, first try to identify whether or not the article is written by a lawyer or an educator. Then try to identify the authors' biases. Then evaluate the evidence presented by each author and contrast that to the evidence I provided in Chapter Two. Which author provides the best argument? Which author uses the strongest evidence?

SELECTED READINGS

Chalk Talk—Religion in the Valedictory
by Caleb McCain

I chose the following article because it continues the debate of religion in schools, begun in Chapter Three. Valedictory speeches are a common tradition in high school graduations. Valedictory speeches also must be approved by school administrators prior to the actual speech. If an administrator previews a valedictory speech that includes religious references, must the administrator require deletion of the religious reference? Would doing so violate the second prong of the Lemon Test, which prohibits schools from inhibiting religious expression? Would not requiring deletion also violate the second prong of the Lemon Test, which prohibits promoting religion?

McCain addresses the Lemon v. Kurtzman *decision, as well as other case law decisions not discussed in Chapter Three. How do these additional cases change the discussion of religion in schools? Do these additional cases negate the power of the Lemon Test for the courts? Is the same true for the use of the Lemon Test for school administrators? How does an educator determine when an action involving religion and schools inhibits or promotes religion? Valedictory speeches are an excellent venue for identifying this fine line.*

I. INTRODUCTION

Every year at graduation time, school administrators struggle to balance the Establishment Clause with their students' freedom of speech. This struggle centers on students' religious speech before the captive audience of the graduating class. Because religion is a preeminent aspect of American life, it is naturally present at important moments like graduation.

But how should a public school administrator handle valedictories and analogous situations? She knows that, constitutionally, the government may not "establish" a state religion. However, she does not want to violate students' free speech or render students' expressions meaningless by excessive editing or censorship. This note will endeavor to help the public school administrator better understand the law in this area.

To begin, it is easy to get lost when delving into the minutiae of Supreme Court opinions. However, here, the Supreme Court cases on the subject provide a good framework. When one steps back and looks at the cases with a broad view, a theme unfolds that will help our administrator frame good policies. Unfortunately, the circuits are divided on this issue. Some are mindful of the aforementioned theme. Other circuits, however, are caught up in the minutiae and have not grasped it. A look at two cases, one from the Ninth Circuit and one from the Eleventh Circuit, will help clarify the theme. Finally, the pending case of Ms. Brittany McComb provides good facts whereby the Supreme Court may finally establish clarity in this area of the law.

II. AFFIRMATIVE PROMOTION IS PROHIBITED; PERMISSIBLE ACCOMMODATION IS ALLOWED

A. The Affirmative Promotion

The seminal case regarding the Establishment Clause and public schools is *Lemon v. Kurtzman*. That case established a three-part test for determining whether or not a statute (or in our case, a school policy) violates the Establishment Clause. Under this test, the policy must have a secular purpose. Second, it must not inhibit or further religion. Third, the policy must not foster an excessive entanglement of the school with religion.[5]

Next, *Lee v. Weisman* and *Santa Fe v. Doe* are the most recent court cases in this area of the law. In *Lee*, the Supreme Court considered the question of whether a public school could have a rabbi deliver a prayer at graduation.[6] In *Santa Fe*, the Court considered whether a school policy providing for invocations before football games established a religion.[7] In both cases, the Court found that the schools' actions violated the Establishment Clause.[8]

Moreover, in both cases, the Court focused solely on whether the schools' policies, whereby religion entered the public school arena, had a secular purpose. In both cases, the Court found that the policies were *affirmatively promoting* religion.[9] That is, the *Lee* and *Santa Fe* school policies had religious, not secular, purposes.

Lee presented a clear case. The school scheduled a time in the graduation program for a prayer and asked a religious leader to deliver the prayer. The school in its official capacity purposefully promoted religion and forced a religious activity onto the graduates.[10]

Santa Fe presented more subtle facts, but the affirmative promotion of religion was still present. The Santa Fe School District had a longstanding practice of providing time for a prayer before football games. However, after the *Lee* decision was issued, the Santa Fe School District reacted by redrafting their policies regarding the pre-game prayers. The new policies seemed to formalistically comply with *Lee*, but in reality, the practice of praying before the games could continue unabated.[11]

In the end, three facts combined to doom the Santa Fe School District's policies. First, the district had a long history of promoting prayer before the games. This history caused the Court

---

5   *Lemon v. Kurtzman*, 403 U.S. 602, 91 (1971).
6   *Lee v. Weisman*, 505 U.S. 577, 580 (1992).
7   *Santa Fe v. Doe*, 530 U.S. 290, 301 (2000).
8   *Lee*, 505 U.S. at 599; Santa Fe, 530 U.S. at 317.
9   *Lee*, 505 U.S. at 599 (Blackmun, J., concurring); Santa Fe, 530 U.S. at 313.
10   *Lee*, 505 U.S. at 581–83.
11   *Santa Fe*, 530 U.S. at 315.

to cast a wary eye upon the school's policies subsequent to *Lee*.[12] Second, the new policies used words like "invocation" and "solemnize" as formalistic devices to avoid the word "prayer" while nevertheless intending prayer.[13] Finally, the effect of the new policy was no different than that of former policies which explicitly provided for prayer.[14] Generally, it was obvious that the purpose behind the school board's actions was to provide a vehicle whereby prayers might be delivered; the school board affirmatively promoted religion, and the Court forbade the surreptitious manner in which it was attempted.[15]

B. The Permissible Accommodation

In *Lee*, the Court noted at the beginning of its opinion that it would *not* consider the entire *Lemon* test regarding impermissible accommodations of religion. Indeed, the blatant affirmative promotion in *Lee* obviated the need for a detailed analysis of whether the prayer policy was a permissible accommodation.[16] If one affirmatively promotes an idea, then one goes well beyond merely accommodating that idea. Thus, an accommodation analysis was rendered superfluous.

In *Santa Fe*, the Court followed its reasoning in *Lee*. Again, in *Santa Fe*, the blatant affirmative promotion of religion again obviated the need for an accommodation analysis.[17]

The Court in *Lee* did not address the issue of whether the policy was a constitutional accommodation of religion because the facts were so one-sided; the outright purpose of the policy was to affirmatively promote religion.[18] However, the Court implied that in a case where the facts did not show an outright affirmative promotion, it would perform a complete Lemon analysis of whether the policy would constitute a permissible accommodation of religion.[19]

Two Circuit Opinions after Santa Fe

The Ninth Circuit in *Cole v. Oroville Union High School District* concluded that if a valedictorian makes religious utterances during the valedictory, then those utterances would violate the Establishment Clause.[20] Accordingly, the Ninth Circuit held that the school was correct to edit the students' speeches for religious content and refuse a student's delivery of such a speech.[21] The Ninth Circuit in *Cole* focused particularly on the coercive nature of religious speech before a captive audience, noting that it is not reasonable to give a student a choice between attending and

---

12 *Id.* at 309.
13 *Id.* at 299.
14 *Id.* at 315.
15 *Id.* at 308.
16 *Lee*, 505 U.S. at 586–87.
17 *Santa Fe*, 530 U.S. at 302.
18 *Lee*, 505 U.S. at 586–87.
19 *Lemon v. Kurtzman*, 403 U.S. 602, 91 (1971).
20 *Cole v. Oroville Union High Sch. Dist.*, 228 F.3d 1092, 1103 (9th Cir. 2000).
21 *Id.* at 1105.

not attending graduation.[22] However, *Lee* noted that religion cannot be totally eliminated from graduations.[23] Indeed, it is hard to imagine a more neutral method than the valedictory whereby religion might permeate the graduation ceremony.

The Ninth Circuit in *Cole* stated: "The critical inquiry under *Santa Fe* and *Lee* to determine if religious activity at a major public school event constitutes impermissible coercion to participate is whether 'a reasonable dissenter ... *could* believe that the group exercise signified her own participation or approval of it.'"[24] First, the Ninth Circuit places too much reliance on this coercion standard as it was only a factor or a means of evaluating a set of circumstances.[25] Second, the Ninth Circuit's application of the standard is questionable due to a difficult fact: The purely objective selection criteria of being a valedictorian. The reasonable dissenter does not seem very reasonable. Third, the Ninth Circuit derived little guidance from *Lemon*, which is still the current law.[26] Finally, the Ninth Circuit stated that, because the school district edited speeches, the "reasonable dissenter" would feel like the district had approved the speech.[27] But it is a tautology to require censorship to prevent unconstitutional speech that derives its unconstitutionality from that very censorship.

The Ninth Circuit felt that *Santa Fe* mandated its holding.[28] However, *Cole* was distinguishable from *Santa Fe*. *Santa Fe* was a case where the purpose of the school policy was clearly not secular. In *Cole*, the purpose of the school policy was arguably secular; there is nothing purposely religious about allowing a valedictorian to speak as a reward for her accomplishment. Thus, it behooved the Ninth Circuit in *Cole* to proceed through the rest of the *Lemon* analysis. Under that test, allowing a valedictorian to deliver a speech based on her accomplishment and as an example of educational excellence is a policy with a clearly secular purpose. Also, such a policy clearly neither inhibits nor furthers religion. Finally, under *Lemon*, such a policy does not cause the school to become entangled with religion.

The Eleventh Circuit in *Adler v. Duval County School Board* considered a policy whereby the student body voted whether or not to have a student deliver an opening or closing message at graduation.[29] In reviewing the policy in light of *Santa Fe*, the Eleventh Circuit found that the policy did not affirmatively promote religion.[30] The Eleventh Circuit in *Adler* went on to reiterate that it upheld the constitutionality of the policy on the basis of *Santa Fe, Lee*, and *Lemon*, all of which are the law in Establishment Clause cases regarding schools.

The policy in *Adler* presented the same danger of a student making religious utterances as did the policy in *Cole*. Nevertheless, the Eleventh Circuit felt that the policy did not violate the

---

22 *Id.* at 1104.
23 505 U.S. at 598–99.
24 *Id.* (quoting Lee).
25 *Lee*, 505 U.S. at 593.
26 *Cole*, 228 F.3d at 1104.
27 *Id.* at 1103.
28 *Id.* at 1102.
29 *Adler v. Duval County Sch. Bd.*, 250 F. 3d 1330, 1332 (11th Cir. 2001).
30 *Id.* at 1342.

Establishment Clause. Any religious utterances a student might have made would have been incidental to the policy instead of being an intended result of the purpose of the policy. Furthermore, one could argue that a policy whereby only religious speech is forbidden would violate a student's freedom of speech and expression as well as the Establishment Clause. The policy would violate the second and third prongs of the *Lemon* test; it would inhibit religion, and would foster excessive entanglement with religion by requiring the school to make judgments about what is and what is not permissible religious speech.

III. A New Case

Finally, the pending case of Brittany McComb provides the facts necessary whereby the Court can clarify its theme in the Establishment Clause cases. In this case, we are again presented with a school policy that allows for the school administration to censor valedictories that contain religious material.[31] The difference is that when Ms. McComb delivered her speech, she felt compelled by conscience to deliver the excised portions, and when she began to do so, the plug was pulled on her microphone.[32] The roughshod manner with which Ms. McComb was treated portrays in sharp relief the nature of the civil rights with which we are concerned. The school administration conveyed in a public and embarrassing way that Ms. McComb's opinions were not to be tolerated. No doubt the administrators acted in good faith, fearing an Establishment Clause violation, but they can no more establish a form of anti-religion than they can religion. The Supreme Court in this case can articulate the law using facts that clearly show where the Establishment Clause and free speech intersect.

IV. Conclusion

In summary, the Court stated in *Lee* and *Santa Fe* that schools cannot affirmatively promote religion. But neither opinion held that any religious utterance in front of a captive audience would automatically constitute an Establishment Clause violation. Both *Lee* and *Santa Fe* presented examples of policies with clearly religious rather than secular purposes. However, in a case where the school's policy is not obviously religious, a reviewing court should perform the rest of the *Lemon* analysis. The Eleventh Circuit went through the *Lemon* analysis and came to a sound result in the case of *Adler v. Duval County School District*. Ms. McComb's case should rise in the Ninth Circuit, and if the Ninth Circuit continues to hold that censorship of student religious speech is required, the Supreme Court should take up the case and clarify this area of the law.

---

31   Compl. of Pet. at 5-6, *McComb v. Crehan*, Case 2:06-cv-00852, (D. Nev. 2006) (Filed 07/13/2006).
32   Compl. of Pet. at 12, *McComb v. Crehan*, Case 2:06-cv-00852, (D. Nev. 2006) (Filed 07/13/2006).

When Evolution and Creationism Are on the American Docket, the Verdict Winds Up Far from Unanimous
by Perry A. Zirkel

In the following article, another timely topic regarding religion and schools is examined: Evolution versus creationism. An initial definition of terms is helpful when examining the debate regarding teaching evolution in schools. Evolution is a scientific theory with the premise that humans originated from biological changes in former animals through a process referred to as natural selection. Evolution is a biological term which posits that changes or modifications of descendants (natural selection) led to various species, but all animals come from one common ancestor.[33] Creationism is a religious theory that claims God created humans. When referring to creationism, the common reference is the description of God's creation of man in the first book of the Bible, Genesis. However, this is the creation story of the Judeo-Christian tradition; many other versions of creationism also exist.

Defining intelligent design is much more controversial. According to the National Center for Science Education, "ID and creation science share the belief that the mainstream scientific discipline of evolution is largely incorrect. Both involve an intervening deity, but ID is more vague about what happened and when."[34] According to the Center for Science and Culture, "Intelligent design refers to a scientific research program as well as a community of scientists, philosophers and other scholars who seek evidence of design in nature. The theory of intelligent design holds that certain features of the universe and of living things are best explained by an intelligent cause, not an undirected process such as natural selection."[35]

Understanding these terms is important because the debate is not always between evolution and creationism. In the second page of the following article, Zirkel refers to a case that occurred in Pennsylvania in 2005. Though not named in the article, the case was Kitzmiller v. Dover.[36] At issue was whether or not intelligent design could be taught in a science class. The district court ruled that "ID cannot uncouple from its creationist, and thus religious antecedents."[37]

T he American dilemma over church-state issues and the more specific quandary over the role of evolution in public education are reflected in the crucible of the courts.

33 "An Introduction to Evolution," Evolution 101, retrieved July 31, 2011, from http://evolution.berkeley.edu/evolibrary/article/0_0_0/evo_02

34 "'Intelligent Design' Not Accepted by Most Scientists," National Center for Science Education, retrieved July 31, 2011, from http://ncse.com/creationism/general/intelligent-design-not-accepted-by-most-scientists

35 "Definition of Intelligent Design," Intelligence.org, http://www.intelligentdesign.org/whatisid.php

36 In the United States District Court for the Middle District of Pennsylvania, *Kitzmiller et al. v. Dover Area School District*, Case No. 04cv2688, retrieved July 31, 2011, from http://www.pamd.uscourts.gov/kitzmiller/kitzmiller_342.pdf

37 Ibid.

The story starts with the legal equivalent of the Bible: The Constitution. The first of the constitutional commandments, or the First of the Amendments, is the mandate that the government not establish a national religion and yet not infringe on either the free exercise of religion or freedom of expression. These First Amendment directives—the Establishment Clause, the Free Exercise Clause, and Freedom of Expression—initially applied to the federal government and, after the Fourteenth Amendment, to state governments and, thereby, the public schools.

The subsequent chapters of the story moved from 1) a famous Tennessee trial court that put the general issue on the map; to 2) a pair of successive U.S. Supreme Court decisions specific to the role of evolution in public schools; to 3) the culminating application of these constitutional precedents in a series of recent lower court decisions.

During the 90 or so years from the opening chapter to the latest developments, various other related Supreme Court precedents also marked the transforming application of the three pertinent parts of the Constitution. For example, a long but fluctuating line of Supreme Court decisions continued to redefine the height of the metaphorical "wall of separation" between church and state that some use to symbolize the Establishment Clause.

Since its crystallization in *Lemon v. Kurtzman* (1971), the primary but not exclusive set of legal criteria that the courts have used in Establishment Clause cases has been the "tripartite test," which examines, in flowchart-like fashion:

1. Whether the purpose of the challenged governmental policy or practice is secular
2. If so, whether its primary effect is religious
3. And if not, whether it represents excessive entanglement between church and state

In recent years, the second criterion has predominated in terms of whether the challenged government action appears to a reasonable observer to be governmental endorsement of religion; the first criterion has proven to be relatively easy to hurdle; and the third has largely withered away.

THE WELL-KNOWN BEGINNINGS: THE SCOPES TRIAL FROM THE 1920S

The first chapter was at the lowest legal level and not based on the Constitution, but it marked-the first major judicial recognition of the conflict between the secular scientific view represented by evolution and the equally entrenched religious view opposed to teaching evolution in the public schools.

As recited and analyzed in a multiplicity of other sources in the literature, this case arose when high school science teacher and football coach John Scopes taught evolution in his biology class despite the prohibition in Tennessee's "Monkey Law."

In a well-publicized trial in 1926 pitting Clarence Darrow (representing the defense) against William Jennings Bryant (representing the prosecution), the jury convicted the 24-year-old Scopes of violating this criminal law, and the judge fined him $100.

The publicity did not accompany the decision, on appeal, a year later. The state's highest court rejected Darrow's challenges based on the state's constitution but reversed Scopes' conviction on the grounds that the jury, not the judge, should have assessed the fine of $100; however, since Scopes was no longer in the state's employ, the court's remedy was limited to nullifying his prosecution, reasoning that there was "nothing to be gained by prolonging the life of this bizarre case."

SUPREME COURT CASES THAT EVENTUALLY FOLLOWED

The next chapter of the story didn't arise until four decades afterwards; it consists of two Supreme Court decisions, the first in 1968 and the next not until 19 years later, concerning the constitutionality of two successive state laws that addressed the subject of evolution in the public schools.

In the first of these two decisions, *Epperson v. State of Arkansas* (1968), the Court held that a state law prohibiting the teaching of evolution in the public schools (and in public colleges) violated the First Amendment's religion clauses, because its sole reason was a particular religious doctrine, thus violating the First Amendment's principle of "governmental neutrality between religion and religion, and between religion and nonreligion."

Viewed with a rearview mirror attuned to the tripartite test, the Court's opinion appears to rely on the first criterion (i.e., whether the purpose of the challenged governmental policy or practice is secular). Specifically, noting that the Arkansas statute was an adaptation of Tennessee's anti-evolution law, the Court reasoned:

> Perhaps the sensational publicity attendant upon the Scopes trial induced Arkansas to adopt less explicit language. It eliminated Tennessee's references to "the story of the Divine Creation of man" as taught in the Bible, but there is no doubt that the motivation for the law was the same: To suppress the teaching of a theory which, it was thought, "denied" the divine creation of man.

Although the Court's opinion was without dissent, three of the nine Justices wrote separate concurrences that showed disagreement with the majority's reasoning.

The strongly held religious views of another segment of the Bible belt—the state of Louisiana—responded to *Epperson* in 1981 by enacting the "Balanced Treatment for Creation-Science and Evolution-Science in Pubic School Instruction" Act, which required that if a public school provided instruction in either theory, it must also provide instruction in the other one.

In *Aguillard v. Edwards* (1987), the Supreme Court rejected the legislature's avowed intent of protecting academic freedom, concluding instead that the purpose of the Act was religious, specifically "to restructure the science curriculum to conform with a particular religious view-point." The Court viewed the Act as part of the history of anti-evolution statutes recited and rejected in *Epperson*.

In dicta, which amount to side comments, the majority clarified: "We do not imply that a legislature could never require that scientific critiques of prevailing scientific theories be taught." Moreover, the growing lack of unanimity was evident.

RECENT LOWER COURT CASES

The first of the subsequent lower court cases amounted to a corollary to the Supreme Court's *Edwards* decision. In this 2001 case, an appellate court in Georgia ruled that a high school biology text that briefly and cautiously mentioned both evolution and creationism did not violate the Establishment or Free Exercise Clauses.

The other relatively recent relevant cases fit into two clusters. One was a group of cases that focused on school district limitations on teachers' promotion of creationist views. The other was a trio of decisions that focused on school district disclaimers of the evolutionist view.

1. Teacher cases

In a cluster of decisions, various lower courts upheld the constitutionality of a school district's directive to a recalcitrant biology teacher requiring him to teach the evolutionist theory and to refrain from promoting the creationist view. The plaintiff-teachers relied, without success, on the Establishment, Free Speech, and/or Free Exercise Clauses.

2. Disclaimer cases

The pertinent disclaimer cases started at about the same time as the teacher cases. In the first such case, the Fifth Circuit Court of Appeals, which covers various states in the Southwest, ruled in 2000 that a school board policy that required teachers to read aloud a disclaimer immediately before teaching evolution violated the Establishment Clause because the disclaimer's wording was not sufficiently neutral.

In the next and most widely publicized of this pair of cases, a federal trial court in Pennsylvania held in 2005 that a school district policy requiring biology teachers to read a disclaimer about evolution and intelligent design violated the Establishment Clause. In a detailed analysis of the language and history of the disclaimer, the court concluded that the policy violated both the purpose and effect prongs of the tripartite test and, alternatively applied as a separate test, served as a governmental endorsement of religion in the eyes of an objective observer. The case did not proceed to the federal appellate court because a newly elected school board agreed to discontinue the disclaimer.

Finally, in a less well-known and anticlimactic 2006 decision that did reach the next judicial level, the Eleventh Circuit Court of Appeals in Atlanta, Ga., vacated a similar ruling by a federal trial court in Georgia, remanding the matter for further factual findings. The parties' subsequent settlement of the case precluded a definitive federal appellate decision on this modern issue.

Conclusion: Continuing Controversy

The end of this article is not the end of the controversy. For example, Louisiana recently passed a Science Education Act that permits teachers to use "supplemental textbooks and other instructional materials to help students understand, analyze, critique, and review scientific theories in an objective manner." Although seemingly innocuous on the surface, the 2008 Act's legislative history suggests that it represents the latest chapter in the interaction between state legislatures, representing a majoritarian process, and the courts, representing the individual protections in the Constitution. Critics of the Act have reportedly characterized it as "an attempt to inject religious doctrine into the classroom under the red herring of academic freedom," whereas "[p]roponents of creationism and its ideological successor, intelligent design, are hailing the decision as a 'victory.'"

The current state of the law in terms of the constitutional boundaries of the Establishment, Free Exercise, and Free Speech Clauses appears to be that 1) state or local governmental authorities may not ban evolution or endorse creationism, and 2) teachers do not have the "academic freedom" to denigrate evolution or promote creationism.

However, these conclusions are conditional because the decisions to date depend to a significant extent on the particular facts of each case and the changing doctrine for these First Amendment clauses.

The successive approaches of governmental authorities, ranging thus far from banning evolution to disclaiming it for the purported purpose of balanced treatment or academic freedom, reflect the irrepressible id of the religionist, predominantly Christian majority, led by the Fundamentalists. The gradually fluctuating composition of the Supreme Court, currently seemingly shifting from a separationist to an accommodationist view, also reflects the tension in the super ego of our society.

Everyone appears to agree on the principle of neutrality, but the applications of this principle to the teaching of evolution and to the competing role of creationism defy objectivity and stability, which are desired but not always achieved features of the judiciary. The American ambivalence about the interrelationship of government and religion inevitably means an evolving legal status of evolution that—depending on your perspective—may be an intelligent design.

Constitutional and Indispensable Legislation:
Mandatory Random Steroid Testing for High School Athletes
by Cynthia Sysol

In the following article, the author addresses another timely issue, one not addressed at all in the previous chapter—privacy. Do students in schools have the right to privacy? A clear violation of privacy is the practice of drug testing athletes, which involves watching an athlete urinate into a medical container for the purpose of testing for drugs. However, is this clear violation of privacy a violation of the U.S. Constitution? By choosing to be an athlete, does a student waive his or her right to privacy? According to the Fourth Amendment to the Constitution, people have the right "to be secure in their persons, houses, papers, and effects against unreasonable searches and seizures."[38] Is mandatory drug testing a violation of this right? Do students in schools have this right, in general? Sysol examines these questions, as well as case laws that addressed these questions in the courts.

I. INTRODUCTION

The crack of a bat changed baseball and the controversy surrounding steroids forever. As thousands of cameras flashed and a million more eyes watched on television, Barry Bonds broke the all-time Major League home run record. A crowning achievement marked with an asterisk.[39] The controversy surrounding athletes' steroid use has been at the forefront of professional sports, but it has now seeped its way into the high school locker room.

According to the American Medical Association, high school steroid use has increased from 2.1 percent in 1999 to almost double at 4 percent in 2002.[40] The increase in steroid use among high school athletes has led some states to enact legislation requiring random steroid testing. The legislation, which some argue is a violation of privacy rights, is not only constitutional but necessary to eradicate the growing problem of youth steroid use. States around the nation need to evaluate student steroid use within its borders and many should follow New Jersey's lead and enact similar legislation to eliminate high school steroid use.

---

38   Cornell University of Law School, Legal Information Institute, retrieved July 31, 2011, from http://topics.law. cornell.edu/constitution/billofrights

39   Marc Ecko, the owner of Barry Bonds record breaking ball, set up an online poll to allow fans to decide the fate of the ball. Fans decided that ball should be marked with an asterisk to suggest that the record was tainted due to steroid use. Christina Boyle, Poll results say Barry Bond's ball will have asterisk,www.nydailynews.com (Sept. 27, 2007).

40   Jan Dennis, Illinois High School Association considers random steroid testing, Chicago Tribune (Sept. 7, 2006).

II. EXPLANATION AND ANALYSIS

A. Recent Legislation

New Jersey became the first state to mandate random steroid testing for high school students.[41] Other states, such as Texas and Florida, are in the process of implementing legislation that requires the testing as well. Still other states like Illinois are working along with their high school athletic association in considering steroid testing legislation.[42] Each of these testing programs applies different penalties for steroid violations, including various suspension times based on offense and a complete ban if a student refuses testing.[43] Students and parents across the country have sued school districts on an individualized basis claiming that steroid testing is a violation of privacy rights. However, courts have repeatedly held that random steroid testing is not a violation of the federal or state constitutional right to be free from unreasonable searches.[44] While no one has yet challenged the new legislation, the laws are constitutional under the Fourth Amendment based on prevailing case law and the pressing need to eliminate steroid use by high school athletes.

B. Fourth Amendment

1. Fourth Amendment Test

The Fourth Amendment emphasizes: "The right of the people to be secure in their persons, houses, papers, and effects, against unreasonable searches and seizures ..." The Fourth Amendment is the hallmark of privacy rights providing protection against unreasonable interferences. Thus, the ultimate measure of the constitutionality is based on the reasonableness of the search. The law defines reasonableness by a balancing test in which a person's Fourth Amendment right to privacy is weighed against the promotion of a legitimate governmental interest.[45] Students have a reasonable expectation of privacy in their own bodies and a valid argument that the government may not force uninvited steroid testing. However, the government may nonetheless intrude upon a student's privacy when a legitimate concern exists, such as preventing high school steroid use. Put another way, the right to privacy can be evaluated by the nature of the privacy interest and the character of the intrusion imposed.[46] Each side of individual privacy and governmental concern must be considered to determine the ultimate reasonableness, and thus the constitutionality of a search.

---

41   Christopher Lawlor, New Jersey adopts statewide steroid testing policy, USA Today (June, 15, 2006).
42   Id.
43   Chris Hamby, Texas and Florida on verge of mandating random steroid testing, www.stateline.org (June, 15, 2007).
44   Vernonia Sch. Dist.47J v. Acton, 515 U.S. 646, 646 (1995).
45   Vernonia Sch. Dist. 515 U.S at 652.
46   Bd. of Educ. ofIndep. Sch. Dist No. 92 of Pottawatomie County v. Earls, 536 U.S. 822 (2002).

2. Reasonableness

a. Privacy Interest: Nature of Interest

Students, as persons, have a federal and state constitutional right to privacy and personal autonomy. Moreover, students do not "shed their constitutional rights at the schoolhouse door."[47] However, schools create a special context in which to view constitutional issues. Schools cannot disregard "their custodial and tutelary responsibility for children," but at the same time, schools must respect the rights of students.[48] Students are not forced, but choose to compete in athletic activities and, therefore, are reasonably subject to regulations for such sports. Students have few expectations of privacy within the school setting, and even lesser expectations in an athletic school setting.[49] Courts have held that "a finding of individualized suspicion may not be necessary when a school conducts drug testing."[50] Thus, a national problem of drug use is enough to trigger school policies of drug testing. Ultimately, the nature of the intrusion in high school steroid testing comes down on the side of reasonable as contemplated by the Fourth Amendment.

b. Character of Intrusion

Courts have held that searches are reasonable when "the invasion of the student's privacy is not significant, given the minimally intrusive nature of the sample collection and the limited uses to which the test results are put."[51] The legislation in place requires a urine sample from random students.[52] Urine samples are collected by a student going into the restroom while a faculty monitor "waits outside the closed restroom stall for the student to produce a sample and must listen for the normal sounds of urination."[53] The court has called this type of intrusion "negligible" and identical to conditions normally encountered in a public restroom which school children use daily.[54] Other courts have not only allowed urine samples, but held that blood tests do not "constitute an unduly extensive imposition on an individual's privacy and bodily integrity."[55]

Furthermore, the results of the drug test are kept confidential, away from any academic records, and not turned over to law enforcement. The results are only released on a need-to-know basis, with no academic discipline, only exclusion of the activity sought to be regulated, such as athletics.[56] Constitutional privacy rights protect an individual's interest in avoiding disclosure of personal matters because injury can occur when personal information is released. However,

---

47   Tinker v. Des Moines Indep. Community Sch. Dist., 393 U.S. 503 (1969).

48   Joye ex. rel. Joye v. Hunterdon Central Regional High Sch. Bd. of Educ., 353 N.J. Super 600 (2002).

49   Kathleen M. Dorr, Validity, under Federal Constitution, of regulations, rules or statutes allowing drug testing of students, 87 A.L.R. Fed. 148, 150 (1988).

50   Id.

51   Pottawatomie, 536 U.S. 822, 823.

52   Anna Scott, Florida high school athletes subject to random drug testing for anabolic steroids, Sarasota Herald-tribune (May 2007).

53   Pottawatomie, 536 U.S. 822, 823.

54   Vernonia Sch. Dist., 515 U.S. 646, 650.

55   Hedges v. Musco. 204 F.3d 109 (N.J. 2007).

56   Pottawatomie, 536 U.S. 822, 823.

although it may be embarrassing to undergo drug testing, it is hardly such a burden on an individual's privacy rights as to cause any measurable damage. The drug test is also administered randomly, and not based on individualized suspicion. Thus, the stigma of undergoing a drug test is by pure chance and not due to a certain athlete's behavior. The search is unobtrusive and limited in scope, providing schools with a legal and reasonable search. Once a test is determined to be reasonable, it must be balanced with the state interest.

c. Legitimate Government Interest

i. Protection of students

Schools nurture and mold students into responsible adults, and have an interest in protecting students from harm. Steroids are a drug and create problems of mental and physical health. The use of steroids leads to physical problems such as improper liver functioning, damage to male and female reproductive systems, damage to cardiovascular health, and stunted growth. Steroid users can also suffer from psychological side effects, such as mood swings, irritability, depression, and aggression.[57] These effects can be long term and the school years are the time when the physical, psychological, and addictive effects of drugs are most severe."[58] Furthermore, "children grow chemically dependent more quickly than adults, and their record of recovery are depressingly low."[59] The physical, psychological, and emotional rollercoaster that teenagers usually experience is only exacerbated by the use of steroids. Athletes who are under the influence of intoxicants perform poorly and endanger not only themselves, but also others on the playing field.[60] Clearly, the state has a compelling interest in preventing the harm that steroid use causes to students.

The rise of steroid use in professional sports demonstrates the growing problem with steroid usage in the United States. This is highlighted by the controversy surrounding Barry Bonds' home run record and other notable athletes being accused of using steroids such as Marion Jones and Lance Armstrong. Professional athletes serve as role models and icons for youth, especially youths who play sports. Students fall into the idea that fame and money are easy to gain and that consequences do not apply to athletes. Furthermore, student athletes see steroids as a way of achieving their goals of prominence through athletic ability. Drug use must be curbed and deterred at a young age and schools must play a role in reducing the use of steroids in sports. Student athletes also serve as role models for their peers and their community at large.[61] The court has even stated "that [there is] a drug problem largely fueled by the role model athletes' drug use." The court has further stated that this "drug problem" can be "effectively addressed by making sure that athletes do not use drugs." The damaging side effects are profound and with the national

---

57 Audiey C. Kao M.D, PhD, Diagnosing Anabolic Steroid Use, Ethics Journal of the Am. Med. Assn, Vol. 6, Num. 7 (2004).

58 Vertwnia Sch. Dist., 515 U.S. 646, 661, citing Hawley, The Bumpy Road to Drug-Free Schools, 72 Phi Delta Kappa 310, 314 (1990).

59 Id.

60 Dorr, 87 A.L.R. Fed 148 at 154.

61 Id.

spotlight on steroid use, legislation mandating steroid testing is indispensable as a stepping stone to eradicate steroid usage by our youth.

ii. Costs of drug testing

While random steroid drug testing for high school athletes is constitutional under the reasonable analysis, one major government concern is the cost associated with administering the tests. In New Jersey, the cost of each test is around $150 to $200 with the state and school board each allotting $50,000 for the cause.[62] Florida's legislature has allotted $100,000 while Texas has given $3 million a year for testing.[63] While costs are a chief concern, the American Medical Association (AMA) notes that some states, such as Illinois, are "looking into private grants and others sources and will not pass the cost onto school members."[64] AMA president, Dr. Ron Davis, further comments that schools need to "beef up" educational programs, but "insists testing still needs to be considered."[65] Steroid testing is just another facet in the fight for educational funding, and can be achieved with the help of state legislation and private grants. The cost of drug testing, while high, pales in comparison to the importance of maintaining the health and welfare of students, not only in their school years, but also in the future.

III. CONCLUSION

The recent legislation passed in several states requiring steroid testing of high school athletes requires a delicate balance of privacy rights and the growing problem with steroid usage by athletes. The test for whether a search is constitutional rests in the reasonableness of the search, including the nature and the character of the intrusion.[66] Although students have an expectation of privacy, it is reduced in the school setting. Also, the intrusion is minimal and limited in scope.[67] Schools have a legitimate government interest in protecting students from health risks and preventing the use of steroids within our society. The cost of implementing random steroid testing is expensive, but the test itself is easily administered and the benefit clearly outweighs the cost. Allotting a large sum of money up front to prevent drug use makes more economic sense than paying for the repercussions and effects of drug use over a long period of time.

Students choosing to participate in sports surrender certain rights and must be subjected to any legislation that regulates sports. Schools should randomly test high school athletes for steroid use and apply the appropriate suspension from athletics based on the offense. If schools fail to implement testing, then the school should suspend their athletic programs or suffer expulsion from state high school athletic associations. Every state should pass legislation requiring random

---

62   Lawlor, supra n. 3.
63   Hamby, supra n. 5.
64   Dennis, supra n. 2.
65   Id.
66   Id.
67   Pottawatomie, 536 U.S. 822, 823.

steroid drug testing for high school athletes to protect teenagers from the effects of drug use and help to eliminate the national use of steroids.

The so called "War on Drugs" has been fought for years in the United States and the focus has been retroactive instead of proactive. The best way to solve the epidemic is to stop drug use in the first place; a simple plan of prevention. Schools must step into more parenting roles and enforce the no tolerance policy of steroid use. Not only must schools and state legislation assist in the fight, but the media and professional athletes must lend a hand as well. Professional athletes need to call out their fellow teammates, denouncing the use of steroids. Records must be erased, medals must be stripped, and money must be reduced because of steroid use at the professional level. The media needs to deplore the conduct, not just report the incidents. Public service announcements should be made to inform children that these so called role models are shameful and should not be emulated.

Furthermore, parents must be just that: Parents. Education begins at home and parents must inform children of the risk of steroids and not require unrealistic athletic achievement from their children. Steroid use has become an overgrown weed on the field. State legislation, schools, professional athletes, the media, and parents must work together to eradicate steroid use in teenagers. Only when steroid use is eliminated can sports accurately reflect true talent and achievement.

DISCUSSION QUESTIONS:

4. Did you examine the footnotes of the authors yet? What are the strengths of the sources each author used? What are the weaknesses of the sources each author used? For example, must an article regarding educational law cite actual laws? Or is it OK to defer to another expert when discussing educational laws?

5. What was the bias or biases of each author? Part of the bias of each author can be found within his or her writings. Also, researching the author can help one understand the biases of the author. What else has the author published? Is there a theme within the topics of the author's writings? Does the author tend to examine all topics from one perspective? For example, in the Sysol article, does the author seem to believe students should have Fourth Amendment protection? Or does she side more with the concept of *in loco parentis* (schools acting in place of parents)?

6. In addition to sources utilized and the bias of the author is the actual argument of the article, for every piece of scholarly writing is an argument. The argument begins with the initial research question. For example, in the McCain piece, the author discusses a theme seen is Supreme Court decisions. Finding a pattern or designing a model is an act of scholarship that lends itself to professional respect. Does McCain succeed in identifying the pattern? In the title of the Zirkel piece, the author uses the phrase "the verdict winds up far from unanimous," suggesting that he believes that court rulings are controversial, even within the

courts. Did he prove this point successfully in the article? In the Sysol article, the author's introduction included the phrase, "the increase in steroid use among high school athletes…," which suggests she views steroid use as a problem. In scholarship, when presenting a problem, an assumption exists that at least part of the solution will also be discussed. Did Sysol do so? If so, are her solution suggestions compelling? If not, would the proposal of a solution strengthen her argument, or weaken it?

ACTIVITIES

1. Compare and contrast the educational law presented in Chapter Two with the educational law presented in this chapter. Examine the arguments presented, the evidence utilized to support their positions, and the bias of each author. What do you know as a result of this examination?

2. Below is a list of professional journals that are likely to publish educational law articles. Examine each site to determine the bias of the editorial board. The first five are law journals; the second five are education publications. How do law and education publications differ? Who is on the editorial boards of the journals? Does the journal provide the names and biographies of the editorial board? What is the location in which the journal is published? Is it a university, or another location? What other sources might you use to further evaluate the validity of the journal?

ONLINE RESOURCES

1. Education and Law Journal   http://www.law2.byu.edu/jel/
2. Journal of Law and Education   http://www.law.sc.edu/jled/
3. The Yale Law Journal   http://yalelawjournal.org/the-yale-law-journal/content-pages/education,-equality,-and-national-citizenship/
4. Journal of Law & Education   http://www.law.louisville.edu/jle
5. ABA Journal   http://www.abajournal.com/blawgs/topic/education+law
6. American School Board Journal   http://www.asbj.com/TopicsArchive/SchoolLawArchive
7. Edweek   http://www.edweek.org/ew/index.html
8. NEA Today   http://www.nea.org/home/1814.htm
9. American Educator   http://www.aft.org/newspubs/periodicals/ae/
10. Phi Kappa Phi forum   http://www.phikappaphi.org/web/Publications/PKP_Forum.html

CHAPTER FIVE
LEGAL AND ORGANIZATIONAL CONTEXT OF SCHOOLING: AN OVERVIEW

WHY DO I NEED TO KNOW THIS?

Though case laws make up much of educational law, legislation at the federal level today also plays a key role—and that role is growing. The success of schools is now largely dependent on teachers and school administrators understanding the particulars and nuances of two federal education policies: No Child Left Behind (NCLB) and the Individuals with Disabilities Education Act (IDEA). The responsibility for whether or not a child passes or fails a test has been largely separated from the home of the child. Teachers are responsible to overcome the obstacles to learning that originate at home, as well as physical, cognitive, and emotional disabilities.

Historically, teachers were responsible for teaching, students were responsible for learning, and parents were responsible for making sure that their children did what was necessary to learn. Teachers were responsible for the class environment and controlling student behavior, as well as presenting information, but whether or not that led to learning was not an evaluation of the teacher or the school. Children received report cards, not schools. This shift in responsibility that changed the structure and organization of schools is primarily due to two federal education policies—the Individuals with Disabilities Education Act and No Child Left Behind.

WHAT ARE THE LEGAL AND ORGANIZATIONAL STRUCTURES OF SCHOOLS?

Two seemingly contradictory sets of words characterize the structure of schooling in the United States: decentralization and democracy versus paternalism and patriarchy. Decentralization is associated with democracy and grassroots politics. In contrast, paternalism is associated with patriarchy and male totalitarianism. The marriage of these seemingly contradictory words in our national psyche can be traced to our Founding Fathers, who famously wrote, "All men are created equal," meaning males, specifically white males. They believed that white males possessed rationality, and therefore, could self-govern. They did not, however, extend this belief to women or ethnic minorities. In many respects, this belief continues to shape the structure and organization of schools today.

Decentralization and Democracy in Schooling

A strong belief tied to schooling in the United States is the belief in local control of schools, which is why, in many respects, schooling continues to be a decentralized operation.[1]

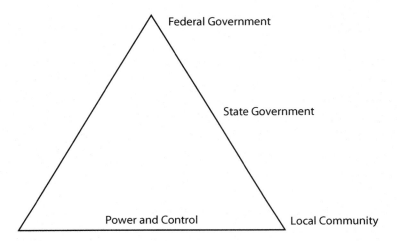

In 1867 the federal Department of Education was established "to collect information on schools and teaching that would help the States establish effective school systems."[2] One year later, as the result of a battle over states' rights versus "federal encroachment,"[3] the Department of Education was downgraded to the Office of Education within the Department of the Interior.[4] The Office of Education was moved within federal departments until 1976, when President Jimmy Carter again elevated it to a department level.[5]

Even though the federal Department of Education as we know it today originated in 1976, state departments of education began gaining strength much earlier. From 1838–1853, "most states in the Northeast (Maine to Maryland) and the 'old' Northwest (Ohio, Indiana, Illinois, Iowa, Michigan, and Wisconsin) authorized the position of state school superintendents…"[6]

---

1 Carl Kaestle, Victory of the Common School Movement, U.S. Department of Education, Historians on America, posted April 3, 2008, retrieved September 27, 2011, from http://www.america.gov/st/educ-english/2008/April/200804 23212501eaifas0.8516133.html

2 "The Federal Role in Education," U.S. Department of Education, retrieved July 31, 2011, from http://www2. ed.gov/about/overview/fed/role.html

3 Ibid.

4 Ibid.

5 Ibid.

6 Carl Kaestle, Victory of the Common School Movement, U.S Department of Education, Historians on America, posted April 3, 2008, retrieved September 27, 2011, from http://www.america.gov/st/educ-english/2008/April/200804 23212501eaifas0.8516133.html

However, as Kaestle maintains, "The local control retained to this day by local, elected school boards in the United States is unique among the industrial nations of the world and testifies to how dearly the concept of local control of school curricula and their budgets still appeals to the average American."[7]

Remember, the Founding Fathers, for the most part, were opposed to public education. Nothing regarding schooling is mentioned in the U.S. Constitution. As a result, for much of our history, public schooling was a local and state issue, and differences existed regarding the definition of schooling from state to state and from community to community. The Common School Movement, which swept much of the nation, was engaged state by state and community by community.[8]

As the following graph demonstrates, local control of schools parallels funding of schools:

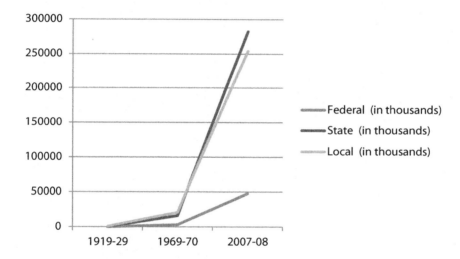

Though the federal government has increased its financial contribution to schools, local and state governments continue to carry the bulk of school funding. Money, however, is not the only reason why Americans embrace the idea of local control of schools. We do not control the administration of entitlement programs such as unemployment payments, food stamps, Social Security, Medicare, or Medicaid. We do not have a say when we go to war or when a war will end. Our elected officials who represent us in this republic make those decisions. One of the few places where democracy actually exists in this country is at the local level and in our schools. Thus, historically, resistance has existed toward state or federal control of schools. State control has gained strength via increases in state funding of schools proportionally.

The practice of the federal government determining education policy for the nation is a recent development and could be a trend or phase, rather than a permanent practice. As recently as the

---

7 Ibid.
8 For more detailed information on the Horace Mann and Common School Movement, see http://www.america.gov/st/educ-english/2008/April/20080423212501eaifas0.8516133.html

2011 presidential campaign, political candidates have called for the federal government to get out of the business of schooling. On September 22, 2011, Republican presidential candidates debated many domestic issues. All of the candidates except one called for dramatically shrinking the power and size of the federal Department of Education or totally eliminating it. The only candidate who did not make this claim was Governor Jon Huntsman of Utah, who stated that unfunded federal mandates must end.[9]

Calling for the elimination of unfunded federal mandates would, in effect, shrink the power and control of the federal Department of Education. IDEA and NCLB are both underfunded federal mandates, which means that the federal government only supplies part of the funding necessary for compliance with the law. When enacted, IDEA was supposed to provide 40 percent of the extra funding necessary to educate students with disabilities. But as of 2011, the federal government only provided 26.3 percent of the necessary funding; states and school districts have received 50 percent of the funding necessary for NCLB.[10]

Despite being underfunded, IDEA and NCLB dramatically changed the national practice of a decentralized public school system. The belief in local control of schools is why all federal legislation is administered, enforced, and interpreted by two levels of bureaucracy before it reaches the level of a school building. The first level is the state education agency (SEA), (commonly referred to as a Department of Education and formerly known as a State Board of Education); the second level is the local education agencies (LEAs), commonly referred to as a Board of Education and/or school district.[11]

Patriarchy and Paternalism in Schooling

Local control of schools has traditionally been in the hands of the men in a local community, even though teachers were primarily women, thus giving schools a patriarchal and paternalistic structure.

---

9   Transcript of Fox News-Google GOP Debate, September 22, 2011, retrieved September 27, 2011, from http://www.foxnews.com/politics/2011/09/22/fox-news-google-gop-2012-presidential-debate/

10   Federal Funding for Education, Wisconsin Associations of School Boards, retrieved September 27, 2011, from http://www.wasb.org/websites/advoc_gov_relations/File/federal_updates/FUNDING_(1)_-_Title_I_and_IDEA_-_WASB_%20Letterhead.pdf

11   Public Law print of PL 107-110, the No Child Left Behind Act of 2001, January 8, 2002, retrieved August 24, 2011, from http://www2.ed.gov/policy/elsec/leg/esea02/107-110.pdf.

POWER AND CONTROL

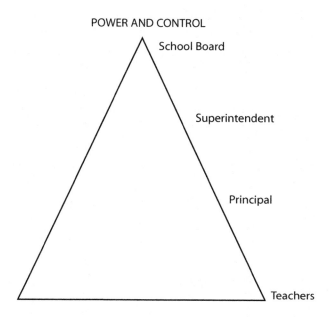

At issue is who is in charge—the masses, or the person or group at the top? From the national perspective, historically, it was the masses; from the school district perspective, it was the person or board at the top. Federal education policy has radically changed the national perspective. The perspective from the school district level has changed very little. At the school district level, patriarchy is the governing ideology. As defined by Lerner:

> Patriarchy refers to the system, historically … in which the male head of the household had absolute legal and economic power over his dependent female and male family members … its wider definition means the manifestation and institutionalization of male dominance … It does not imply that women are either totally powerless or totally deprived of rights, influence and resources.[12]

Paternalism is "the relationship of a dominant group, considered superior, to a subordinate group considered inferior, in which the dominance is mitigated by mutual obligation and reciprocal rights."[13]

A number of factors came into play in why "women teach and men manage" in schools.[14] Women became teachers because some believed that they were better suited to be teachers due to their temperament.[15] Women could also be paid less. A man filling the position of principal or superintendent, especially in urban areas, was an intentional component of the establishment

---

12   Lerner, *The Creation of Patriarchy*, p. 240.
13   Ibid.
14   Strober and Tyack, "Why Do Women Teach and Men Manage? p. 494.
15   Altenbaugh, *The American People and Their Education.*

of administrative positions. Strobe and Tyack explain, "Hiring male managers also assisted urban school boards in the maintenance of bureaucratic control."[16] This suggests that a conscious decision was made that patriarchy would shape the structure of schools and administrative styles of school officials.

Today, 59 percent of public elementary principals are female, but only 29 percent of secondary principals are female.[17] The majority of teachers continue to be female, with 84 percent at the elementary level and 59 percent at the secondary level. At the superintendent level, only 14–24 percent of superintendents are women.[18] Furthermore, according to the American Association of School Administrators, men continue to make up the majority of school board members.[19] Teachers' unions have played a key role in giving teachers more of a voice in schools (a point discussed in more detail in Chapter Seven), but patriarchy continues to play a central role in the ideology of school districts.

Though schools have traditionally been decentralized, democratic, patriarchal, and paternalistic, two federal policies have also dramatically changed the organization of schools. The Individuals with Disabilities Education Act (IDEA) opened the doors of schools to children with disabilities; No Child Left Behind (NCLB) empowered the federal Department of Education and state departments of education in determining what would be taught in schools, as well as creating consequences for schools and teachers who did not meet their standards.

INDIVIDUALS WITH DISABILITIES EDUCATION ACT (IDEA)

In the 1970s, one outcome of the civil rights movement and the *Brown v. Board* decision was that parents began demanding educational services for their disabled children.[20] In *Pennsylvania Association for Retarded Children (PARC) v. Pennsylvania* (PA, 1971) and *Mills v. Board of Education* (DC, 1972), "the courts established the right of children with disabilities to a free, appropriate public education in the least restrictive environment by interpreting the equal protection guarantee of the 14 Amendment."[21]

Prior to these case laws, millions of children were excluded from educational services and often placed in institutions. One such child was Allan, who was placed on the steps of an institution for

---

16   Ibid., p. 499.

17   S. Aud, W. Hussar, G. Kena, K. Bianco, L. Frohlich, J. Kemp, and K. Tahan (2011). *The Condition of Education 2011* (NCES 2011-033). U.S. Department of Education, National Center for Education Statistics. Washington, DC: U.S. Government Printing Office, Glossary, indicator 33.

18   "Where Are All the Women Superintendents?" June 2000, American Association of School Administrators, retrieved October 1, 2011, from http://www.aasa.org/SchoolAdministratorArticle.aspx?id=14492; Holland, "Gender gap is narrowing in ranks of school chiefs," stltoday.com, retrieved October 1, 2001, from http://www.stltoday.com/news/local/metro/article_ff3df347-9f24-5b7e-88d6-bde2873ae7c0.html

19   "Where Are all the Women Superintendents"

20   "Background & Analysis," Federal Education Budget Project, retrieved August 14, 2011, from http://febp.newamerica.net/background-analysis/individuals-disabilities-education-act-overview

21   Ibid.

children with mental retardation. In this institution he was fed and clothed, but never assessed for educational services. Eventually Allan went blind from banging the side of his face with his fist. At the age of 35, following the legal requirements to educationally assess all children, personnel discovered that Allen was not mentally retarded and actually had an average intelligence. He learned, at an early age, to smash his fist into face by watching other patients (perhaps in an attempt to gain some attention).[22]

With the passage of the above case laws, millions of children previously excluded from public education began attending public schools, which placed a cumbersome financial strain on local school districts. In 1975 Congress enacted the Education for All Handicapped Children Act (Public Law 94-142), which allowed federal funds to be used to supplement school budgets, partially paying for special education services.[23]

Public Law 94-142, Education for all Handicapped Children Act, now known as the Individual's with Disabilities Education Act, became law in 1975.[24] The name change was also a philosophical change. The word handicapped is indicative of limitations. As such, the phrase "handicapped children" means imperfect children. In contrast, "individuals with disabilities" implies a whole person who happens to have a weakness in some area of his or her life. Taking this one step further, it could be argued that the spirit of IDEA is that all children learn differently and therefore, it recognizes individual differences in the classroom.

As with all federal legislation, there are many parts to the law. In IDEA, Part B is the portion directly associated with requirements of local school districts.[25] A key to understanding the requirements of Part B of IDEA is deciphering the acronyms and key phrases of IDEA:

- FAPE—Free and Appropriate Education
- LRE—Least Restrictive Environment
- IEP—Individual Education Plan.[26]

Free and appropriate education means that a child with a qualifying disability receives services with no financial burden to his or her family. Under IDEA, all disabilities are not equal. The qualifying disabilities are as follows: autism, deaf-blindness, deafness, developmental delay, emotional disturbance, hearing impairment, intellectual disability, multiple disabilities, orthopedic impairment, other health impairment, specific learning disability, speech or language impairment, traumatic brain injury, and visual impairment including blindness.[27]

22 "Archived: A 25 Year History of IDEA," Special Education & Rehabilitative Services, U.S. Department of Education, retrieved August 14, 2011, from http://www2.ed.gov/policy/speced/leg/idea/history.html
23 Ibid.
24 "Building the Legacy: IDEA 2004," U.S. Department of Education, retrieved August 24, 2011, from http://idea.ed.gov/
25 Ibid.
26 Council for Exceptional Children, retrieved August 2, 2011, from http://www.ldonline.org/article/6086
27 "Categories of Disability under IDEA," National Dissemination Center for Children with Disabilities, April 2009, retrieved August 2, 2011, from http://nichcy.org/disability/categories

The U.S. Department of Education requires that the following be included in an IEP:

Current performance. The IEP must state how the child is currently doing in school (known as present levels of educational performance). This information usually comes from the evaluation results such as classroom tests and assignments, individual tests given to decide eligibility for services or during reevaluation, and observations made by parents, teachers, related service providers, and other school staff. The statement about "current performance" includes how the child's disability affects his or her involvement and progress in the general curriculum.

Annual goals. These are goals that the child can reasonably accomplish in a year. The goals are broken down into short-term objectives or benchmarks. Goals may be academic, address social or behavioral needs, relate to physical needs, or address other educational needs. The goals must be measurable—meaning that it must be possible to measure whether the student has achieved the goals.

Special education and related services. The IEP must list the special education and related services to be provided to the child or on behalf of the child. This includes supplementary aids and services that the child needs. It also includes modifications (changes) to the program or supports for school personnel—such as training or professional development—that will be provided to assist the child.

Participation with nondisabled children. The IEP must explain the extent (if any) to which the child will not participate with nondisabled children in the regular class and other school activities.

Participation in state and district-wide tests. Most states and districts give achievement tests to children in certain grades or age groups. The IEP must state what modifications in the administration of these tests the child will need. If a test is not appropriate for the child, the IEP must state why the test is not appropriate and how the child will be tested instead.

Dates and places. The IEP must state when services will begin, how often they will be provided, where they will be provided, and how long they will last.

Transition service needs. Beginning when the child is age 14 (or younger, if appropriate), the IEP must address (within the applicable parts of the IEP) the courses he or she needs to take to reach his or her post-school goals. A statement of transition services needs must also be included in each of the child's subsequent IEPs.

Needed transition services. Beginning when the child is age 16 (or younger, if appropriate), the IEP must state what transition services are needed to help the child prepare for leaving school.

Age of majority. Beginning at least one year before the child reaches the age of majority, the IEP must include a statement that the student has been told of any rights that will transfer to him or her at the age of majority. (This statement would be needed only in states that transfer rights at the age of majority.)

Measuring progress. The IEP must state how the child's progress will be measured and how parents will be informed of that progress.[28]

Least Restrictive Environment (LER) concerns the practice of inclusion, and is perhaps the most controversial part of the IDEA:

> To the maximum extent appropriate, children with disabilities, including children in public or private institutions or other care facilities, are educated with children who are not disabled, and special classes, separate schooling, or other removal of children with disabilities from the regular educational environment occurs only when the nature or severity of the disability of a child is such that education in regular classes with the use of supplementary aids and services cannot be achieved satisfactorily.[29]

Thus, a child with a disability should be included in a regular education classroom whenever possible and only removed if his or her educational needs cannot be met in that classroom.

The controversy with LER is that it only addresses the rights of the child with a disability in a classroom. It does not address the rights of other students in a classroom or the teacher of a classroom. In other words, the determination of whether or not a child with a disability should be placed in a traditional classroom is contingent on what is best for that one child. Whether or not placement of the child in the classroom will interfere with the learning experience of other children is not taken into consideration. Whether or not the classroom teacher has any experience or training to work with children with disabilities is also not necessarily taken into consideration, especially in schools unable to hire intervention specialists or enough intervention specialists to truly assist each child with a disability.

The U.S. Department of Education has placed strict requirements on the qualifications of highly qualified intervention specialists (also referred to as special education teachers), but via

28 "My Child's Special Needs: A Guide to the Individualized Education Program," archived information U.S. Department of Education, retrieved August 24, 2011, from http://ed.gov/parents/needs/speced/iepguide/index. html#contents

29 "Building a Legacy: IDEA 2004," U.S. Department of Education, retrieved August 2, 2011, from http://idea. ed.gov/explore/view/p/,root,statute,I,B,612,a,5,

the practice of inclusion, a child could be placed in a traditional classroom, but an intervention specialist may not be in that same classroom. The reason why an intervention specialist may not be in a traditional classroom is multifold. One, there is an intervention specialist shortage nationally.[30] Two, school districts cannot afford to hire enough intervention specialists for placement in every traditional classroom; this is especially true in financially struggling school districts. Three, intervention specialists must now be highly qualified in every content area they teach. Thus, a school may have five intervention specialists, but only one highly qualified in math. Thus, the language arts classes would be more likely to have placement of an intervention specialist than a math class. Lastly, a child's IEP is tied to specific content areas. As a result, a child might have an IEP addressing reading difficulties and as a result has an intervention specialist in his or her language arts class, but not in any other class, even though those other classes involve reading.[31]

In a traditional classroom, then, a teacher with one or more students on an IEP must give that child extra services and attention, thereby taking time away from other children in the classroom. Sometimes this extra service is extra time on a test. If there is some place in the school where the child can take tests and someone to supervise the child in doing so, it occurs outside of the traditional classroom. If no such place or personnel are available, the extended time to take the test continues in the traditional classroom. Such an event may or may not dramatically change the learning experience of other students in the classroom. Much is contingent on the creativity of the traditional classroom teacher in finding other learning activities to occur for other children as the student on the IEP completes the test. Other issues involving students on an IEP are much more difficult to resolve, and they often involve disciplinary issues. Another problem is when a child needs a test read to him. If no other space is available, the classroom teacher must read the test to the child, at the same time as maintaining silence so that other students can contemplate the test problem they are trying to solve. If more than one child needs a test to be read, the situation becomes even more complicated, and the individual creativity of a classroom teacher may not be enough to create the optimum test-taking environment for all children in the class.[32]

If a child has an emotional or behavior disability, what would be described as misbehavior for one child may actually be a manifestation of another child's disability. Emotional disturbance is one category covered by IDEA. A child with an anger management disability can be quite difficult to control in a classroom with 28 other children. This is particularly true when the child is not considered accountable for his or her actions because disruptive behavior is part of his or her disability. Under IDEA, when a child violates a school's code of conduct, the school is restricted from removing the student from the classroom if the behavior is a manifestation of his or her disability:

---

30 "Teacher Shortage Areas Nationwide Listing, 1990–91 thru 2011–2012," U.S. Department of Education, March 2011, retrieved August 24, 2011, from http://www2.ed.gov/about/offices/list/ope/pol/tsa.html
31 Conversations with Nancy Robitaille, Math Clinician, Sixth Grade Math Teachers, Streetsboro City Schools, 2001–2011.
32 The views in this paragraph are those solely of the author and do not represent those of the teachers identified previously.

School personnel under 34 CFR 300.530 may remove a child with a disability who violates a code of student conduct from his or her current placement to an appropriate interim alternative educational setting, another setting, or suspension, for not more than ten consecutive school days (to the extent those alternatives are applied to children without disabilities), and for additional removals of not more than ten consecutive school days in that same school year for separate incidents of misconduct (as long as those removals do not constitute a change of placement under 34 CFR 300.536).[33]

In "December 2004, IDEA was amended, with final regulations published in August 2006 (Part B for school-aged children)."[34] Some of the changes that occurred in IDEA addressed discipline issues and children on IEPs.

Special circumstances—School personnel may remove a student to an interim alternative educational setting for not more than 45 school days without regard to whether the behavior is determined to a be a manifestation of the child's disability if the child

1. Carries a weapon to or possesses a weapon at school, on school premises, or to or at a school function under the jurisdiction of a [state department of education or local school district];
2. Knowingly possesses or uses illegal drugs, or sells or solicits the sale of a controlled substance, while at school, on school premises, or at a school function under the jurisdiction of [state department of education or local school district];
3. Has inflicted serious bodily injury upon another person while at school, on school premises, or at a school function under the jurisdiction of a [state department of education or local school district].[35]

Though these changes did ease some of the pressure in schools regarding children with disabilities and school discipline, in some respects they caused additional burdens. When a child with a disability is removed from a traditional school setting, regardless if the behavior is a manifestation of his or her disability or not, the school is responsible for providing home instruction for the child. This adds another financial burden to schools, which may already be struggling financially.[36]

The Individuals with Disability Education Act clearly changed classrooms across America in public schools. For children like Allan, who would have previously been dumped and forgotten in an institution, the law is literally a lifesaver; for teachers dealing with a child with an anger management disability, the change is likely viewed much less favorably. The change in classrooms is theoretical as well as practical. With the passage of IDEA, we as a nation basically declared all

33 "Building a Legacy: IDEA 2004," U.S. Department of Education, retrieved August 24, 2011, from http://idea.ed.gov/explore/view/p/%2Croot%2Cdynamic%2CTopicalBrief%2C6%2C

34 "IDEA: Individuals with Disabilities Education Act," National Dissemination Center for Children with Disabilities, retrieved September 11, 2011, from http://nichcy.org/laws/idea

35 Ibid.

36 Ibid.

children are worthy of educational services. The enforcement of least restrictive environment requirements took this one step further and declared that not only are all children worthy of educational services, but when it benefits a child with a disability to be in a traditional classroom, that will occur. In other words, we proclaimed that as a nation, when possible, we are going to give less abled children priority.

No Child Left Behind (NCLB)

The reauthorization of the Elementary and Secondary Education Act in 2001, also known as No Child Left Behind, indicated additional educational priorities in our nation. The new focus was that every child should learn the same academic material at the same rate, regardless of disability, knowledge of the English language, ethnicity, or social class. One could argue that this is an extension of the national priority to give more to less abled students and expanded it to give priority also to ethnic minority children, English language learners (ELLs), and children living in poverty. Another way to look at it is that, in some respects, it is intended to achieve the promise made, but not achieved, via *Brown v. Board*.

The "Statement of Purpose" of NCLB begins with, "to ensure that all children have a fair, equal, and significant opportunity to obtain a high-quality education and reach, at a minimum, proficiency on challenging State academic achievement standards and State academic assessments."[37] The statement continues by claiming, "This purpose can be accomplished by:[38]

1. Ensuring that high-quality academic assessments, accountability systems, teacher preparation and training, curriculum, and instruction materials are aligned with challenging State academic standards so that students, teachers, parents, and administrators can measure progress against common expectations for academic achievement;
2. Meeting the educational needs of low-achieving children in our Nation's highest-poverty schools, limited English proficient children, migratory children, children with disabilities, Indian children, neglected or delinquent children, and young children in need of reading assistance;
3. Closing the achievement gap between high- and low-performing children, especially the achievement gaps between minority and nonminority children, and between disadvantaged children and more advantaged peers.[39]

---

37 P.L. 107-110, the No Child Left Behind Act of 2001, "Statement of Purpose," retrieved August 25, 2011, from http://www2.ed.gov/policy/elsec/leg/esea02/pg1.html#sec1001
38 NCLB provides 12 bullet points regarding how to achieve its goals; only the first three are listed here. The additional bullet points address school accountability and authority, parental involvement, and distribution of resources; ibid.
39 Ibid.

Within NCLB, the word "accountability" was utilized 80 times in reference to schools and teachers. The word "measure" was used 134 times and the word "standards" was used 412 times. The phrase "academic achievement" was mentioned 303 times and the word "improve" was used 476 times. The basic assumption was that teachers needed to be more accountable to the public, and that was going to occur via raising academic standards and measuring progress toward meeting those standards. In other words, an assumption existed at the passage of NCLB that teachers' expectations of students were too low and that teachers could not be trusted to raise expectations via reaching standards established by each state. An additional assumption was that states could not be trusted to raise standards, either. Many have questioned the accuracy of these assumptions. Regardless, the stage was set for changes in the public school system.

Like IDEA, understanding NCLB requires understanding acronyms and key phrases:

- Title I Grants
- Achievement Gap
- LEA: Local Education Agency
- SEA: State Education Agency
- NAEP: National Assessment of Educational Progress
- AYP: Annual Yearly Progress
- Needs Improvement
- Highly Qualified Teachers
- SI: School Improvement
- Supplemental Educational Service
- Public School Choice (PSC)
- Vouchers
- Charter Schools
- Report Cards

Title I grants are the funds set aside in the federal budget given to the education agency (i.e., department of education) of each state (SEA) to supplement the school budgets in low-income communities. Each SEA then distributes this grant money to local education agencies (LEAs), commonly referred to as school districts, which are categorized as Title I schools.[40] The designation of Title I school is an LEA in which 40 percent of the student population is from a low-income family. Children are most often identified as from a low-income family when they qualify to receive a free or reduced lunch from the school.[41]

---

40   Public Law print of PL 107-110, the No Child Left Behind Act of 2001, January 8, 2002, retrieved August 24, 2011, from http://www2.ed.gov/policy/elsec/leg/esea02/107-110.pdf.

41   "No Child Left Behind Requirements for Schools," retrieved August 25, 2011, from http://www.greatschools. org/about/aboutUs.page; "What is Title I and What Type of Students Does it Serve," National Center for Educational Statistics, U.S. Department of Education Institute of Education Sciences, retrieved August 25, 2011 from http://nces. ed.gov/fastfacts/display.asp?id=158; "Public School Choice USDE Guidance," Public School Choice (PSC), retrieved

Shortly after the signing of NCLB by President George W. Bush, an amendment was added, P.L. 107-279. This amendment put in place the mechanism for ensuring that all schools—not only those receiving Title I grants—would be required to engage in federal school improvement policies.[42] The amendment to NCLB established the Institute of Education Sciences, the National Center for Education Research, the National Center for Education Statistics, and the National Center for Education Evaluation and Regional Assistance.[43] An additional requirement made by this amendment was the following:

> Any state that wishes to receive a Title I grant must include in the state plan it submits to the Secretary of Education an assurance that beginning in the 2002–2003 school year the state will participate in the biennial state-level National Assessment of Educational Progress (NAEP) in reading and mathematics at grades 4 and 8. State participation in NAEP other than reading and mathematics in grades 4 and 8 shall be voluntary.[44]

Not surprising, beginning in 2003, all states have participated in NAEP assessments for reading and mathematics. As of 2007, 46 states participated in the science and writing assessments. NAEP assessments are achievement tests separate from state achievement tests, but they strongly influence state achievement tests. Each year NAEP publishes the National Report Card, which ranks states based on academic standards. The findings of the NAEP assessment are compared to each state's assessment to determine if state standards are high or low. For example, if Ohio were to have 85 percent proficiency in fourth grade mathematics on state tests, but only 65 percent on the NAEP assessment, it would be interpreted that the state of Ohio's mathematical standards at the fourth-grade level are lower than national standards at the fourth-grade level. Conversely, if on the state assessment in Ohio for fourth-grade mathematics 45 percent of students were assessed as proficient, but NAEP determined via their assessments that 65 percent of fourth-grade students in math were proficient, it would be interpreted that the academic standards in Ohio in regard to fourth-grade mathematics were higher than the national standards. These results also allow for state-to-state comparisons and rankings.

In addition to the National Report Card are State Report Cards, SEA report cards, and buildings within an SEA report card. The federal government evaluates state standards and produces a report commonly referred to as the National Report Card. Each state also produces a report, which publicizes the scores of students on standardized tests, as well as graduation and dropout rates. The National Report Card makes comparisons of states based on standards set by

September 17, 2011, from http://www.ode.state.oh.us/GD/Templates/Pages/ODE/ODEDetail.aspx?page=3&TopicRelationID=1782&ContentID=2516&Content=107696

42   Title III—National Assessment of Educational Progress, Sec. 301., Short Title, retrieved August 25, 2001, from http://www.nagb.org/who-we-are/naep-law.htm

43   H.R. 3801, One Hundred and Seventh Congress of the United States of America, at the second session, retrieved August 25, 2001, from http://www2.ed.gov/policy/rschstat/leg/PL107-279.pdf

44   "Important Aspects of No Child Left Behind Relevant to NAEP," National Assessment of Educational Progress, retrieved August 25, 2011, from http://nces.ed.gov/nationsreportcard/nclb.asp

the National Assessment Governing Board, which is an "independent bipartisan board" that is "made up of 26 members, including governors, state legislators, local and state school officials, educators and researchers, business representatives, and members of the general public."[45]

On the National Report Card, each state is rated as Basic, Proficient, or Advanced. The Basic achievement level means "partial mastery of prerequisite knowledge and skills that are fundamental for proficient work at each grade."[46] The second benchmark is the Proficient level, which "represents solid academic performance. Students at this level have demonstrated competency on challenging subject matter. Proficiency."[47] Advanced signifies superior performance.[48] Perhaps one of the most confusing aspects of the National Report Card is that proficient "is not synonymous with grade level performance."[49] In the 2009 National Report Card, the word proficient is used 50 times, but the definition of proficient is not clearly explained. Instead the above, rather obscure definitions are provided. Furthermore, only one state, on one indicator, reached the proficient level. Massachusetts achieved proficiency in math at the eighth grade level.[50]

In each state report card, a different set of descriptors may be utilized. For example, in Ohio six categories of ranking exist: 1) Excellent with Distinction; 2) Excellent; 3) Effective; 4) Continuous Improvement; 5) Academic Watch; and 6) Academic Emergency.[51] Whereas the federal ratings are based on NAEP testing as well as graduation and dropout rates, in Ohio these ratings are obtained via four separate measures, the first being a state indicator of academic achievement:

- Meeting or exceeding the goal of 75 proficient or above on

3rd grade achievement tests: reading, mathematics

4th grade achievement tests: reading mathematics

5th grade achievement tests: reading, mathematics, science

6th grade achievement tests: reading, mathematics,

7th grade achievement tests: reading, mathematics

8th grade achievement tests: reading, mathematics, writing, science, social studies

- Meeting or exceeding the goal of 85 proficient or above on Ohio Graduation Test—Cumulative 11th grade, reading, mathematics, writing, science, social studies
- Meeting or exceeding the 90 percent state requirement in Graduation Rate

---

45 "Overview," National Assessment Governing Board, retrieved September 18, 2011, from http://www.nagb.org/who-we-are/overview.htm

46 Mapping State Proficiency Standards onto the NAEP Scales: Variation and Change in Standards for Reading and Mathematics, 2005–2009, P. 9, U.S. Department of Education, NCES 2011–458, retrieved September 18, 2011, from http://nces.ed.gov/nationsreportcard/pdf/studies/2011458.pdf

47 Ibid., p. 30.

48 Ibid., p. 30.

49 Ibid

50 Ibid.

51 "2010–2011 State Report Card," Ohio, retrieved September 20, 2011, from http://education.ohio.gov/GD/Templates/Pages/ODE/ODEDetail.aspx?page=3&TopicRelationID=115&ContentID=34744

- Meeting or exceeding the 93 percent state requirement in Attendance Rate.[52]

The second academic achievement indicator in Ohio is the Performance Index, which ranks students' test scores as limited, basic, proficient, accelerated, and advanced. The third academic achievement indicator is Value Added, which is whether or not each student gained one year in academic achievement since the previous year, as indicated on the previous year's achievement tests. The final indicator is Adequate Yearly Progress (AYP), which is whether or not a school is making adequate yearly progress (AYP) toward the NCLB goal of 100 percent proficiency by spring of 2014.[53]

A key to understanding the rather complicated school ranking system of Ohio is that it is one state's attempt to meet the federal requirements of NCLB. Though one could argue that Ohio is clearly making attempts to meet the requirements of NCLB, they failed. As of 2009:

> At the fourth-grade reading level—Ohio ranked 38th out of 49, compared to other states in the nation and scored below the basic level of academic achievement.
> At the eighth-grade reading level—Ohio ranked 34th out of 49, compared to other states, but above the basic level and below the proficient level of academic achievement.
> At the fourth-grade math level—Ohio ranked 37th out of 49, compared to other states and below the basic level of academic achievement
> At the eighth-grade math level—Ohio ranked 31st out of 49, compared to other states and exactly at the basic level of academic achievement.

All of this testing, measurement, and labeling is not simply for the purpose of bragging rights or even understanding the academic achievement of students within a state. Within NCLB are another list of ranks, and with these ranks come consequences for individual schools. Academic achievement tests, previously referred to as proficiency tests, existed prior to the passage of No Child Left Behind and gained strength with the passage of Goals 2000 by President Bill Clinton, but the federal legal requirement that all states have some form of academic achievement testing occurred with the passage of NCLB and had their own consequences for school districts not doing well on these tests.[54]

The key is AYP (Adequate Yearly Progress): Is a school district making progress toward reaching 100 percent proficiency by 2014? Whether or not a school is deemed as meeting AYP varies from state to state and has led to various strategies by states to remedy the situation:

---

52   "Guide to Understanding Ohio's Accountability System, 2010–2011, p. 2, Ohio Department of Education, retrieved September 20, 2011, from http://education.ohio.gov/GD/Templates/Pages/ODE/ODEDetail.aspx?page=279
53   "Accountability and Local Report Card Frequently Asked Questions," Ohio Department of Education, retrieved September 17, 2011, from http://www.ode.state.oh.us/GD/Templates/Pages/ODE/ODEDetail.aspx?page=3&TopicRelationID=115&ContentID=46854&Content=110534; "Adequate Yearly Progress," *Education Week*, retrieved September 17, 2011 from http://www.edweek.org/ew/issues/adequate-yearly-progress/.
54   Patrick J. McGuinn, *No Child Left Behind and the Transformation of Federal Education, 1965–2005*, University Press of Kansas, 2006.

To keep their schools from failing, some states began lowering their cutoff scores, which determine whether a student is deemed "proficient." Others took advantage of the "safe harbor" provision of the law, which gives schools credit for making AYP if they see a 10 percent decline in the proportion of students who aren't proficient within a particular subgroup, even if they fail to meet that year's target. Meanwhile, other states, including California and Illinois, increased their annual performance targets and saw their failure rates rise. In California, 61 percent of schools failed to make AYP in 2010, up from 34 percent in 2006—an increase of nearly 3,000 schools. In Illinois, 51 percent of schools missed their targets in 2010, up from 18 percent in 2006, and the numbers could have been higher, since 15 percent of the state's schools made AYP solely because of the law's safe-harbor provision (McNeil, April 28, 2011; Center on Education Policy, 2011).[55]

Schools' AYP is measured overall, building by building in a district, as well as regarding the following student subgroups: 1) students with disabilities; 2) economically disadvantaged students; 3) racial ethnic groups (African American, Asian, Hispanic, multiracial, Native American, and white), and English language learners.[56] If any one of those subgroups within a school does not meet AYP and/or the school as a whole does not meet AYP, the school is placed into School Improvement (SI) status. The following is the list of consequences for schools given this status:

School Improvement Year I occurs after AYP is not met for two consecutive years and is also referred to as *needs improvement*.
1. Offer Public School Choice (PSC) to all students
    a. Districts not having PSC options shall, to the extent practicable, establish a cooperative agreement with other school districts in the area for a transfer;
    b. Districts may offer Supplemental Educational Services (SES) as an alternative to Public School Choice for schools in SI Year 1 if either (a) there are no qualified schools available to which to transfer, or (b) the parents choose to decline the transfer school assigned for their child.
2. Develop a school improvement plan to cover a three-year period
    c. The plan must be developed within three months of being put into SI status.
3. Spend not less than 10% of the building's Title I funds on professional development
4. Promptly notify parents (in a language they can understand) and explain:
    a. What identification means;
    b. How the school compares in terms of academic achievement to other schools in the district and state;

55 "Adequate Yearly Progress," *Education Week*, retrieved September 17, 2011, from http://www.edweek.org/ew/issues/adequate-yearly-progress/.

56 "Accountability and Local Report Card Frequently Asked Questions," Ohio Department of Education, retrieved September 17, 2011, from http://www.ode.state.oh.us/GD/Templates/Pages/ODE/ODEDetail.aspx?page=3&TopicRelationID=115&ContentID=46854&Content=110534

    c. Reasons for the identification and what the school, district and state are doing to address the problem of low achievement;

    d. How the parents can become involved in addressing the academic issues that caused the school to be identified for school improvement;

    e. An explanation of the parent's options to transfer the child.

School Improvement Year II occurs after AYP is not met for three consecutive years, and is also referred to as *needs improvement.*

    1. All of the above plus—

    2. Make Supplemental Educational Services available to students from low-income families (giving priority to the lowest achieving children from this group if there are inadequate resources).

School Improvement Year III occurs after AYP is not met for four consecutive years and is also referred to as *corrective action.* The school is now in year one of Corrective Action. The district must publish and disseminate information regarding corrective actions to the public and to parents of each student enrolled in the corrective action school. The district must ensure that the identified school implements the following:

    1. All of the above plus—

    2. Take corrective action by taking at least one of the following measures:

        a. Replace school staff relevant to the failure;

        b. Institute and implement a new research-based and professionally-developed curriculum;

        c. Significantly decrease management authority at the school level;

        d. Appoint an outside expert to advise the school in its progress;

        e. Extend the school year or school day for the school;

        f. Restructure the internal organization structure of the school.

School Improvement Year IV occurs after AYP is not met for five consecutive years and is also referred to as *restructuring.*

    1. All of the above plus—

    2. Prepare a restructuring plan, to take effect within a year, to do one or more of the following:

        a. Reopen the school as a public charter school;

        b. Replace all or most of the staff (which may include the principal) who are relevant to the failure to make adequate yearly progress;

        c. Enter into a contract with an entity, such as a private management company, with a demonstrated record of effectiveness to operate the public school;

        d. Turn the operation of the school over to the ODE, if permitted by State law and agreeable to the SEA;

e. Any other major restructuring of the school's governance arrangement that makes fundamental reforms, such as significant changes in the school's staffing and governance, to improve student academic achievement in schools and that has substantial promise of enabling the school to make adequate yearly progress.

f. NOTE: Rural districts of less than 600 students in average daily attendance … may request assistance from the Secretary for implementing this portion of the law.

School Improvement Year V occurs after AYP is not met for six consecutive years and is also referred to as *restructuring*.

1. All of the above plus—
2. Implement the restructuring plan developed in SI Year 4.[57]

The reference to "Supplemental Educational Services" above means resources outside of the school district, but paid for by the school district, such as tutoring. In other words, these are educational services provided by organizations and individuals not employed by the school.[58] During School Improvement Year I, these services are available only for low-income families who attend Title I schools; following School Improvement Year I, they are available to all students, but students from low-income homes are given priority. Once a parent selects a company to provide service, members of that organization meet with school officials to determine how academic progress will be measured.[59]

"Public School Choice (PSC)" refers to the requirement to provide parents the opportunity to transfer their children to another public school not needing improvement and may include public charter schools.[60] When parents are provided this option, with more than one choice, LEAs decide which students are permitted to go to which school and must give priority to "lowest achieving students from low-income families."[61] In some states, school choice means that students are given vouchers, which pay for all or part of the tuition for a private school, but not for other costs such as uniforms or school supplies. Regardless, if a student transfers to another public school or a

---

57 Center for School Finance, Office of Federal Programs School Improvement/District Improvement Questions and Answers, p. 2 of 7. Revised 10/8/2004 as cited in "School Improvement/District Improvement, Questions and Answers, Center for School Finance, Office of Federal Programs, Ohio Department of Education, retrieved September 17, 2011, from http://www.ode.state.oh.us/GD/Templates/Pages/ODE/ODEDetail.aspx?page=3&TopicRelationID=132&ContentID=2151&Content=109538

58 "Supplemental Educational Services," Ohio Department of Education, retrieved September 17, 2011, from http://www.ode.state.oh.us/GD/Templates/Pages/ODE/ODEDetail.aspx?page=3&TopicRelationID=1781&ContentID=1908&Content=111551

59 "Supplemental Educational Services Brochure," U.S. Department of Education, retrieved September 17, 2011, from http://www2.ed.gov/parents/academic/involve/suppservices/index.html

60 "Public School Choice USDE Guidance," p. 12, retrieved September 18, 2011, from http://www.ode.state.oh.us/GD/Templates/Pages/ODE/ODEDetail.aspx?page=3&TopicRelationID=1782&ContentID=2516&Content=107696.

61 Ibid., p. 18.

private school, under the school choice provisions, the original LEA must provide transportation to the new school."[62]

The last key component of NCLB is that students are not the only ones now taking tests. Teachers must also take tests to gain the title of "Highly Qualified Teacher." Prior to NCLB, teacher qualifications were different from state to state. The certification of teachers at the state level continued to be a national practice, but two requirements were added if a teacher were to be given the title of "highly qualified teacher." First, to achieve this title, a teacher must possess a bachelor's degree. Second, teachers must demonstrate knowledge of content area prior to obtaining certification or licensure. Approximately 40 states use tests created by Educational Testing Services (ETS) to evaluate the knowledge of preservice teachers.[63] ETS is a nonprofit organization that creates the NAEP tests and the SAT, as well as 50 million other assessment tests including the PRAXIS tests used.

CONCLUSION

Much controversy surrounds IDEA and NCLB. Some of those controversies will be explored further in the discussion questions below. Regardless of the controversy surrounding these two federal policies, they have changed the structure and organizational context of teaching and learning in this nation. Historically, from the national perspective, schools exemplified the idea of democracy via their decentralized nature. Their patriarchal and paternalistic nature, from the school system perspective, mirrored our Founding Fathers' belief that "All men are created equal." IDEA and NCLB have, in many respects, diminished the democratic perspective and strengthened the paternalistic perspective. School authorities and building principals have been given a proverbial rod to bend teachers to their will. However, an even stronger rod has been given to education officials at the state and federal level to bend the will of school authorities and building principals.

NCLB and IDEA are underfunded federal mandates. They are enforced via threats of removal of federal funding for schools, yet they are costing states and school districts more money than they receive from the federal government. To use a phrase by former first lady Nancy Reagan, why do they not "just say no"? IDEA has the backing of case law for enforcement purposes; NCLB does not. So why do states continue to follow its mandates? Could it be because if they do not they will lose their rod? Individual school districts cannot continue to function if they lose state funding and thus must follow the dictates of their state departments of education. States are at risk of violating the Fourteenth Amendment to the U.S. Constitution (see Chapter Three) if they do not follow NCLB; however, the degree to which they follow the mandates varies. Some

---

62   Ibid., p. 28.
63   "ETS Fast Facts," retrieved September 17, 2011, from http://www.ets.org/about/fast_facts; "Who Are We," retrieved September 17, 2011, from http://www.ets.org/about/who

states, such as Ohio, have embraced the mandates of NCLB, and one could easily argue, taken it even further than the original mandates. Why?

I will be the first to admit that when it comes to the motivations of politicians and policy maker, my beliefs are extremely negative. I embrace the idea that every decision they make is for selfish personal reasons. Their first priority is staying in office. Their second priority is to make a name in history and/or money. With this stated, it is not surprising that I am suspect of all federal policies, especially education policies. I tend to view political debates and discussions regarding education as simply a means of changing the political discussion away from real issues facing our nation for which there are no simple solutions. It is easy to bash teachers and argue that they must be held more accountable. It is easy to say that our educational system is in crisis. As I will discuss in later chapters, I believe that, if there is a crisis, it is one created by politicians, policy makers, and parents, not teachers. Scapegoating teachers, however, has become a national pastime and has gotten many politicians elected and/or kept them in office. It has also increased the wealth of private citizens who donate to political campaigns, but has it done anything to benefit our nation's children?

In addition to my suspicions regarding the motivations behind federal education policy, I am greatly concerned that NCLB and IDEA convey opposing messages regarding the purpose of education in the United States. The Individuals with Disabilities Act, in practice and the letter of the law, focuses our national attention on the idea of equality for all in our public schools. In writing, the No Child Left Behind Act sounds like it is also about achieving equality in our public schools, but it is more about striving for excellence in our public schooling. Those states and schools that strive for and/or achieve excellence are ranked higher and given bragging rights; those states—and particularly schools—that do not achieve excellence, are punished.

Regardless of my cynicism regarding politician and policy makers, or my beliefs regarding federal education policies, I believe IDEA and NCLB have dramatically changed the legal and organizational context of schooling in America. Further, though I oppose the bashing of teachers, federal education policies, especially NCLB, have brought schooling to the forefront of national debates. In doing so, these paternalistic policies have led to dialogues which are central to the practice of democracy. Even if NCLB is repealed or weakened, it has changed discussions regarding schooling in the United States and implemented structures that may change, but are unlikely to disappear. Personally, I would like to see the creation of special education schools in every county of this nation, so that we could better meet the needs of children with disabilities and interfere less with the learning of students without disabilities. However, doing so would lead to separation and segregation of students, and would also be decidedly undemocratic.

DISCUSSION QUESTIONS

1. In this chapter, I was much more forthright with my bias. Is my conclusion consistent with the information in this chapter? Did my sources strengthen my arguments? Should I have used other sources? Did I succeed in my final arguments regarding what these two laws say about the purpose of education in the United States? Did the sources I utilized support this argument? Did the quotes I provided and or the organization of this chapter lead you to this same conclusion?

2. If you return to the first two chapters of this book, you will note that throughout the history of our nation, the purpose of schools has been a moral purpose of education. Given this premise, what is the moral purpose of education in the United States if one were only to read IDEA and examine school practices as a result? What is the moral purpose of education in the United States if one were only to read and examine the practices of NCLB? Are they contradictory, as I suggest?

3. Using the information in this chapter examine following questions (Hint: None of these questions has a simple "yes" or "no" answer):
   a. If a child with a disability is disruptive in a class, is a school permitted to restrict that child from a traditional classroom?
   b. If the majority of students in school pass the state academic achievement tests, but children with disabilities in that school district do not, is the school considered proficient?
   c. Are teachers at schools with excellent ratings paid more than teachers at schools where fewer students pass proficiency tests?
   d. If a teacher's students fail state achievement tests, is the teacher fired?
   e. If a child has an anger management disability and punches a teacher, can the school punish that child? Must the teacher continue working with the violent child?

4. How would public education be different if we did not have IDEA?

5. How would public education be different if we did not have NCLB, the Bilingual Education Act, the Civil Rights Act, and Title IX?

CLASS ACTIVITIES

1. In the links below are resources that will help in gaining a better understanding of the Bilingual Education Act, the Civil Rights Act, and Title IX. Examine these links to get a better understanding of each; compare and contrast how these laws are similar and different from IDEA and NCLB.

2. A significant focus of NCLB, as well as the explanation above, is on accountability. NCLB, however, also addresses other areas of schooling. Using the resources below, what aspects of NCLB are not included in this chapter?

3. Debate in class what should be the purpose of public education in the United States and whether or not it should be to strive for equality or excellence. If equality, for whom and how so? If excellence, how so? Use information from this chapter as well as the links below to defend your position.

4. As indicated above, many controversies surround NCLB and IDEA. Use the links below and the following questions to explore these controversies.

    a. Are schools being evaluated fairly?

    b. Are the standards too low, or are they too high?

    c. Are the various people who are determining academic standards at the federal and state level qualified to do so?

    d. Is more money needed to achieve the goals set, or is money not the key to academic achievement?

    e. Are we as a nation putting too much pressure on students and teachers, or are our expectations too low?

    f. Should tax dollars meant to pay for public schooling be given to private schools and private organizations or companies?

    g. Will such practices lead to the privatization of public school in the United States? Should we move more into the direction of privatization?

    h. Should we give priority in our schools to the disabled, economically deprived, English language learners, and ethnic minority students?

    i. Is all of this an effort to fulfill promises not fulfilled by laws such as Brown v. Board, or do other reasons exist for these federal education policies?

Online Resources

National Center for Education Statistics   http://nces.ed.gov/

"The Condition of Education 2012," National Center of Educational Statistics
    http://nces.ed.gov/pubsearch/pubsinfo.asp?pubid=2011033

U.S. Department of Education   http://www.ed.gov/

Building the Legacy: IDEA 2004   http://idea.ed.gov/

Elementary and Secondary Education Act, U.S. Department of Education   http://www.ed.gov/esea

No Child Left Behind   http://www2.ed.gov/policy/elsec/leg/esea02/index.html

Individuals with Disabilities Education Act (IDEA): Overview of Major Provisions, CRS Report for Congress   http://www.law.umaryland.edu/marshall/crsreports/crsdocuments/RS20366_01112002.pdf

Individuals with Disabilities Education Improvement Act of 2004   http://frwebgate.access.gpo.gov/cgi-bin/getdoc.cgi?dbname=108_cong_public_laws&docid=f:publ446.108

State Education Agencies   http://wdcrobcolp01.ed.gov/Programs/EROD/org_list.
cfm?category_ID=SEA

EdWeek, Topics   http://www.edweek.org/topics/index.html?intc=thed

Bilingual Education: An Overview, CRS Report for Congress   http://www.policyalmanac.
org/education/archive/bilingual.pdf

The Bilingual Education Act: Twenty Years Later   http://www.ncela.gwu.edu/files/rcd/
BE021037/Fall88_6.pdf

The Office of English Language Acquisition   http://www2.ed.gov/about/offices/list/oela/
index.html

Office of Civil Rights   http://www.hhs.gov/ocr/

Civil Rights Act (1964): National Archives   http://www.archives.gov/education/lessons/
civil-rights-act/

Title IX and Sex Discrimination   http://www2.ed.gov/about/offices/list/ocr/docs/tix_dis.
html

CHAPTER SIX

FEDERAL EDUCATION POLICY SCHOLARSHIP AND THE LEGAL AND ORGANIZATIONAL CONTEXT OF SCHOOLING

WHY DO I NEED TO KNOW THIS?

In Chapter Five, NCLB and IDEA were explained in detail. Understanding the specifics of each federal policy is necessary for all educators, but that does not mean they are not controversial. As indicated in the conclusion of Chapter Five, a central issue of that debate is whether or not the two policies are compatible in practice or contradictory philosophically and pedagogically. In this chapter, scholars discuss how to balance the competing requirements, what must be done to enable teachers to meet these goals, and what has not been done, but should be done to ensure that both policies may be fulfilled.

At the end of Chapter Five, I suggest that we as a nation must choose educational equity or educational excellence, that these two goals are not possible to achieve together. I also suggest that, in trying to achieve these competing educational ideologies, we have lost our focus on the moral purpose of education in the United States. The articles in this chapter take a very different position and instead assume that both federal policies can exist side by side, but that some changes must occur for that goal to be achieved. I disagree, but I want the reader (and my students) to come to their own conclusions, which is why I have included articles that approach these federal polices from a very different perspective than mine. While reading these articles, I encourage all readers to identify the assumptions of each scholar and compare their conclusions to those I made in Chapter Five.

WHAT IS FEDERAL EDUCATION POLICY SCHOLARSHIP?

In Chapter Four, when discussing case law scholarship, I identified two primary sources: legal scholars and educational scholars. In this chapter, a new type of educational scholar is introduced—the practitioner scholar. Teacher education is a professional education, much like law school and medical schools. However, it primarily begins at the undergraduate level. As a result, training for teachers simultaneously addresses scholarship and practice. The two cannot and should not be separated. As a result, within educational scholarship is the voice of practitioners and teachers as well as the voices of non-practitioner scholars, who often serve as the critics of education. It is the critics who ask what might be described as deeper questions, such as, "What does this policy indicate regarding the moral purpose of education?" while practitioners ask, "Now that this policy exists, how do we make it happen?" Both types of scholarship are vital in understanding the dynamics of education in a democratic society; both are represented in this chapter.

I fall into the category of a critic of education. My PhD is in a field called Cultural Foundations. We examine educational issues from a multidisciplinary perspective: historical, sociological, philosophical, anthropological, political science, etc. As I tell my students, I represent the public in public education. Former teachers should teach methods courses and should have experience "in the trenches," but someone should also represent the public in teacher education programs. That is my role. Some argue that only former teachers should teach in teacher education programs. I clearly disagree.

When reading the articles in this chapter, do not simply look for the bias of the author, but also the position of the author. Is this author an outside critic? Is this author someone who has "worked in the trenches?" Does it matter, and if so, why? In Chapter Seven, teacher professionalism will be explored. Part of the debate in regard to teacher professionalism is who should teach in teacher education programs. Before getting to that chapter, examine this question while reading the articles in this chapter.

SELECTED READINGS

Determining Appropriate Testing Accommodation: Complying with NCLB and IDEA
by Spencer J. Salend

In this article, Salend provides recommendations on appropriate alternative testing for students with disabilities. He begins by discussing problems that teachers, administrators, and parents experience due to the competing requirements of NCLB and IDEA. He also updates the reader on changes to legislation that occurred in 2007. Salend identifies nine steps that must be addressed for compliance of IDEA and NCLB to exist: 1) Create a diverse multidisciplinary team (MDT); 2) determine which students should receive testing accommodations; 3) understand the elements of valid testing accommodations (access, not altering); 4) be aware of a range of testing accommodations; 5) gather information to inform decision making; 6) comply with state and district policies; 7) select appropriate testing accommodations; 8) implement accommodations; and 9) evaluate testing accommodations and processes. Salend also provides additional resources for the reader, as well as outlines of the issues, regulations, and testing accommodations. This article clearly gives the reader much to consider and possibly implement, but does it resolve all of the issues tied to the competing practices and philosophies of IDEA and NCLB?

I know I need testing accommodations to pass and graduate. I think they help me show others what I have learned. But some of them are embarrassing and unnecessary. I hate it when they make me leave the classroom to take a test with the special education teacher. It makes me feel different and the other kids always ask me why I have to leave.
    —A student with a disability

Many of our students' families are very savvy. They are used to getting what they want, and many of them want their children to have the advantage of having testing accommodations when they take tests to improve their chances of getting into college.
    —A special education teacher

Although I understand the need for some testing accommodations, many of them are inappropriate and unfair. They change the nature of my tests and give students with disabilities an advantage over other students. I wish they would consult me and consider the other students when making decisions about testing accommodations.
    —A general education teacher

I was very disappointed, confused, and angry. I worked with the IEP team to identify the testing accommodations my son should receive. We listed them in the IEP and I assumed he would receive them, especially for the state tests. Then they told me the state says he can only use state-approved testing accommodations when taking the state tests. What about the other testing accommodations he's supposed to receive? He uses them to take his teachers' tests. Why can't he use them for the state tests?
    —A parent of a student with a disability

Although it has caused us to focus more on students with diverse and special needs, NCLB places an over-reliance on standardized testing, and forces schools to adopt a one-size-fits-all approach. The judging of a school's success at making adequate yearly progress based on the results of standardized tests for different groups of students with special needs can make these students scapegoats, particularly students with disabilities. Testing accommodations related to IDEA help us level the playing field for some of our students with special needs, and many of them are testing quite well. Unfortunately, many are falling farther behind.
    —A school administrator

The movement toward high-stakes testing and the implementation of testing provisions associated with the No Child Left Behind Act of 2001 (NCLB) and the Individuals With

- Complying with NCLB and IDEA.
- Differentiating between high-stakes (standardized) and teacher-made tests.
- Addressing disproportionate representation; who receives which testing accommodations?
- Understanding the elements of valid testing accommodations.
- Having a decision-making process regarding testing accommodations.
- Ensuring implementation.
- Examining issues of fairness, appropriateness, and effectiveness.
- Considering the acceptability (stigma) of testing accommodations.

Figure 1. Issues Related to Testing Accommodations

Disabilities Education Improvement Act of 2004 (IDEA) have generated a variety of issues that challenge our educational system (see Figure 1) and evoke strong reactions from educators, family members and students (Ysseldyke et al., 2004). NCLB mandates that most students with disabilities will participate in high-stakes testing programs aligned with statewide learning standards, and take the same general grade-level assessments as their classmates without disabilities. However, in lieu of taking general grade-level assessments, students with significant cognitive disabilities may be allowed to complete alternative assessments (e.g., portfolio assessment) based on *alternate achievement standards* that are not as complex as grade-level achievement standards (Browder, Karvonen, Davis, Fallin, & Courtade-Little, 2005; Yell, Katsiyannas, & Shiner, 2006). Further, students who do not have significant cognitive disabilities but whose disabilities affect their ability to achieve grade-level proficiency in the same timeframe as other students are now allowed to take alternate assessments based on *modified academic achievement standards* (see box, "What Do the Regulations Say About Assessing Students With Disabilities?"). Recognizing that many students with disabilities need accommodations in order to participate in high-stakes assessments, IDEA requires that students' individualized education programs (IEPs) delineate testing accommodations for state, district, and teacher-made tests. These testing accommodations help incorporate the principles of universal design for learning into the testing process, fostering the design and administration of testing materials that are accessible to students of a wide range of ability levels and unique strengths and challenges (McGuire, Scott, & Shaw, 2006).

Many multidisciplinary teams (MDTs) experience difficulties in determining which students should receive testing accommodations (see box, "Who Receives Testing Accommodations?"), and in selecting and consistently implementing valid testing with disabilities educated in colleges and universities (see Brinckerhoff & Banerjee, 2007, for additional information about testing accommodations and higher education).

WHAT DO THE REGULATIONS SAY ABOUT ASSESSING STUDENTS WITH DISABILITIES?

In April 2007, the U.S. Department of Education proposed new regulations for assessing students with disabilities under NCLB and IDEA that define the use of modified academic achievement standards for certain students with disabilities and guide how alternate assessment results based on such standards may be used for adequate yearly progress (AYP) purposes. These regulations allow states to

- Develop modified (challenging but less difficult) academic achievement standards that relate to mastery of grade-level content.
- Create alternate assessments based on these modified academic achievement standards that address the same grade-level content but are less difficult than the general assessments taken by students without disabilities.
- Use the principles of universal design for learning to create and administer alternate assessments.

For example, students being assessed using alternate assessment based on modified standards might take less rigorous grade-level content tests that have multiple-choice items with fewer choices and fewer passages to read.

These modified standards and alternate assessments are designed for use with students with disabilities who (a) do not have a significant cognitive disability, (b) have access to grade-level content instruction, and (c) are not likely to reach grade-level proficiency in the same timeframe as their classmates without disabilities. Therefore, states are also required to provide guidelines for IEP teams to use in identifying students with disabilities who will be assessed via alternate assessments based on modified academic achievement standards. The new regulations do not establish limits on the number of students who may take an alternate assessment based on modified achievement standards. However, when calculating AYP under NCLB, states can only count proficient and advanced test scores on these alternate assessments for up to 2.0% of all students with disabilities in the grades assessed (along with 1.0% of proficient and advanced assessment scores based on alternate achievement standards assessments administered to students with severe cognitive disabilities).

Other aspects of the new regulations include:

- Students who take alternate assessments based on modified standards can graduate with a regular high school diploma.
- Test scores of students with disabilities who have been exited from special education programs can be counted in the special education subgroup for up to 2 years after they have stopped being classified as receiving special education services, which parallels the regulations for students moving out of programs for English language learners.
- Students with disabilities can take state assessments multiple times and their highest scores can count for AYP calculations.

CREATE A DIVERSE MULTIDISTIPLINARY TEAM

As described under IDEA, MDTs make important decisions concerning the education of students with disabilities. The MDT determines if students are eligible for special education services under IDEA or Section 504 of the Rehabilitation Act, and develops an IEP or 504 accommodation plan for eligible students, which includes any testing accommodations that students need in order to participate in high-stakes assessments and take teacher-made tests. The MDT also determines which students with disabilities will take alternate assessments based on modified academic achievement standards and which ones (with significant cognitive disabilities) require alternate assessments based on alternate achievement standards. For example, when determining whether a student with a disability should take alternate assessments based on modified academic standards, the MDT should (a) be reasonably certain that, even if significant growth occurs, the student will not achieve grade-level proficiency in the year covering the student's IEP; (b) include goals addressing grade-level content standards in the student's IEP; and (c) use multiple and objective measures to assess the student's achievements including state- and district-wide assessments and classroom assessments (e.g., teacher-made tests).

The MDT should comprise a diverse group of professionals, typically students' teachers; other professionals who have knowledge of the state and district learning standards, educational assessment, curriculum and instruction; and administrators who can ensure that the testing accommodations are implemented. Including family members and students on the team also can provide important information; including culturally sensitive professionals and community members allows the team to consider cultural, experiential, and linguistic factors in assessing and instructing students (Figueroa & Newsome, 2006; Garcia & Ortiz, 2006). Therefore, in the case of second language learners, it is a good practice for the MDT to include bilingual educators and/ or English as a second language teachers.

UNDERSTAND THE ELEMENTS OF VALID TESTING ACCOMMODATIONS: ACCESS, NOT ALTERING

Because what constitutes a valid testing accommodation is often misunderstood, it is critical for all members of the MDT to understand that valid testing accommodations are designed to provide students with access to tests without altering the tests. Thus, valid testing accommodations are changes in the testing administration, environment, equipment, technology, and procedures that allow students with disabilities to participate in testing programs and do not change the nature of the test (Cox, Herner, Demczyk, & Nieberding, 2006; Sireci, Scarpati, & Li, 2005). For example, although having a proctor read test items would not be a valid testing accommodation on a reading test, as it changes the nature of the test to listening comprehension (Edgemon, Jablonski, & Lloyd, 2006), it might be appropriate for use on a mathematics test that is not designed to assess reading. Whether students are taking state, district, or teacher-made tests, the MDT should

WHO RECEIVES TESTING ACCOMMODATIONS?

Although students of color and students from lower socioeconomic backgrounds tend to be overrepresented in terms of being placed in special education, they tend to be underrepresented with respect to receiving testing accommodations. A recent study by The College Board found that affluent students with disabilities who attended private schools and public schools in the wealthiest communities were more likely to receive testing accommodations than their counterparts who attended schools in less affluent communities (Lewin, 2003). The study also reported that students with disabilities who received 24% of the accommodations for students nationwide attended less than 1% of our nation's high schools.

recognize that an essential element defining a valid testing accommodation is that it must not change the test's content, format, constructs, and results.

BE AWARE OF A RANGE OF TESTING ACCOMMODATIONS

Because of the varied purposes of testing and the unique qualities of students, it is important for members of the MDT to be aware of a range of possible testing accommodations (Ketterlin-Geller, Alonzo, et al., 2007; Salend, in press). Testing accommodations (see Figure 2) are usually categorized as relating to presentation and response mode formats; to timing, scheduling, setting alternatives; and to linguistically based factors (Edgemon et al., 2006). *Presentation mode* testing accommodations involve changes in the ways test questions and directions are presented to students (Elbaum, 2007). *Response mode* testing accommodations refer to changes in the way students respond to test items or determine their answers (Cox et al., 2006). *Timing, scheduling, and setting* testing accommodations provide alternatives to where, when, and with whom students take tests (Cohen, Gregg, & Deng, 2005; Elliott & Marquart, 2004). When language proficiency might affect a student's test performance, *linguistically based* accommodations can address the unique abilities and challenges of second language learners (Abedi & Hejri, 2004; Albus, Thurlow, Liu, & Bielinski, 2005; Herrera, Murry, & Cabral, 2007). Recent advances in technology-based testing provide new ways to assess student learning and offer novel ways to design and implement all types of testing accommodations (Ketterlin-Geller, Yovanoff, & Tindal, 2007; Thompson, Quenemoen, & Thurlow, 2006); they provide alternatives to traditional testing formats and allow for the implementation of customized testing accommodations for individual students.

Gather Information to Inform Decision Making

Instead of assuming that all students with disabilities need testing accommodations, decisions regarding the need for specific testing accommodations should be based on information about individual student characteristics, strengths, and challenges, and the accommodations that support their learning (Edgemon et al., 2006). For instance, the need for timing, scheduling, and setting testing accommodations may be based on information that reveals that students (a) have problems with processing information and staying on task; (b) require additional time to use specialized testing techniques (such as dictating answers or reading test items aloud); (c) need specialized testing conditions (such as special lighting, acoustics or equipment/furniture); (d) have physical conditions that cause them to tire easily; (e) experience test anxiety; or (f) take medications which work only for a limited amount of time or have side effects that affect performance.

Because testing accommodations should parallel instructional accommodations regularly used by students in their classrooms, MDTs also need to identify the teaching accommodations to be used in daily classroom instruction (Cox et al., 2006; Ketterlin-Geller, Alonzo, et al., 2007). There is a variety of ways to collect data on students' skills, strengths, challenges, learning and testing styles and preferences, self-concept, attitudes, and health, and effective strategies that support their learning (Brinckerhoff & Banerjee, 2007). MDTs can review assessment data and student work, tests, and records, and observe students in classroom and testing situations. Interviewing students, teachers, family, and ancillary support personnel, or asking these individuals to complete a checklist, survey, or rating scale, are also excellent ways to gather information about students and the factors that affect their learning (Ketterlin-Geller, Alonzo, et al., 2007). Some basic questions can guide MDTs in analyzing student information to determine possible testing accommodations, including:

- Does the student exhibit academic and social behaviors that interfere with his or her learning or the learning of others? If so, what are these behaviors and what strategies and resources are used to address them?
- What instructional methods, approaches, strategies, specialized equipment, technology, materials, and/or classroom designs have been successful in supporting the student's learning?
- What strategies and resources are used to help the student understand directions and respond to classroom activities?
- What are the student's learning and testing style preferences?
- Does the student have sensory, medical, and/or attention conditions that affect classroom performance?
- Does the student require extended time to complete assignments?
- Does the student need additional motivation to complete assignments?

Figure 2. Testing Accommodations

Presentation Mode Accommodations

- Reading directions and items aloud
- Clarifying/simplifying language
- Repeating directions as necessary
- Listing directions in sequential order
- Providing a sample of each item type
- Highlighting changes in the directions
- Presenting only one sentence per line
- Using markers/masks to maintain place
- Presenting tests via screen readers, audio recordings, and verbal descriptions of pictorials
- Providing students with sound amplification devices and closed-captioning, sign, or pictorially based test presentation formats
- Using reminders
- Highlighting key words or phrases

- Organizing/sequencing items appropriately and logically
- Increasing the spacing between items
- Placing fewer items on a page
- Providing a reading proctor
- Offering aid in turning pages and maintaining place
- Presenting tests via signing and/or Braille
- Providing students with graphics, tactile and photo-enlarged materials, visual magnification aids, and color acetate overlays
- Using technology to give students choices about the presentation modes used to administer tests (e.g., print size, color, backgrounds, spacing and pacing, etc.)

Response Mode Accommodations

- Responding via native language/preferred mode of communication
- Providing extra space
- Using lined/grid paper
- Using enlarged answer bubbles/blocks
- Providing a proctor to monitor place and the recording of answers
- Allowing students to respond via technology (e.g., voice recognition and augmentative communication systems, touch screens, adapted switches and keyboards, word processors, Braille writers, pointers, spell and grammar checkers, word prediction and cueing programs, electronic dictionaries/thesauri, digital recorders, etc.)

- Writing answers on the test/test booklet
- Allowing students to dictate answers
- Fewer items per page
- Using multiple-choice items
- Providing a scribe
- Allowing students to use memory aids (e.g., calculators, glossaries, software programs, mathematics tables, and PDAs, etc.) and to access strategy reminders and motivational enhancements
- Embedding error minimization techniques

Timing and Scheduling Accommodations

- Giving more time or untimed tests
- Providing shorter versions of tests
- Allowing breaks as needed
- Adjusting the testing order

- Eliminating items/sections
- Varying the times of the testing sessions
- Scheduling shorter testing sessions
- Administering tests over several days

Setting Accommodations

- Taking tests in small groups/individually in separate locations
- Allowing movement and background sounds
- Providing preferential seating arrangements (carrels)

- Providing adaptive furniture/equipment
- Eliminating visual and auditory distractions
- Delivering reinforcement
- Providing specific environmental arrangements (lighting, acoustics, sound amplification)

Linguistically Based Accommodations

- Using understandable and familiar language
- Repeating orally based directions/items
- Teaching the language of academic testing
- Pairing items/directions with graphics/pictures
- Translating tests
- Allowing responses in native languages/dialects
- Offering review sheets and lists of important vocabulary
- Allowing use of bilingual materials (glossaries/dictionaries)

- Providing context clues
- Providing alternate ways to demonstrate mastery of test material
- Providing translators to administer tests
- Using technology to give students choices about the language in which the test is administered and whether to access bilingual materials and pop-up translations.

COMPLY WITH STATE AND DISTRICT POLICIES

The MDT can use information gathered about students and their classroom accommodations to determine if individual students need testing accommodations to participate in high-stakes assessments and/or to take teacher-made tests. For students who need testing accommodations to participate in high-stakes assessment, the MDT must comply with state and district policies regarding approved accommodations (Ketterlin-Geller, Alonzo, et al., 2007; Thurlow, Lazarus, Thompson, & Morse, 2005). In making these determinations, states often consider whether the accommodation is appropriate and valid and would eliminate "a barrier due to a disability without changing the construct being tested" (MacArthur & Cavalier, 2004, p. 55). Therefore, accommodations related to high-stakes testing must be consistent with state and district policies on approved testing accommodations and provided under certain testing situations (Elliott & Thurlow, 2006). For instance, some states mandate that a testing accommodation be employed for a specific period of time before it can be used during high-stakes assessments (Thurlow et al., 2005).

Some states also have provisions that allow MDTs to seek permission to allow individual students to use accommodations that are not listed as approved. Because accommodations allowed in one state may not be allowed in other states and policies vary from state to state, educators should obtain information about their state's testing accommodations policies by contacting their state education department or visiting its Web site (see box, "Additional Resources").

Testing accommodations should parallel instructional accommodations regularly used by students in their classrooms.

MDTs generally have more flexibility when identifying testing accommodations for students taking districtwide assessments and teacher-made tests. For example, although a state may not approve the use of a thesaurus for its standardized writing test, the MDT may determine that it is an appropriate testing accommodation for teacher-made tests in a range of content area classes. MDTs also need to be aware of any districtwide testing policies. Therefore, it is important to differentiate between testing accommodations used during the administration of teacher-made, districtwide, and state assessments, and to make this distinction explicit when identifying testing accommodations on students' IEPs or 504 accommodation plans. However, even when students are taking teacher-made and districtwide tests, testing accommodations should not alter the constructs or content upon which tests are based. Furthermore, in the vast majority of cases, the testing accommodations used for teacher-made tests and high-stakes tests should be similar to allow educators both to assess student performance on high-stakes assessments and so that students can become more familiar with the conditions they will encounter when taking high-stakes tests.

SELECT APPROPRIATE TESTING ACCOMMODATIONS

Rather than being disability-specific, testing accommodations for students should be individually determined, consistent with state and district policies, proven to be effective, and appropriate for the testing context. Valid testing accommodations also should be selected and implemented so that they do not violate the constructs and content upon which the test is based (Salend, 2008). In addition, students may benefit from more than one testing accommodation and therefore may require packaging or combining different types of testing accommodations (Edgemon et al., 2006). Resources to assist MDTs in selecting testing accommodations for students with a wide range

Additional Resources

National Center on Educational Outcomes (NCEO)

(http://cehd.umn.edu/nceo)

This site offers information, research, and resources on a variety of aspects related to the involvement of students with disabilities and English language learners in national and state testing programs. It offers access to publications, presentations, teleconferences, projects, statewide policies, bibliographies, and related Web sites on such topics as testing accommodations, alternate assessments, reporting testing results, and universal design.

Center for Research on Evaluation, Standards, and Student Testing (CRESST)

(http://www.cse.ucla.edu)

This site disseminates current research, newsletters, policy briefs, and resources for educators and families addressing evaluation issues such as testing techniques, technology, and interpretation of test scores.

Center for Educational Assessment

(http://www.umass.edu/education/cea/main.htm)

This center disseminates research reports and policy analysis related to educational assessment.

Practical Assessment, Research, and Evaluation (PARE)

(http://www.pareonline.net)

This site provides educators with access to an online journal presenting articles addressing assessment, research, and evaluation.

National Center for Fair and Open Testing (Fairtest)

(http://www.fairtest.org)

This site, designed to make sure that educational assessment is conducted in fair, open, valid and educationally sound ways, includes helpful features such as fact sheets, publications, and links to resources.

of disabilities include the Survey of Teacher Recommendations for Accommodation (Ketterlin-Geller, Alonzo. et al., 2007); Assessment Accommodation Checklist (Elliott, Kratochwill & Schulte, 1998); and the Dynamic Assessment of Test Accommodations (Fuchs & Fuchs, 2001).

When selecting testing accommodations, another important factor to consider is acceptability—the extent to which a specific accommodation is easy to implement, effective, appropriate for the setting, fair, and reasonable (Edgemon et al., 2006). Reasonableness can be assessed by examining the accommodation in terms of how much time, money, and resources are needed to implement it, and whether it will require important changes in the tests or their administration.

In general, educators are more likely to choose accommodations that they perceive are practical, easy to use, effective, and consistent with their philosophy.

An important aspect of acceptability is the impact of the accommodation on specific students and their peers, so it is important for MDTs to ensure that accommodations do not adversely affect either the students or their classmates. Testing accommodations should not give students with disabilities an advantage over other students; if implemented for a group of students, these accommodations should have little effect on the test performance of students without disabilities (Elliott & Marquart, 2004; Sireci et al., 2005).

IMPLEMENT TESTING ACCOMMODATIONS

MDTs also should consider students' and educators' reactions to and perceptions of testing accommodations, which can impact the extent to which testing accommodations are implemented appropriately and consistently. Both students and educators prefer testing accommodations that are fair, useable, age appropriate, and do not embarrass or isolate students. For example, students may not like to take tests in separate locations because it may make them different from their classmates. It also is important for MDTs to consider students' and educators' prior experiences with and concerns about accommodations as well as the training they need to implement specific accommodations (Cox et al., 2006). For instance, although dictation can be an effective accommodation, many students may need training and experience in dictating to a scribe to use it successfully (MacArthur & Cavalier, 2004). Similarly, when proctoring an exam for students, educators should be taught how to proctor exams effectively and appropriately and to avoid giving students cues and additional information that may affect their answers.

Therefore, when identifying testing accommodations, the MDT should consider the factors that foster implementation by delineating on IEPs and 504 accommodation plans (a) which individuals will be responsible for implementing the testing accommodations; (b) what materials, resources, technology, locations, and equipment will be needed to implement the testing accommodations; and (c) what training students and educators will need to implement the testing accommodations (Salend, in press). Thus, if the MDT determines that an appropriate testing accommodation is the services of a proctor or scribe, the team must also determine who will be the scribe as well as what training the proctor/scribe and the student will need to receive.

EVALUATE TESTING ACCOMMODATIONS AND THE PROCESS

Testing accommodations should be continually evaluated to assess if they are valid, effective, useful, and fair (Cox et al., 2006); it is important to examine their impact on students, educators, family members and other relevant parties. Primarily, the impact of testing accommodations should be assessed by examining student learning data such as increased mastery of learning standards,

- Did we have a diverse multidisciplinary team?
- Did we determine whether the student was eligible for special education services?
- Did we determine whether the student should take general grade-level assessments, alternate assessments based on modified academic achievement standards, or alternate assessments based on alternate achievement standards, or a combination of those assessments?
- Did we understand and consider the elements of valid testing accommodations?
- Did we use a variety of methods and sources to collect data to determine:
  - How the student's disability affects his or her educational performance?
  - Which effective classroom-based instructional accommodations support the student's learning?
  - Whether and to what extent the student needs testing accommodations to access state and district testing programs and/or teacher-made tests?
- Did we identify a range of testing accommodations, including:
  - Presentation mode accommodations?
  - Response mode accommodations?
  - Timing, scheduling, and setting accommodations?
  - Linguistically based accommodations?
  - Technology-based accommodations?
- Does the student's IEP/504 plan contain testing accommodations that:
  - Allow tests to assess the student's abilities rather the student's disability?
  - Do not change the validity and integrity of the test's content, format, constructs, and results?
  - Parallel accommodations that the student uses regularly in daily classroom instruction?
  - Are delineated as approved for state and district testing?
  - Are delineated as only appropriate for teacher-made tests?
  - Are valid, effective, easy to use, appropriate for the setting, and reasonable?
  - Do not adversely affect either the student or classmates?
  - Are fair, age-appropriate, and do not embarrass or isolate students?
  - Have limited impact on the performance of others?
- Did we identify:
  - Which individuals are responsible for implementing the testing accommodations?
  - What materials, resources, and equipment are needed to implement the testing accommodations?
  - What training is needed by students and educators to implement the testing accommodations?
  - Which strategies will be used to gradually fade out testing accommodations so that students take tests in the same ways as their peers without disabilities?
- Did we continually assess the effectiveness, validity, efficiency, fairness, acceptability, and continued need of the student's testing accommodations and make changes based on these data?
- Which aspects of the testing accommodations determination process went well? Which were problematic?
- What steps could we take to improve our testing accommodations determination process?

Note. From Salend, S. J., *Creating Inclusive Classrooms: Effective and Reflective Practices* 6/e, ®2008, p. 501, Reprinted by permission of Pearson Education, Inc., Upper Saddle River, New Jersey.

Figure 3. Evaluating the Testing Accommodations Determination Process

changes in student grades, and improved state and districtwide exam results. In addition to assessing the positive impact of testing accommodations on student performance, MDTs also should consider possible cautions associated with the testing accommodations (Edgemon et al., 2006; Ketterlin-Geller, Alonzo, et al., 2007), For example, having items read aloud can make some test items more difficult and make the testing session longer. Effective testing accommodations can be continued, and others gradually faded out so that students take tests in the same ways as their peers without disabilities. Similarly, efforts should be made to make sure that effective testing accommodations used for teacher-made tests match those allowed for high-stakes tests so that students can become more familiar with the conditions they will encounter when taking high-stakes tests. Testing accommodations that are not achieving their intended outcomes should be revised to make them more effective or discontinued if they continue to be unsuccessful.

MDTs also should consider the perceptions of students, educators, and family members regarding testing accommodations for overall effectiveness, efficiency, and acceptability. Examining issues of equity helps determine the extent to which various testing accommodations are available and accessible to individual students as well as different groups of students. Teachers might reflect upon the impact of testing accommodations on the teaching and learning process, including success in fostering student performance, availability for a range of students, impact on other students, and the time and training it takes to implement the accommodations. Students and family members can also share their perceptions to help identify successful and unsuccessful testing accommodations, and make recommendations for improvement. Tools such as Elliott and Marquart's survey (2004) can solicit student feedback and preferences regarding the effectiveness and acceptability of testing accommodations used.

Finally, MDTs also need to evaluate the testing accommodations determination process itself. Reflection (see Figure 3) is a particularly good way for MDTs to evaluate their processes and think critically about their professional practices (Salend, 2008). These reflections can serve as a framework for identifying the team's strengths, challenges, and misunderstandings as well as determining the steps that can be taken to improve effectiveness.

LEARN MORE ABOUT ASSESSMENT AND TESTING ACCOMMODATIONS

Special education is a field that is constantly changing as new research, model programs, assessment and instructional strategies, and legislation related to formal and informal assessment and testing accommodations continue to evolve. Effective professionals strive to keep abreast of new developments and continue to develop their skills. There is a variety of ways to learn more about current research findings, techniques, issues and changes—from reading journal articles and books such as those in this article's reference list to visiting Web sites (see box, "Additional Resources") that offer information and resources addressing issues related to assessment and testing accommodations.

Final Thoughts

Educators, students, and families face many challenges in responding to the testing mandates of the NCLB and IDEA, including providing students with disabilities with individualized, approved, valid, effective, and acceptable testing accommodations. There are guidelines and resources that MDTs can use to identify, select, and evaluate appropriate testing accommodations for individual students. In addition to providing students with valid testing accommodations, educators can help students perform at their optimal levels on tests by offering instruction that aids students in developing test-taking skills. Educators also can carefully examine and tailor the format, content, and readability of their tests to address their students' unique learning characteristics (Salend, 2008). It also is important for educators to supplement traditional testing with informal ongoing classroom-based techniques such as observations, curriculum-based measurement, and portfolio assessment to provide a complete picture of student performance, to examine and improve the effectiveness of their instructional programs, and to demonstrate accountability.

References

Abedi. J., & Hejri, F. (2004). Accommodations for students with limited English proficiency in the National Assessment of Educational Progress. *Applied Measurement in Education*, 17, 371–392.

Albus, D., Thurlow, M., Liu, K., & Bielinski, J. (2005). Reading test performance of English language learners using an English dictionary. *The Journal of Educational Research*, 98, 245–253.

Brinckerhoff, L. C., & Banerjee, M. (2007). Misconceptions regarding accommodations on high-stakes tests: Recommendations for preparing disability documentation for test takers with learning disabilities. *Learning Disabilities Research & Practice*, 22, 246–255.

Browder, D. M., Karvonen, M., Davis, S., Fallin, K., & Courtade-Little, G. (2005). The impact of teacher training on state alternate assessment scores. *Exceptional Children*, 71, 267–282.

Cohen, A. S., Gregg, N., & Deng, M. (2005). The role of extended time and item content on a high-stakes mathematics test. *Learning Disabilities Research & Practice*, 20, 225–233.

Cox, M. L., Herner, J. G., Demczyk, M. J., & Nieberding, J. J. (2006). Provision of testing accommodations for students with disabilities on statewide assessments: Statistical links with participation and discipline rates. *Remedial and Special Education*, 27, 346–354.

Edgemon. E. A., Jablonski, B. R., & Lloyd, J. W. (2006). Large-scale assessments: A teacher's guide to making decisions about accommodations. *TEACHING Exceptional Children*, 38(3), 6–11.

Elbaum, B. (2007). Effects of an oral testing accommodation on the mathematics performance of secondary students with and without learning disabilities. *The Journal of Special Education*, 40, 218–229.

Elliott, J. L., & Thurlow, M. L. (2006). *Improving test performance of students with disabilities … On district and state assessments* (2nd ed.). Thousand Oaks, CA: Corwin Press.

Elliott, S. N., Kratochwill, T. R., & Schulte, T. R. (1998). The assessment accommodation checklist. *TEACHING Exceptional Children*, 31(2), 10–14.

Elliott, S. N., & Marquart, A. (2004). Extended time as a testing accommodation: Its effects and perceived consequences. *Exceptional Children*, 70, 349–367.

Figueroa, R. A., & Newsome, P. (2006). The diagnosis of LD in English learners: Is it nondiscriminatory? *Journal of Learning Disabilities*, 39, 206–214.

Fuchs, L. S., & Fuchs, D. (2001). Helping teachers formulate sound test accommodation decisions for students with learning disabilities. *Learning Disabilities Research & Practice*, 16. 174–181.

Garcia, S. B., & Ortiz, A. A. (2006). Preventing disproportionate representation: Culturally and linguistically responsive prereferral interventions. *TEACHING Exceptional Children*, 38(4), 64–67.

Herrera, S. G., Murry, K. G., & Cabral, R. M. (2007). *Assessment accommodations for classroom teachers of culturally and linguistically diverse students.* Boston: Allyn & Bacon.

Ketterlin-Geller, L. R., Alonzo, J., Braun-Monegan, J., & Tindal, G. (2007). Recommendations for accommodations: Implications of (In)consistency. *Remedial and Special Education*, 28, 194–206.

Ketterlin-Geller, L. R., Yovanoff, P., & Tindal, G. (2007). Developing a new paradigm for conducting research on accommodations in mathematics testing. *Exceptional Children*, 73, 331–347.

Lewin, T. (2003, November 8). Change in SAT procedure echoes in disability realm: Looking closer at requests for more time. *The New York Times*, A10.

MacArthur, C. A., & Cavalier, A. R. (2004). Dictation and speech recognition technology as test accommodations. *Exceptional Children*, 71, 43–58.

McGuire, J. M., Scott, S. S., & Shaw, S. F. (2006). Universal design and its applications in educational environments. *Remedial and Special Education*, 27, 166–175.

Salend, S. J. (2008). *Creating inclusive classrooms: Effective and reflective practices* (6th ed.). Columbus, OH: Merrill/Prentice Hall.

Salend, S. J. (in press). *Inclusive testing, assessment, and grading practices: Informing instruction and supporting student learning.* Thousand Oaks, CA: Corwin Press.

Sireci, S., Scarpati, S., & Li, S. (2005). Test accommodations for students with disabilities: An analysis of the interaction hypothesis. *Review of Educational Research*, 75, 457–490.

Thompson, S. J., Quenemoen, R. F., & Thurlow, M. L. (2006). Factors to consider in the design of inclusive online assessments. In M. Hricko & S. L. Howell (Eds.), *Online assessment and measurement: Foundations and challenges* (pp. 102–117). Hershey, PA: Information Sciences Publishing.

Thurlow, M. L., Lazarus, S. S., Thompson, S. J., & Morse, A. B. (2005). State policies on assessment participation and accommodations for students with disabilities. *The Journal of Special Education*, 38, 232–241.

Yell, M. L., Katsiyannas, A., & Shiner, J. G. (2006). The No Child Left Behind Act, adequately yearly progress, and students with disabilities. *TEACHING Exceptional Children*, 38(4), 32–39.

Ysseldyke, J., Nelson, J. R., Christenson, S., Johnson, D. R., Dennison, A., Triezenberg, H., et al. (2004). What we know and need to know about the consequences of high-stakes testing for students with disabilities. *Exceptional Children*, 71, 75–94.

Reauthorization of NCLB: A Postscript on Voices from the Field
by Olusegun A. Sogunro, Judith Faryniarz, and Anthony Rigazio-DigiLio

I chose this article because of the authors' use of language, which is more clearly biased than most scholarly papers. The assumptions of the authors are plainly stated with phrases such as "deteriorating status of American education"[1] and "reactionary measure to the following decadence in American public education."[2] Prior to the authors explaining what teachers reported, the word "apathetically"[3] was used to describe these research participants. No such words are used to describe parents or administrators.

Another noteworthy aspect of this article is that it highlights the tension between federal and state education policies. Prior to the passage of NCLB, Connecticut legislators and school administrators began their own testing system. They fear that their own creation, which is "psychometrically clean examinations,"[4] will be put aside for the commercially developed assessments of NCLB.

Another advantage of this article is that it highlights the political nature of federal policies. The authors discuss motivations of Republicans and Democrats in voting for NCLB, as well as the fear of a push to privatize public education. Finally, the authors provide suggestions on how to improve NCLB.

Enacted on January 8, 2002 by President George W. Bush Jr., the No Child Left Behind Act was commissioned to revitalize the deteriorating status of American education by raising the educational performance of all school children in America. In its intent and caprices, the NCLB is a brain child of the Elementary and Secondary School Act (ESEA) of 1965 which has come with more intensity to link Federal funding to specific result-oriented educational goals. However, hardly had the euphoria that greeted the enactment of the law died down than grievous inadequacies in the law started unfolding. In other words, while the NCLB philosophy has been idealistically embracing and fascinating, its objectives have been unrealistically unattainable in many regards. The situation is likened to a very good prescription following a diagnosis of an ailment but without provision for adequate and affordable medication to cure the ailment.

The NCLB Act was a Federal Government policy crafted as a reactionary measure to the following decadence in American public education:

- That about 70 percent of inner city fourth graders is unable to read at a basic level on national reading tests.
- That American high school seniors trail most countries on international math test.

---

1 Italics added, Olusegun A. Sogunro, Judith Faryniarz, and Anthony Rigazio-DigiLio, "Reauthorization of NCLB: A Postscript on Voices from the Field," *New England Reading Association Journal*, 2009, vol. 44 (2), p. 54.
2 Ibid.
3 Ibid., p. 56.
4 Ibid., p. 57.

- That the academic achievement gap between the rich and poor, Anglo and minority gets widened at an alarming rate (Bush, 2001).

Consequently, the policy continues to be implemented nation-wide through mandatory standards, accountability and sanctions. However, without adequate funding, the outcomes of the policy's high expectations for academic success are rather becoming counter-productive. Thus the most contentious and recurring question is, "Does this legislation offer real opportunities for all American children to learn at challenging levels, or has it ironically resulted in 'Lost Opportunities Left Behind?'" This poses a critical concern in salvaging the debasing nature of American education. The crux of the matter is that while not all the states have the capability to assist the increasing number of underperforming schools, the federal government is not providing adequate funding to assist the states to alleviate the problems.

On Friday, April 15, 2004, under the auspices of the Central Connecticut State University's (CCSU) Chapter of Phi Delta Kappan, two groups of Connecticut public school administrators (superintendents and principals) representing diverse school communities across the state were engaged in two sessions of focus group interviews to voice their opinions regarding the law and its impact on their schools and districts. The event was jointly coordinated by the Departments of Educational Leadership and Reading and Language Arts at CCSU.

FOCUS GROUP DISCUSSIONS AND INTERVIEWS

Eight focus groups were used to engage participants in a face-to-face dialogue over some of the pertinent issues, concerns, and challenges from their varied experiences in implementing the NCLB policy. As recommended by Worthen, Sanders, and Fitzpatrick (1997), our role as organizers was "to facilitate discussion through posing initial and periodic questions and by moderating the responses of more vocal members and encouraging response of quieter members" (p. 383).

School superintendents and principals across the state of Connecticut constituted the two main groups of school leaders involved in the focus group interviews and discussions held on April 15, 2004 at Central Connecticut State University. With the intention of forming two sub-groups of each main group, 12 superintendents and 12 principals were selected randomly from among the state's 169 school districts representing rural, suburban and urban school settings. The selection also reflected the state's nine Education Reference Groups (ERG). Other than the ERG and location factors, the focus group of principals was a composition of representatives from elementary, middle, and high schools. However, since only 9 out of the 12 superintendents and 7 out of the 12 principals invited were in attendance, the superintendent's group was divided into two sub-groups of five and four while the seven principals present formed a separate focus group. The superintendents' session was held in the morning (8–10:30am) while the principals' session was held in the afternoon (11am– 1:30pm). Both sessions were preceded with breakfast and lunch, respectively. Each session was assigned one moderator. The task of the moderators was to facilitate the discussions by clarifying the purpose of the forum, setting ground rules, posing stimulating questions (as already identified) and guiding the trend of discussions to ensure fairly equal participation of all members.

Each focus group discussion ran for about 90 minutes. The superintendent sub-groups met for about one hour each and another 30 minutes for a joint session to summarize common themes and ideas. Each of the sessions was paper and tape recorded.

Flip charts were also used to record discussion highlights. Transcripts from the focus groups were content analyzed by coding, categorizing, and theming. The emerging and recurring or isolated themes and issues are discussed later in this paper.

Following the superintendents' and principals' focus groups of April 15, 2004, data were also collected from eight convenient samples of teachers in the Spring, Summer, and Fall semesters of 2004. These groups of teachers were enrolled in the master's degree program in Educational Leadership at CCSU. In all 176 teachers were engaged in discussions in four focus groups. In other words, each class represented a focus group. That is, 28, 20, and 18 teachers from the Administration class in Spring, Summer, and Fall semesters of 2004, respectively; 19, 22, and 27 teachers from the Supervision class in Spring, Summer, and Fall semesters of 2004, respectively; 25 teachers from Education Motivation and the Learning Process class in Spring semester of 2004; and 17 teachers from the Curriculum Leadership Class in Fall semester of 2004.

Fifteen parents from Title I inner city schools in Hartford, New Britain, and New Haven were involved in one-on-one interviews. Seven of the parents were Black, six were Latino, and two were White. There were five Black, three Latino, and two White Males in the parent group. Single parents from the group were three Black (one man, two women), three Latino (three women) and one White woman.

Emerging Themes

Inadequate Funding of Supporting Initiatives

Concern for how NCLB might negatively impact schools and communities, or require interventions for which there are no funds, was expressed across the eight focus groups. Both superintendents and principals saw the need for extended instructional opportunity. As one principal noted, "We're not an agrarian society any more and we need to look at the architecture of the school calendar to support learning." The superintendents discussed extended year models currently being implemented in urban districts. There is no doubt that the burgeoning of initiatives requires adequate funding in order to be successful. In addition, educators were concerned about the law's impact on school initiatives that support other types of valuable learning experiences, such as critical thinking and problem solving, developing school culture, or educating the whole child. At the school level, principals and teachers asserted that addressing the emotional needs of children was also a necessary priority, especially for students who live in "generational poverty." One of the principals pointed out, "Schools should not be expected to make bricks without straw."

NCLB's Impact on Children and Schools

Both superintendents and principals concurred that while NCLB might be well-intentioned, implementation of the provisions of the law was problematic and, in fact, "antithetical to the intent." Both groups expressed the concern that educators had limited input into the design of the law and felt that mandates at the federal level were "too far removed from the classroom," where the most effective assessment and instructional decisions are enacted.

Focus group participants reiterated that the mechanism by which the law seeks to improve student performance is an array of sanctions, based on the belief that penalties will improve the work of educators, in their words "punishing toward excellence." Unfortunately, the effect on children, teachers, and administrators has been less than motivating as more and more schools, even high performing schools, make the "list" for one inadequacy or another. Superintendents noted that energy and resources were beginning to shift from instruction and learning to meeting the provisions of the law. Principals also expressed concern about the increased stress for teachers and the negative effects on children. "When students lack skills, and the school does not have the resources to intervene, and the students continue to fail, the law becomes discriminatory," said one principal, who noted the need for social reform, not just educational reform. Another school building leader remembered picking up a child at home to bring him in for testing in an effort to meet NCLB's standard for participation rate. "It was the first time I've seen fear on the face of a child who was afraid to fail," recalled the principal. Children and teachers care about their school and are anguished when their own performance is poor and their school carries a negative label, despite their efforts to succeed.

Teachers' Perceptions About NCLB

Following the discussions in the classrooms with eight focus groups of 176 teachers, about 93% of the teachers were concerned about the compelling pressure of the NCLB Act on their work. Apathetically, the general feeling was that it is just one more thing they have to do and perhaps one more thing that may not last. As one teacher put it, "The NCLB Act has come like a powerful hurricane of category 7 magnitude! It came overnight to discredit virtually all our efforts. Now we are being asked to work harder than ever before without adequate remunerations." Another teacher agreed, "When students do not do well, accusing fingers are pointed at us as if we don't teach well enough. They forget that it is one thing to take a presumably thirsty horse to water, it is another thing to make the horse drink it." This teacher further lamented,

Some students are just not prepared to learn. For example, in an attempt to enhance learning, we were told to adopt the principle of constructivism in teaching, especially in an attempt to encourage students to self-discover learning and be more responsible for their own learning. Whereas for constructivism to be effective, it requires small classroom settings where individualized attention and differentiated instruction are practicable. One could imagine how hectic it is to teach five subjects in a day with an average class size of 25–30 for each of the classes!"

In buttressing the above conjecture, a teacher asked, "If we believe in a constructivist teaching and its effects on enhancing learning and we have research to support our ideas, why do you think it has not been embraced by the US education system and why do we continue to focus on standardized testing and teaching to the test?" Another teacher added, "The NCLB Act is not making us teach the whole child anymore. The high-stake testing and unending demands for accountability are only good at making us teach to the test simply to make students pass the standardized tests and avoid our schools being labeled as failing or in need of improvement."

About 95% of the teachers were concerned about the role of media being indulged in orchestrating standardized test results, especially through haphazard and misleading ranking of schools. One teacher argued, "The portrayal of teachers in negative images is just not fair. While these make us lose our integrity to the public, the real estate agents often use the ranking of the test scores to boost the housing business, especially for districts that have been publicized for doing better than others." Another teacher claimed that the publicity of state and district achievement data is also responsible for the apparent "flight" of parents and their wards from low-performing to high-performing school districts. "The media's negative image of low-performing schools and the ensuing flights of students present an ugly impression that teachers in such school districts are ineffective and marginal."

Parents' Perceptions About NCLB

Parent perceptions about NCLB range broadly among different districts and communities. Some focus group participants felt that many parents do not fully understand the law. Other parents are frustrated when NCLB provisions, such as requesting a transfer to another school, do not result in marked differences in educational opportunity. Still other parents worry about increased time for testing and decreased time for learning. Parents in one community even felt that the law was irrelevant—only one more tool designed to encourage skepticism toward public education. In one- on-one interviews with 15 parents (7 Blacks, 6 Latinos, 2 Whites), especially from Title I inner city schools in Hartford, New Britain, and New Haven, concerns were expressed that the NCLB sanctions against low-performing schools would soon engulf their children's schools. One hundred percent (100%) of the parents claimed that the low-performance of their children were due to inequitable access to educational opportunities, including funding inequalities and substandard conditions of teaching and learning in their school districts.

Superintendents and principals agreed that at the end of the day, the score that meant the most to students and parents was the SAT (Scholastic Aptitude Test) score, something not reported under NCLB. In the words of one superintendent, "When high school students are applying to the colleges and universities of their choice, they ask for three or four things, and the SAT is usually one of them."

Lost Opportunities

While NCLB focuses on sanctions, there were other ways to have crafted the legislation in order to achieve its objectives. According to participating superintendents, the law does not embrace the notion of systemic reform. A superintendent described the school as the largest unit of reform and each school exists within a community context with local strengths and needs best understood and addressed by local decision makers. Thus, efforts toward school improvement must not only be grounded in valid, relevant research and practice, but must also reflect the contextual needs of each school.

Another point of discussion was the respective organizational capacities of the federal government, state government, and school districts to collaborate efforts on behalf of student learning. One participant asserted that, far more than states or districts, the federal government has "a tremendous capacity to do work in terms of creating and disseminating effective research" to improve instruction. He noted that although exciting things were happening through grants and other initiatives, for example, in reading, this information rarely reaches the typical first grade teacher who could "integrate it, understand it, and apply it." Developing a repertoire of scientifically-based but varied pedagogical methods would also allow classroom teachers to contextualize their decisions regarding instruction and assessment to the needs of their students.

Worse yet, superintendents and principals worried that debating the pros and cons of the specific provisions of the law diverted energy and resources away from student achievement, another consequence of the burden of implementation detail. "The irony is that we may lose [NCLB] as a public policy and sustaining that public policy because of the weight, the political weight, of the detail," noted one superintendent.

Impact of NCLB on CMT and CAPT

The irony of NCLB within the Connecticut context was also not lost on local superintendents. They recalled the state's informed and inclusive efforts to develop the Connecticut Mastery Test (CMT) and the Connecticut Academic Performance Test (CAPT). An understanding of these assessments begins with their history, which included input by both local educators and outside professionals. Today, in contrast to the commercially developed assessments used years ago, the CMT and CAPT are recognized by Connecticut educators as relevant, "psychometrically clean examinations" which measure important content and offer a basis for comparison across the state's schools and districts. As a result, the tests are the centerpiece of assessment in Connecticut and inform the development of district and classroom assessments across the state. Superintendents and principals alike worry that the demands of NCLB will sidetrack Connecticut's vision and direction.

No Politics Left Behind

The breadth of the political support for NCLB was clearly understood, as evidenced by comments in the focus group discussions among Superintendents. The fact that 80% of the legislatures at the national level passed the law demonstrated that the legislation was grounded in the "fundamental beliefs that are ... embraced by America today," including equitable educational experiences and school accountability. At first, it appeared that support was bi-partisan, as well, until educators began to learn more about why political leaders voted for passing the law. One superintendent recalled hearing a speaker at a recent conference address the issue directly: "The Republicans were behind this because of the voucher model; Democrats were behind it because they thought it would initiate court-mandated funding changes." Superintendents were also concerned that "the more virulent provisions of the law ... [were] a kind of set up, leading to privatization in general."

In Connecticut, congressional legislators have been convening superintendent task forces and focus groups to obtain feedback about the continuing implementation of the law. Participating district leaders noticed that, while some politicians seemed more defensive of the law, others continue to agitate for its modification.

Future Advocacy for NCLB

In the present economic climate, districts and schools are caught in the crosswinds of constricted local budgets and un-funded or under-funded federal and state mandates. Nonetheless, while advocating for the reauthorization of the NCLB Act, superintendents and principals in the CCSU focus groups did not hesitate to suggest some modifications that might more positively support student learning. These included:

- stronger equitable fiscal support for all schools to serve the needs of all students;
- clarification of our educational goals. How do we want children to learn and grow?;
- preservation of the intent of NCLB;
- an understanding of what we need to do to scale up improvement of student performance;
- stronger dissemination of research-based instructional strategies to close the achievement gap;
- implementation of a family-oriented resource model which would provide high quality interventions for parents and high quality early interventions for their children;
- a strong federal role in universal pre-school programs, beginning as early as 1.8 years of age;
- extended instructional opportunities for low performing students to prevent learning loss;

- stronger policy support for the mandates of the Individuals with Disabilities Education Act;
- making all public schools more attractive to parents and students, especially through provisions of standard learning conditions, equitable resources, and high quality teachers;
- reducing average class size to below 20 pupils across all schools in the state in order to reap the benefits of small classes, including enhanced learning conditions and student achievement.

Further to this advocacy, the organizers of the event have called for further research into alternatives to closing schools and assigning students as well as strategies for achieving the seven performance-based titles addressed in the NCLB blueprint: Improving the academic performance of disadvantaged students; boosting teacher quality; moving limited English proficiency students to English fluency; promoting informed parental choice and innovative programs; encouraging safe schools for the 21st century; increasing funding for impact aid; and encouraging freedom and accountability (Bush, 2001).

Conclusion

In this paper, we have presented the voices from the field regarding the challenges of the NCLB Act. Although we are keen advocates of educational excellence, we would not want to claim that the NCLB Act as implemented today, readily offers any appreciable fundamental solution. Rather, it manifests a knee-jerk reaction.

As generally agreed upon by the participating school administrators at the CCSU's focus group interviews, each of the evolving themes and initiatives requires advocacy for more manageable policies and adequate funding. In addition, accomplishing real and meaningful progress in reducing the achievement gap and attaining 100% proficiency on state tests for all students by the 2013-2014 school-year as mandated by the Act will demand significant changes to the fiscal structure in Connecticut and at the federal level. Whether or not the states and the federal government are able to make these resources and programs an imperative may well be the deciding factor in whether this ambitious law will be left behind.

Overall, while the authors of this paper agree with the intent of the NCLB policy to strengthen American educational system and make schools more accountable for the education of every child, we detest the law that forces schools to "teach to the test" just for the sake of not losing funding. For all practical and positive result- oriented purposes, the authors believe in an educational system that is driven by achievable goals and what Susan Ohanian (2004) has referred to as "standards of conscience" rather than deceitful philosophical slogans. Finally, without necessary modification and adequate funding, it is apt to conclude that the NCLB is simply a white elephant which does nothing other than to put a cog in the wheel of the American educational system.

REFERENCES

Bush, G.W. (2001). *Executive summary of the No Child Left Behind Act 2001*. Washington, DC: White House, http://www.ed.gov/nclb/overview/intro/ execsummary.html. Retrieved 3/30/04.

Ohanian, S. (2004, March 13). Children: More than a test score. Conference organized by the Department of Reading and Language Arts, Central Connecticut State University, New Britain, CT.

Worthen, B.R., Sanders, J.R., & Fitzpatrick, J.L. (1997). *Educational evaluation: Alternative approaches and practical guidelines* (2nd ed.). White Plains, NY: Longman.

"Some Benefit" or "Maximum Benefit": Does the No Child Left Behind Act Render Greater Educational Entitlement to Students with Disabilities?
by Philip T. K. Daniel

This article brings the discussion of the legal and organizational context of schooling full circle. In Chapter Three, the emphasis was on case laws pertaining to freedom of speech, religious freedom, and educational access. In Chapter Four, more case laws were introduced pertaining to student rights in schools, such as the right to privacy. Chapter Five focused on the specifics of IDEA and NCLB. The first two articles in this chapter focused on school practice in regard to NCLB and IDEA. The following article returns to case law. As the following diagram demonstrates, schools interpret federal policies and case laws, implement them into their organization, and the issue returns to the courts for reexamination. In this article, Daniel brings the conflicts of IDEA back to the level of case law and asks if the spirit and practice of FAPE, as outlined in Board of Education of the Hendrick Hudson Central School District v. Rowley, *is being followed.*

I. INTRODUCTION

The No Child Left Behind Act and the congressional reauthorization of the Individuals with Disabilities Education Improvement Act (IDEA) caused researchers to question whether the provision in the IDEA governing Free Appropriate Public Education should be revised to better serve the interests of special needs children. For each student protected by the IDEA, an instrument must be developed to serve the child's unique needs, and part of this requirement is the promotion of participation in the general curriculum. As determined by the national government, standards of achievement measured by assessment instruments are cornerstones of this new approach to education. This study examines federal legislation, including statutes, regulations, and case law interpreting whether a student is entitled to "some benefit" or to a maximum benefit in education. A preliminary analysis suggests that the interpretation found in *Board of Education of the Hendrick Hudson Central School District v. Rowley*[1] has changed little over the past quarter century. The United States Office of Education, however, may have a different opinion. Their recent study states that that further guidelines and research are important to establish before school personnel, parents, children, and the attorneys who represent each have a definitive position on this very important topic.

II. The *Rowley* Decision

The educational rights of students with special needs are created and protected primarily through the Individuals with Disabilities Education Act (IDEA).[2] The Act provides extensive, detailed substantive and procedural rights and protections for disabled children and their parents. The Act's fundamental premise is that all special needs children are entitled to a free appropriate public education (FAPE). Since the enactment of IDEA, there has been a great deal of litigation regarding what constitutes a FAPE. At the heart of this litigation is the definitive U.S. Supreme Court case of *Rowley*, which interpreted IDEA's[3] statutory definition of the term. The Court held that the statute does not require that a particular substantive standard be used to measure whether the education provided a special needs child is appropriate. In *Rowley*, the Court enunciated what it considered to be a "tolerable"[4] standard for regulating the content of educational programs:

> Insofar as a State is required to provide a handicapped child with a "free appropriate public education," we hold that it satisfies this requirement by providing personalized instruction with sufficient support services to permit the child to benefit educationally from that instruction. Such instruction and services must be provided at public expense, must meet the State's educational standards, must approximate the grade levels used in the state's regular education, and must comport with the child's IEP [Individualized Education Program]. In addition, the IEP, and therefore the personalized instruction, should be formulated in accordance with the requirements of the Act and, if the child is being educated in the regular classrooms of the public education system, should be reasonably calculated to enable the child to achieve passing marks and advance from grade to grade.[5]

The Court found that establishing a test for all children covered by the Act would be too difficult[6] and therefore confined its analysis to *Rowley* plaintiff's unique circumstances. The conclusion that education is appropriate if the child is achieving passing grades and advancing from grade to grade is implicit in the Court's reasoning. *Rowley* therefore established that equal access, rather than equal opportunity, was the IDEA'S goal.[7] Through its decision in *Rowley*, the Court established a "basic floor of opportunity" which need only be "individually designed to provide educational benefit to the handicapped child."[8]

Unfortunately, as later lower court opinions confirmed, in attempting to set forth a functional standard for the FAPE element of the IDEA, the *Rowley* Court created more ambiguity than clarity for educators seeking to meet the statutory requirements. Lower courts have been left to struggle with the question of how the benefit is to be measured and how much is required to qualify a disabled child for a free appropriate public education. For example, cases that immediately followed the *Rowley* decision interpreted the "some educational benefit" test as establishing a standard that does not require a school to provide the best education that money can buy.[9] In construing the *Rowley* educational benefit standard, the trend of cases reflect that special education should produce satisfactory or meaningful progress toward achievement of a disabled child's unique educational needs.[10]

III. National Standards in Education

Given the increasing national focus on standards and educational adequacy requirements, it is argued that *Rowley* and the "some benefit" language no longer accurately reflect the FAPE requirements in the IDEA.[11] The catalyst for such a position is featured in the contemporary American experiment in accountability, based on student achievement, involving universal educational standards for each grade level and high stakes proficiency testing for every student.

Accountability and Testing

At one level, accountability represents a response to poor study and work skills, and substandard overall test scores on the part of all students, especially those representing protected populations. In 2002, the United States Congress, relying on the perceived success of programs in states such as Ohio, Texas, and North Carolina, radically restructured federal education funding by imposing new accountability procedures on every state. This new legislation, entitled the No Child Left Behind Act (NCLB), is a federal spending statute, authorizing and combining under one rubric, those funds to be allocated for K–12 education programs.[12] Through the "spending clause" of the United States Constitution,[13] the federal government has extended itself into American education on a national level as never before. As a profound shift of authority over educational policy tilted toward the national government and away from the states, this mandate prescribed accountability guidelines for states, districts, and schools. The Act held states accountable by measuring student performance in state tests based on a state's general curriculum.

Assessment tests, aligned with challenging content and achievement measures for all students, are designed to accomplish accountability. States are required to administer these tests periodically. Within the core of NCLB, a number of measures are designed to drive broad gains in student achievement, and to hold states, school districts, schools and school personnel more accountable for student progress. States must establish "challenging academic content standards" and "student achievement standards" to ensure an adequate education for all students. For example, beginning in the 2002–2003 academic year, states had to furnish annual report cards showing a range of information, including achievement levels for students and targeted ethnic and socioeconomic populations; school-by-school data was also required to demonstrate this report card responsibility.—Furthermore, by the year 2005–2006, states began testing students in grades 3–12 against statewide standards in literacy, mathematics, and science. The tests had to align with state academic standards and each state had to participate in the National Assessment of Educational Progress testing program in reading and math to form year-to-year comparisons of achievement. With the national NCLB mandate, through programming states had to bring all students to a proficient level on state tests. Individual schools must meet state adequate yearly progress targets toward the proficiency level goal (based on a formula spelled out by law) for the student population as and certain demographics.

Students with special needs are a group singled out for protection under NCLB. Early on while enacting the legislation, Congress recognized the need to educate such students using the same standards as those without disabilities. Exposure to the general curriculum was initially required, and determination of progress was assessed with the same testing instruments to determine whether all students were making annual yearly progress.

Organizations supporting the needs of disabled children praised the legislation. The Disability Rights and Education Defense Fund stated that the Act "bolster[ed] the right of special needs students to participate … and make progress … in the general education curriculum … It put[s] an end to the processing and hoop jumping that students … endure … to improve their chances of getting the support they need."[14] Student disability rights organizations supported the notion that the law had an even stronger incentive than some disability statutes to align the education of special needs students with a state's general education content.[15] This meant that such students would integrate more into regular classrooms beyond social opportunities. Most of these students would be expected to reach the same level of proficiency as their non-disabled peers. This legislation was viewed as significant and as representing a noteworthy cause. Hence, few would disagree with the intent of this statute; to help educators and parents reconcile educational approaches with the needs of all students, particularly those with low-achievement scores, so as to substantially improve the chances of academic success.

IV. IDEA 1997 AND 2004 REAUTHORIZATION

The Individuals with Disabilities Education Improvement Act (IDEA) continues to define FAPE as "special education and related services that … meet the standards of the state educational agency."[16] The definition is parallel to the original language of the legislation, but today it carries a more academic-centered meaning. At the time the Supreme Court decided Rowley in 1982, most state standards spoke to the process in which services would be provided to students, but did not involve substantive requirements for provision of the educational services. Today state and federal performance objectives address the essence of what students should know and be able to do. The standards-based reform movement has incorporated language in guidelines to educational institutions regarding curriculum content, expected levels of demonstrated achievement, and benchmarks based on assessment measures. Under current mandates, in order to accomplish FAPE, students without special needs must meet state curricular and achievement standards for their respective grade levels.[17] These standards are based on content and proficiency standards rooted in a core curriculum which each state must create along with specific assessment measures.

The standards-based approach was integrated into the statute in two reauthorized phases. The 1997 IDEA amendments were the first to require demonstrated assessment of students with disabilities, marking a significant shift from the Supreme Court's decision in Rowley. These amendments established high expectations for special needs children to achieve real educational results. The amendments changed the focus of IDEA from merely providing access to an education, as the Court noted in Rowley, to requiring measured educational improvement. These changes were made explicit in the House Committee Report:

> This Committee believes that the critical issue now is to place greater emphasis on improving student performance and ensuring that children with disabilities receive a quality public education.
>
> Educational achievement for children with disabilities, while improving, is still less than satisfactory.
>
> This review and authorization of the IDEA is needed to move to the next step of providing special education and related services to children with disabilities: To improve and increase their educational achievement.[18]

The No Child Left Behind Act, signed into law in early 2002, emphasized high academic standards for all children. As noted, this included disabled children. Under NCLB, state content standards must: 1) specify what children are expected to know and do; 2) contain rigorous content; and 3) encourage the teaching of advanced skills.[19] State achievement standards must be aligned with content standards and must describe two levels of high achievement: Proficient and advanced.[20] A third level of achievement called "basic" is required to provide complete information about the progress of students towards meeting the proficient or advanced levels.[21] NCLB makes it clear that, under federal law, students with disabilities are entitled to and expected to meet the same high academic standards as non-disabled children.

The standards movement assumes that all students can achieve high levels of learning if they receive high expectations, clearly defined standards, and effective teaching to support achievement. These high expectations in state education standards, however, are at odds with the core holding in Rowley that school districts only need to meet the minimalist "some educational benefit" standard. The shift from process to outcome, which is at the heart of the standards-based movement, also contradicts the *Rowley* finding that the purpose of the IDEA is to provide access to education. The movement's emphasis on content and proficiency focuses on what students actually learn, not necessarily the process by which they learn. Special education, on the other hand, has traditionally focused on the process of providing services to students. Therefore, it has been hypothesized that it will be necessary for local and state educational agencies to incorporate state educational content and proficiency standards into the statutory definition of FAPE so that high expectations are included in the IEPs of students with disabilities. It has also been suggested that courts may use content and proficiency standards to assess whether a school has provided a child with a FAPE.

In early 2004, the United States Congress again reauthorized IDEA with the latest version entitled the Individuals with Disabilities Education Improvement Act (IDEA) or IDEA04.[22] This more recent iteration of the legislation retains the basic foundation, but also illustrates the influence of NCLB requirements of academic proficiency for all disabled students. The statute explicitly mandates that states establish performance goals for children with disabilities consistent with the goals and standards set for all children.[23] Specifically, the state must establish goals for the performance of children with disabilities that are the same as the state's definition of adequate yearly progress. This must include the state's objective of progress for children with disabilities consistent, to the extent appropriate, with any other goals and standards for children established by the state.[24] Furthermore, the state must establish performance indicators that assess progress toward achieving the goals described above, including measurable annual objectives for progress by children with disabilities.[25]

The United States Department of Education has only recently issued regulations necessary to ensure compliance with the IDEA statute. These final regulations were not complete until summer 2006 and did not take effect until October of the same year. The guidelines follow NCLB legislation and the IDEA statute with the requirement for "highly qualified teachers." Such teachers must have earned at least a bachelor's degree at an accredited institution, possess a teacher's license for the respective state, and be able to demonstrate knowledge of the content areas for subject matter and grade level.[26] The regulations extend the statutory requirements permitting states to create "high[ly] objective uniform state standard[s] of evaluation" or HOUSSE standards, "by which special education teachers can demonstrate competency in core academic subjects they teach."[27] One researcher further defined such standards:

> [A] single HOUSSE covering multiple subjects is permitted at all grade levels, as long as the separate HOUSSE does not establish a lower standard for content knowledge than is expected of general education teachers. Special educators typically have pedagogical training that is different from that of general educators, and presumably this new standard allows special education methods, assessment procedures, behavior management competencies, and other evidence-based practices to be introduced in a special education HOUSSE. The new standard, however, is unable to address concerns that recruitment and retention of special educators is being harmed by excessively strict academic subject matter competency requirements for special educators.[28]

Other FAPE-related provisions are equally important. The Code of Federal Regulations makes it clear that a child's IEP must include a statement of the child's present levels of academic achievement and functional performance, including how the child's disability affects involvement and progress in the general education curriculum (i.e., the same curriculum that non-disabled children learn).[29] The general education curriculum is presumed to include content and proficiency standards for student achievement; hence, it is necessary for a child's present levels of academic achievement and functional performance in his/her IEP to directly reference the state content and proficiency standards that are articulated in the general curriculum standards for the school district.

The Regulations also specify that a child's IEP must include a statement of measurable annual goals, academic and functional, designed to meet the child's needs that result from the child's disability. This is to enable the child to make progress in the general education curriculum.[30] Again, this language suggests that IEPs now must include a statement of measurable annual goals designed to enable the child to be involved and make progress in the state content and proficiency standards articulated in the general education curriculum.

The Regulations state that an IEP must include a statement of any individual, appropriate accommodations that are necessary to measure the academic achievement and functional performance of the child on state and district-wide assessments. If the IEP team determines that the child must take an alternate assessment other than the state or district-wide assessment of student achievement, a statement of why the child cannot participate in the regular assessment must be clearly articulated.[31]

Finally, regulations of the No Child Left Behind Act state that "[a]ll children with disabilities are included in all general State and district-wide assessment programs, including assessments described under section … [6311 of this title] … with appropriate accommodations and alternate assessments where necessary and as indicated in their respective individualized education programs."[32] Almost immediately exceptions were realized for students with the most severe cognitive disabilities.[33] These are students with severe cognitive disabilities who are unlikely to meet grade level testing with the assessments measuring non-disabled children. As such, NCLB now permits school districts to use alternate achievement standards to evaluate the performance of these students. Beginning in 2003, schools could include the assessments of such students, said to represent approximately 1% of all students, within their annual yearly progress totals. Just recently, Margaret Spellings, U.S. Secretary of Education, also announced new guidelines to allow an additional 2% of students to be tested alternatively.[34] These are the so-called "gap kids" or disabled students with "persistent academic difficulties," who do not fit into the category of children with "significant cognitive difficulties." These students can make significant progress, but may not reach grade-level achievement standards within the state's time frame. Such students are assessed on modified academic standards and take their tests based on these standards. These scores may also be blended in annual yearly progress reports. The two alternative assessments taken together would represent testing for 3% of all students or approximately 30% of students with special needs.

Supporters of special education students have raised concerns based on the 1%/2% testing scheme, suggesting that this would be a facial violation of NCLB and IDEA04 because it could deny students the possibility of participating in the general curriculum. It is more likely, however, that the regulations may alleviate dilemmas for students who could not meet the regular standards other students face. In fact, an argument could be made that the exceptions actually follow the principles established in the legislation, designed for students who need greater intervention; the laws were actually premised upon individualized instruction, and the creation of goals and objectives based on the unique needs of the student.

Concerns about the vast majority of students with special needs, or those presumed to be able to reach state-based achievement standards through educational assessments, represents another story. A real question is whether the new legislation can be interpreted to redefine free appropriate public education where content and proficiency standards of the general curriculum command that special needs students be educated to their maximum abilities. Recall the Supreme Court ruled in the *Rowley* decision that school districts were only obligated to educate the student so as to achieve "some benefit."

V. Interpretations Of FAPE Since *Rowley*

Continued research on interpretations of the standards-based movement, as legislated in NCLB and IDEA, yield the conclusion that emphasizing demonstrated educational accountability does not necessarily translate into an education that enables special needs children to maximize their potential. As noted in previous research, decisions of the courts can be divided into requirements of "meaningful benefit," "some or adequate benefit," and" a mixed standard."[35] Few courts have ruled that that the education statutes and regulations support re-interpretation of Rowley. An analysis of some of the few decided cases follows.

A. "Meaningful Benefit" Standard

In Polk v. Central Susquehanna Intermediate Unit 16[36] the Court of Appeals for the Third Circuit interpreted the *Rowley* standard to require more than a *de minimis* benefit to a special needs student.[37] In *Polk*, parents of a child with mental and physical disabilities wanted direct hands-on therapy from a physical therapist, rather than a teacher, as a related service. Agreeing with the parents about the need for professional treatment, the appeals court ruled that the anticipated benefit must be meaningful and, therefore, more than trivial progress must occur.[38] The *Polk* court stated that the standard was more than a "toothless standard" and declared that a FAPE required more than the mere prevention of regression.[39] In a very recent decision, *Kirby v. Cabell County Board of Education*[40] from the Southern District Court of West Virginia, a federal court followed the "meaningful benefit" standard, stating that IDEA "does not require providing every available service necessary to maximize a disabled child's potential, [and] 'a school district cannot discharge its duty ... by providing a program that provides only *de minimis* or trivial academic achievement.'"[41] The case also notes the importance of students with disabilities participating, as much as possible, in the same activities as students without disabilities. The case involved an eighteen year old student with non-verbal learning disorders: Asperger's disorder, attention deficit disorder, a speech and language disorder, dysgraphia, and specific learning disabilities. The plaintiff in the case challenged the previous decision of the impartial hearing on an independent evaluation, appropriateness of the defendant's IEP, private school placement, and reimbursement. In bringing the claim, the plaintiff contended that NCLB "imposes additional obligations on the District in regards to the level of educational benefit required by IDEA."[42] The court rejected the plaintiff's claim, finding there is "no language in [NCLB] that places additional obligations on the development or assessment of a child's IEP."[43] Rather, the court found that the statute places responsibility on the state to adopt "challenging academic content standards and challenging student academic achievement standards to carry out the state's plan under the Act" and that this obligation applies to *all* students.[44] The court found that NCLB "does not contain specific obligations to children with disabilities nor does it alter the Court's standard of review [of] [IEPs]."[45]

B. "Some or Adequate Benefit" Standard

Federal courts, especially in recent decisions, interpret the floor of "some benefit" to be below the one provided in *Polk* and *Kirby*. In *School Board of Lee County v. M.M*[46] a Florida district court addressed a request for reinterpretation of FAPE in light of NCLB and its impact on IDEA04. The case involved complaints about the adequacy of an IEP for a seven year old student with a specific learning disability, speech and language impairment, attention deficit hyperactivity disorder, and microcephaly. The court followed the "some or adequate benefit" standard, stating that "a child must be provided with 'a basic floor of opportunity' that affords 'some' educational benefit, but the outcome need not maximize the child's education."[47] The court also stated that a "student is only entitled to some educational benefit; the benefit need not be maximized to be adequate."[48] The court noted that, in addition to the "some or adequate benefit" standard, education is a fundamental value in Florida and that it is, therefore, "a paramount duty of the state to make adequate provision for the education of all children residing within its borders."[49] The judgment, nevertheless, rejected the argument brought by the student that references to "high quality education" elevates the substantive component of the FAPE for Florida children and that NCLB establishes a higher state standard which requires that a child's potential be maximized.[50] In evaluating whether a higher standard is applicable, the court differentiated cases where a statute requires a state to ensure every child a fair and full opportunity to reach his full potential. The court found that given the well-established nature of the federal standard, an intent to impose an enhanced requirement for IDEA must be more clearly stated in NCLB and that there are no court decisions finding a requirement in Florida that education be maximized in the IDEA context. These cases, according to the court, continue to impose the *Rowley* standard, followed in Florida precedent, that "there is no requirement to maximize each child's potential."[51]

In *Mr. C. v. Maine School Administrative School District*[52] the Court of Appeals for the First Circuit also applied the "some or adequate benefit" standard with regards to FAPE by declaring that IDEA "does not promise perfect solutions ... [but rather] sets modest goals ... emphasizing] an appropriate, rather than ideal, education; requiring] an adequate, rather than an optimal, IEP."[53] "Appropriateness and adequacy," the court continues, "are terms of moderation."[54] It follows that, although an IEP must afford some educational benefit, the benefit conferred need not reach the highest attainable level or even the level needed to maximize the child's potential.

In drawing this conclusion the court rejected the plaintiff's argument that the 1997 and 2004 amendments to IDEA rendered pre-2004 case law obsolete and raised the bar with respect to the FAPE standard.[55] The court noted that the plaintiffs relied on *J.L. v. Mercer Island School District*[56] and that the First Circuit expressly rejected this argument in 2004. See *L.T., T.B. and E.B. ex rel. N.B. v. Warwick School Community District*[57] ("This court has continued to apply the *Rowley* standard in cases following the 1997 amendments, as have several of our sister circuits. And that is for good reason. The Rowley standard recognizes that courts are ill-equipped to second-guess reasonable choices that school districts have made among appropriate instructional methods.")

The court also rejected the plaintiff's argument that *Winkelman v. Parma City School District*[58] requires that the combination of the 1997 and 2004 amendments supersede the *Rowley* standard. This claim was rejected because the passage cited from *Winkelman* "merely noted the unremarkable fact that *Rowley* happened to have construed the meaning of FAPE in the precursor statute to the IDEA ... [t]he court neither stated nor suggested that the standard set forth in the Rowley decision had been superseded by either the 1997 or 2004 amendments to IDEA."[59]

C. Mixed Standard of the Seventh Circuit

The Court of Appeals for the Seventh Circuit is alone in its use of a mixed standard to determine the legal criteria for FAPE.[60] This is best delineated in *Alex R. ex. rel Beth R. v. Forrestville Valley Community Unit School District Number 221* in the following passage:

> An IEP passes muster provided that it is "reasonably calculated to enable the child to receive educational benefits," or in other words, when it is "likely to produce progress, not regression or trivial educational advancement." The requisite degree of reasonable, likely progress varies, depending on the student's abilities. Under Rowley, "while one might demand only minimal results in the case of the most severely handicapped children, such results would be insufficient in the case of other children." Objective factors, such as the regular advancement from grade to grade, and achievement of passing grades, usually show satisfactory progress.[61]

Board of Ottawa Township High School District 140 v. The United States Department of Education[62] in the Northern District of Illinois follows the same reasoning. The plaintiffs in the case were the school boards of the Ottawa Township High School and Elementary School districts, four special education students, and their parents. Collectively they brought complaints against the United States Department of Education, the Illinois State Board of Education, and the leadership of both agencies. Plaintiffs sought a declaration that portions of NCLB violated the IDEA. The District Court disposed of the case on standing grounds, reaching the merits of plaintiffs' arguments only in *dicta*. With regard to standing, the court held that the plaintiff school districts failed to allege any current or imminent harm. *Id*. Specifically, the court held that those sections of NCLB containing corrective measures did not apply to the first of the two plaintiff school districts because it had not accepted Title I funds, and was therefore exempt from those sections of the Act. *Id*. The court rejected that district's argument that the State of Illinois' acceptance of Title I funds forced the district to comply with NCLB. *Id*.

With regard to the second school district, the court acknowledged that it had accepted Title I funds, but that it still lacked standing because the occurrence of the harms of which it complained—changing curricula and losing local control of the district—were too remote and speculative. Specifically, the school board claimed that NCLB's creation of adequate yearly progress ("AYP"), used to determine the extent to which a district is meeting a states' academic achievement standards, violated IDEA'S requirement that all children with disabilities are entitled to a FAPE. Under NCLB, nearly all students (except for a very small percentage with the most serious cognitive disabilities) are held to the same standard-achievement scores. The Plaintiff failed to make AYP because most of their students with disabilities were tested at grade level standards rather than standards established by their IEPs. The board alleged that, had the proficiency scores of the students with disabilities been excluded from the calculation, it would have made AYP.

The court rejected *in dicta* the argument that NCLB achievement standards harm children with disabilities because those children are held to the same standards as students without disabilities. First, the Court stated that the statutes provide for alternate assessments and alternative academic achievement standards for children with disabilities. Second, the court reasoned that NCLB does not force children, protected by IDEA, to do anything contrary to IDEA's guarantee of a FAPE. The court rejected all of the plaintiffs' positions, relying heavily on alternative assessment allowances in NCLB:

> IDEA requires all disabled children included in statewide assessment programs, including NCLB assessments, to take alternative assessments, if required by their IEPs. 20 U.S.C. §1412 (a)(16)(A). Alternative assessments are allowed for "children with disabilities … who cannot participate in regular assessments under subparagraph (A) with accommodations *as indicated in their respective individualized education programs.*" 20 U.S.C. § 1412 (a)(16)(C)(i) (emphasis added). These alternate assessments must be *aligned* with, not equal, the State's challenging academic content standards and challenging student academic achievement standards; and also measure the achievement of students with disabilities against *alternate academic achievement standards*, if the

State has adopted such alternate academic achievement standards permitted under the regulated promulgated to carry out §6311(b)(l). 20 U.S.C. §1412 (a)(16(C)(ii).[63]

The court also pointed to the reasonable adaptations and accommodations that are available to students with disabilities as reasons to find NCBL did not violate IDEA. The plaintiffs' complaint, in addition, asserted that NCLB only allowed alternate assessments for students with the most "serious cognitive disabilities" rather than all students with disabilities, and that this gap in the alignment of the statutes resulted in violation of IDEA'S main purposes. The court rejected this argument because there had been "no showing that holding disabled children to the same achievement standards as non-disabled children is in itself harmful or violative of IDEA'S guarantee of a [FAPE]."[64] The Court again points to the inclusion of children with disabilities in alternative assessments and the alignment of alternate assessments with the State's content standards as consistent with the purposes state in IDEA.

On appeal, the Seventh Circuit similarly failed to reach the merits of whether IDEA and NCLB impose inconsistent obligations upon school districts, although it acknowledged that both plaintiff school districts had standing to sue. The court accepted the argument that the school districts were required to comply with NCLB by virtue of the state's acceptance of Title I funds, and further reasoned that the districts had standing because satisfying the requirements of NCLB is expensive and may cost more than a district receives in federal grants. The court, nonetheless, declined to address—or to remand for consideration of—the merits of the plaintiffs' argument regarding the alleged inconsistent obligations imposed on the districts by IDEA and NCLB. The court held, as a matter of statutory interpretation, that any inconsistency between the two statutes must be resolved in favor of NCLB, as it was the statute enacted latest in time.[65]

D. The United States Office of Civil Rights

Amy June Rowley, the plaintiff in the Supreme Court case by that famous name, was a profoundly deaf student performing at a well-above-average level even without the accommodation of a sign language interpreter she requested from her school district. Case law above would suggest that not much has changed in 25 years regarding a legal interpretation of FAPE. A recent executive opinion by the United States Department of Education Office of Civil Rights may, however, suggest that students like Amy are entitled to accommodations to meet the achievement levels of NCLB as delineated in their Individualized Education Plans. The opinion originated from a report that some schools and school districts have refused to permit qualified students with disabilities to participate in accelerated and gifted and talented academic programs or that schools condition participation in such programs on the abandonment of special education and related services. The Office of Civil Rights (OCR) found that these practices are inconsistent with Section 504 of the Rehabilitation Act of 1973,[66] Title II of the Americans with Disabilities Act,[67] and the Individuals with Disabilities Improvement Act. Specifically with regard to FAPE, the Office instructed districts where participation by a student with a disability in an accelerated class or program is considered part of the regular education or the regular classes referenced in the Section 504 and the IDEA regulations. Thus, if a qualified student with a disability requires related aids and services to participate in a regular education class or program, then a school cannot deny that student the needed related aids and services in an accelerated class or program.

OCR gave the following example: If a student's IEP or plan under Section 504 provides for Braille materials in order to participate in the regular education program, and she enrolls in an accelerated or advanced history class, then she also must receive Braille materials for that class. The same would be true for other needed related aids and services such as extended time on tests or the use of a computer to take notes. OCR also cautioned school districts that conditioning enrollment in an advanced class or program on the forfeiture of needed special education or related aids and services. OCR noted that this is inconsistent with the principle of individualized determinations, and that the requirement for such determinations is violated when schools ignore the student's individual needs and automatically deny a qualified student with a disability requisite related aids and services in an accelerated class or program.[68]

VI. CONCLUSION

The foregoing discussion demonstrates that the Individuals with Disabilities Education Improvement Act and No Child Left Behind support millions of children with special needs in gaining access to public education. It also alerts us that, for the most part, the education provided offers little in the way of promoting intervention leading toward maximum scholastic benefit. Progress has been made but, by and large, little has changed in the interpretation of a free appropriate public education since the landmark decision of *Board of Education of the Hendrick Hudson Central School District v. Rowley* decided 25 years ago. Congressional action protecting the rights of all students, with particular emphasis on students with special needs, has been necessary and impressive, but reliance on judicial interpretations has resulted in continued burdens on this population, particularly students who can perform at high academic levels. The few court cases addressing whether NCLB has heightened the requirements of FAPE or is violative of IDEA have yielded negative answers.

This article has presented information on the *Rowley* decision, the FAPE standards in IDEA, the national standards fostering a general curriculum, and the NCLB standards for reaching goals, and case law interpreting FAPE. One ray of hope is found in a very recent executive opinion prepared by the United States Office of Education Office of Civil Rights. This executive rendering posits that a possible violation of IDEA, the Americans with Disabilities Act, and Section 504 of the Civil Rights Act of 1973 may occur if qualified students with disabilities are refused the opportunity to participate in accelerated and gifted and talented academic programs or that schools condition participation in such programs on the abandonment of special education and related services. Further research in this area must wait until the OCR opinion prevails.

NOTES

1. Bd. of Educ. of the Hendrick Hudson Cent. Sch. Dist. v. Rowley, 458 U.S. 176, (1982).
2. 20 U.S.C. §§ 1400 *et. seq.*
3. At the time of the Rowley decision, the statute was called the Education for All Handicapped Children's Education Act (EAHCA).
4. *Rowley* 458 U.S. at 203.
5. *Id.* at 203–204.
6. *Id.* at 198
7. *Id.* at 200.
8. *Id.* at 201.
9. Lunceford v. Dist. of Columbia Bd. of Educ., 745 F.2d 1577. 1583 (D.C. Cir. 1984) (IDEA "does not secure the best education money can buy;" rather it requires an "appropriate education" for the child); Hessler v. State Bd. of Educ., 700 F.2d 134. 139 (4th Cir. 1983) (education need not be the best education).
10. *See, e.g.,* Burke County Bd. of Educ. v. Denton. 895 F.2d 973. 980 (4th Cir. 1990) (affirming district court finding that day program constituted FAPE because student made good "educational progress" in that setting); Evans v. Dist. No. 17.841 F.2d 824. 831 (8th Cir. 1988) (*Rowley* directive to allow school district to choose method of instruction means that "if a child is progressing satisfactorily" with the current method, court is not to question whether another method might work better); Abrahamson v. Hershman. 701 F.2d 223. 228 (1st Cir. 1983) ("educational progress" necessary for FAPE).
11. Scott Johnson, *Reexamining Rowley: A New Focus in Special Education Law*, 2003 BYU Educ. & L.J. 561 (2003).
12. 20 U. S.c. §§ 6301 *et. seq.*
13. U.S. Const. article I, § 8.
14. Stephen Rosenbaum, *Aligning or Maligning: Getting Inside a New IDEA, Getting Behind No Child Left Behind and Getting Outside of it All*, 15 HASTINGS WOMEN'S L.J. 1, 27–29 (2004).
15. Southern Disability Law Center, http://www.sdlcenter.orglissues.htm (last visited Feb. 22, 2008).
16. 20 v.s.c. § 1401(9) (2006).
17. 20 v.s.c. § 1401(9)(B).
18. H.R. Rpt. 105–95, at 83–84 (May 13, 1997).
19. 20 V.S.c. § 6311(b)(1)(D).
20. 20 V.S.c. § 631l (b)(1)(D)(ii).
21. *Id.*
22. 20 U.S.c. §§ 1400 *et. seq.*
23. 20 U.S.C. § 1412(a)(15).
24. 20 U. S.c. § 1412(a)(15) (A)(ii, iv).
25. 20 U.S.C. § 1412(a)(15)(B).

26. 20 U. S.C. § 1401(10).

27. Dixie S. Huefner, *The Final Regulations for the Individuals with Disabilities Education Improvement Act*, 217 Educ. L. Rep. 1, 2–3 (2007).

28. *Id.*

29. 34 C.P.R. § 300.320(a)(l)(i).

30. 34 C.P.R. § 300.320(a)(2)(i).

31. 34 c. F. R. § 300.320 (a)(6).

32. 20 U.S.c. § 1412 (16).

33. 34 c. F. R. § 200.13.

34. "U.S. Department of Education, Secretary Spellings Announces New Regulations to More Accurately Assess Students with Disabilities," (April 4, 2007), http://www.ed.gov/printl-news/pressreleases/2007/04/04042007.html. (last visited December 15, 2007).

35. P.T.K. Daniel and Jill Meinhardt, *Valuing the Education of Students with Disabilities: Has Government Legislation Caused a Reinterpretation of a Free Appropriate Public Education?*, 222 Educ. L. Rep. 515 (2007).

36. 853 F.2d 171 (3d Cir.1988), *cert. denied*, 488 U.S. 1030 (1989).

37. *Id.* at 184.

38. *Id.*

39. *Id.* at 179.

40. Kirby v. Cabell County Bd. Of &luc, 2006 WL 2691435 (S. D. W. Va., September 19, 2006).

41. *Id.* at 2, citing Bd. of Educ. of the County of Kanawha v. Michael M., 95 F. Supp.2d 600,607 (S. D. W. Va. 2000) (citations omitted).

42. *Id.* at 6.

43. *Id.*

44. *Id.*

45. *Id.*

46. Sch. Bd. of Lee County, Fl. v. M.M., 2007 W.L. 983274 (M. D. Fla., March 27, 2007).

47. *Id.* at 3, citing Walker Co. Sch. Dist. v. Bennett, 203 F. 3d 1293, 1296 n. 10 (11th Cir. 2(00).

48. *Id.* at 3, citing Devine v. Indian River County Sch. Bd., 249 F. 3d 1289, 1292 (11th Cir. 2001).

49. *Id.* at 3.

50. *Id.* at 4.

51. *Id.*, citing M.H. v Nassau County Sch. Bd. , 918 So. 2d 316, 318 n. 1 (Fla. Dist. Ct. App. 2005).

52. Mr. C. v. Me. Sch. Admin. Dist. No. 6, 2007 WL 4206166 (D. Me., Nov. 28, 2007).

53. *Id.* at 26.

54. *Id.*

55. *Id.* at 27, n. 31.

56. J.L. v. Mercer Island. Sch. Dist., 2006 w,L. 3628033 (W. D. Wash., Dec. 8 , 2006).

57. L.T., T.B. and E.B. ex rel. N.B. v. Warwick Sch. Cmty. Dist., 361 F. 3d 80, 83 (1st Cir., 2004).

58. Winkelman ex. rel. Winkelman v. Parma City Sch. Dist., 127 S. Ct. 1994 (2007).

59. 2007 W.L. 4206166 at 27 n. 3 1.

60. Lester Aron, *Too Much or Not Enough: How Have the Circuit Courts Defined a Free Appropriate Public Education After Rowley*, 39 Suffolk U. L. Rev. 1, 7 (2005).

61. Alex R. ex. rel. Beth R. v. Forrestville Valley Cmty. Unit Sch. Dist. No. 221, 375 F. 3d 603, 615 (7th Cir. 2004), *cert. denied*, 125 S. Ct. 628 (2004)).

62. Bd. of Ottawa Twp. High Sch. Dist. 140 v U.S. Dept. of Educ. , 2007 WL 1017808 (N. D. Ill., March 31, 2007).

63. *Id.* at 7.

64. *Id.* at 8.

65. Bd. of Educ. of Ottawa Twp. High Sch. Dist. 140 v. Spellings, 517 F.3d 922, (7th Cir. 2008).

66. 29 U.S.C. § 794(a).

67. 42 U.S.c. § 12102 *et. seq.*

68. "United States Office of Education: Office of Civil Rights, Access by Students with Disabilities to Accelerated Programs," (December 26, 2007). http://www.ed.gov/about!offices/ list!ocrnetters/colleague-20071226.html (last visited January 2, 2008).

DISCUSSION QUESTIONS

69. The Council for Exceptional Children published the first article above. What is this organization? Who are the members of this organization? Who is on the editorial board of their journal? Who is Spencer J. Salend (besides being the author of the first article)? Based on these questions, what might be the bias of this journal?

70. Are testing modifications for students with disabilities fair? If not, to whom are they unfair? What do you mean by the word "fair?" Do the suggestions by Spencer create more or less fairness in regard to testing accommodations? Support your argument with information from the article.

71. Spencer recommends the following "additional resources": National Center on Educational Outcomes, Center for Research on Evaluation, Standards and Student Testing, Center for Educational Assessment, and Practical Assessment, Research, and Evaluation. What are these organizations? Does recommending these organizations give credence to Spencer's main point? What might be the bias of these organizations?

72. As stated above, the authors of the second article use language that clearly identifies some of their biases. What are their biases? What is the purpose of the authors in describing teachers as apathetic? Do these authors support NCLB? Why or why not?

73. At the beginning of this chapter, you were asked to determine the assumptions of the authors and position of the authors. What are the assumptions and position of each author? Who is the audience of each author, or who do the authors wish would read their articles?

74. A tendency with articles consisting of legalese is to assume not bias, but rather stating "that is just the law." Hopefully, after reading Chapter Four in particular, that assumption has been erased. The bias of Daniel, author of the last article above, can be found in his conclusion. What is that bias?

CLASS ACTIVITIES

1. At the beginning of the second article, the authors cite President George W. Bush's claim regarding public schooling at the passage of NCLB: 1) That about 70 percent of inner-city fourth graders are unable to read at a basic level on national reading tests; 2) That American high school seniors trail most countries on international math tests; and 3) That the academic achievement gap between the rich and poor, Anglo, and minority gets widened at an alarming rate. As will be seen when examining the National Report Card site below, these are very generalized statements for complicated questions. Using the National Report Card site below, give a more accurate description of educational progress in the United States.

2. Using the Digest of Educational Statistics, analyze the state of education in the United States and whether or not NCLB has improved the public schooling in the United States.

3. Another account on education is the Condition of Education, 2011, report. Indicator 25 of this report is "International Comparison of Educational Attainment." Based on this report and indicator, how is the United States doing educationally, as far as international comparisons? In the countries surpassing the United States educationally, what grades are compulsory for all children? How do these other countries meet the educational needs of disabled, economically deprived children who speak languages different from the majority, and ethnic minority children? Do these other countries have the level of diversity as exists in the United States? Do these countries have academic achievement gaps? Do these countries permit children who are disabled in their schools? In what other ways does public education in these countries differ from that of the United States? Should these differences be considered when making international comparisons?

ONLINE RESOURCES

Nation's Report Card   http://nationsreportcard.gov/
Digest of Educational Statistics   http://nces.ed.gov/programs/digest/
The Condition of Education, 2012   http://nces.ed.gov/pubsearch/pubsinfo.asp?pubid=2012045

<u>CIA World Factbook</u>   https://www.cia.gov/library/publications/the-world-factbook/index.html

<u>Global Special Education and Disability Sites</u>   http://www.doe.mass.edu/sped/links/global.html

<u>Nationmaster</u>   http://www.nationmaster.com/index.php

Chapter Seven
Curriculum and Instruction—Biases

Why Do I Need to Know This?

Thus far, in this text, I have discussed identifying biases by checking sources the author uses to defend a position, examining the organization of an argument, and understanding the training of the author (i.e., law versus education). The word "bias," especially when applied to the written word, suggests disingenuous intentionality or even an evil purpose. In some cases, such as Hitler's manifesto *Mein Kampf*, one could easily argue that the purpose was evil. Nonetheless, bias, for the most part, is not pernicious. Instead, it is part of the human condition. We are all biased.

The key for educators is recognizing the bias behind information; doing so allows for a clearer understanding and makes it possible for knowledge to truly become power. In this chapter, you will begin to understand how bias plays a role in the politics of schooling, as well as daily interactions between teachers, parents, administrators, and students. You will learn the origins of educational biases, as well as how to understand categories of bias in your daily life.

What Are Biases?

My PhD is in the academic discipline of Cultural Foundations of Education. We examine educational issues from a variety of perspectives—history, sociology, political science, philosophy, and anthropology. If you were to read a Social Foundations of Education textbook, you would find a chapter on philosophies or theories of education. I disagree with the organization of such chapters, primarily because a distinction is not made regarding types of belief systems. For example, in one text, pragmatism will be referred to as a philosophy; in another text it is a theory of education. Types of belief systems have different roles and should not be confused.

In schools, this confusion also exists. You will more than likely at some point be asked to provide your teaching philosophy, when in reality they want your teaching theory. A philosophy is an all-encompassing belief system with no inherent contradictions; it answers questions such as "What is Truth?" or "How can we know Truth?" Notice that I capitalized the word Truth. I do not mean truth as in honesty. I mean *Truth*, as in the meaning of life or what is beauty or what is goodness or evil.

Humans are walking contradictions; I am a walking contradiction. I believe that there are some people who have walked this earth who lived a philosophy. Jesus of Nazareth, Muhammad, Gandhi, and Martin Luther King Jr. lived a philosophy. Many of us might like to say we live a philosophy, but if we are honest with ourselves, we are quite ideological. An ideology also answers the question "What is Truth?" but has inherent contradictions as part of its belief system. It sounds better to say, "This is my philosophy," than to say, "This is my ideology," because we have put belief systems on a hierarchy that most of us do not achieve.

A third category of belief systems also exists, which again we are less likely to claim—theories. However, the reason for embracing the word philosophy over ideology is different from the reason we might embrace the word "philosophy" over "theories." When ones says, "Well, that's my philosophy!" in an argument, it is similar to saying, "And therefore it is Truth." When someone accuses someone else of being ideological in an argument, it may be similar to saying, "And therefore what you are saying is biased and not the truth." Sometimes we will do the same with the word "theory." However, in an argument when someone says, "Well that's your theory," what they may actually be saying is, "And it's a stupid theory at that, but if you want to believe it, go ahead."

Theories have another burden to overcome. They are often viewed as boring or impractical. When I have interviewed teachers about their teacher education programs, I have often heard the astonishing mantra, "We just learned a bunch of dumb theories." Can you imagine a doctor saying, "We just learned some stupid theories about how the human body works?" Can you imagine a lawyer saying about law school, "We just learned some stupid case laws and theories about the legal system?" What about a religious leader saying, "We just learned about this silly book called the Bible (or the Koran or the Torah)?" No! These professionals would never make such ludicrous statements. To do so would be to undermine their profession. Yet, teachers do so when discussing their teacher education classes.

I suspect teachers verbally negate theories because they do not truly understand those theories, they do not recognize the power of theories, or they do not know how to use the power of theories. In this chapter, I will attempt to show you such power and how to use it. However, before I do so, you need to understand how theories are different from philosophies and ideologies. Theories are the application of a variety of sources of knowledge to one specific topic.

If you were at a party and were asked, "What are you, a feminist?" would you say yes without hesitation? What if your professor, a female, asked you that question; would you say yes? I ask my class this question each semester and the majority initially says no. I then ask them if they think I am a feminist and the majority says yes. We socialize students to determine what the teacher wants and give it back to the teacher. For my students, first semester freshmen, they have been socialized to do so for thirteen or more years, and I am their first education professor. The inner strength my students draw upon to tell their first education professor, who they assume is a feminist, that they are not feminists, is the power of a theory.

Are you a feminist? Do any of the statements below apply to your beliefs regarding males and females?

1. Men and women are the same and equal.
2. Men and women are equal, but different. There are some activities that men do better than women and some activities that women do better than men.
3. Do you believe that in history, and even today, men are paid more than women for doing the same job?
4. Do you believe that what is viewed as a male characteristic (rationality) is more positively viewed in society than characteristics associated with women (being emotional)?
5. Do you disagree with those who believe women are less developed than men (morally, physically, or cognitively)?

If you agree with any of the statements above, you are a feminist. If you believe in more than one statement above you are actually a radical feminist.[1] Feminism is nothing more than a theory; actually, it is multiple theories regarding gender. Feminist theories explain why males and females are different and/or similar and tie those differences to sociological, psychological, political, economic, and historical reasons. Basically, feminists (also known as gender scholars or women's study scholars) use a variety of academic disciplines to explain differences between men and women. Radical feminists believe in more than one theory of gender.[2] However, individuals such as Rush Limbaugh refer to them as feminazis. If you want to demonize anything, attach the word Nazi to it. Feminists are also described as women who hate men. Yet if you go to a gender studies conference, there are men in attendance and most, if not all, of the women there have husbands, sons, and/or fathers they love. Feminism actually has nothing to do with whether one loves or hates men or women. Feminism is simply the study of gender.

Later in this chapter, I am going to discuss educational theories, which are belief systems that answer four primary questions: 1) What is a student? 2) What is a teacher? 3) What should be taught? 4) How should it be taught? These theories, like feminism, are the study of a specific topic, using the lenses of a variety of academic disciplines. Some argue that they are "just theories," but I believe they have power. You need not agree with me, but in some class in your teacher education program you will learn about a theory (hopefully more than one) that you can and should use when you become a teacher. Such is the behavior of a professional teacher.

---

1 Much of my understanding of feminist theory comes from courses I took in my PhD program, and from one book in particular: *Feminist Theory*, by Josephine Donovan. I did not pursue this line of inquiry beyond my course work and am by no means an expert. I use feminist theory here to simply demonstrate the power of theories.
2 Donovan, Josephine. (1992). *Feminist Theory*. New York: Continuum.

PHILOSOPHIES

As indicated above, philosophies are all-encompassing belief systems with no inherent contradictions. Though I have read many philosophical works, I am by no means an educational philosopher. Thus, my approach to philosophy is different than what one might traditionally read in philosophical writings. My approach to philosophy is "How can I use this?" or "Can this be used by teachers?" Thus, for those interested in the topic of educational philosophy, I will recommend sites at the end of this chapter that will provide a broader and more in-depth view of educational philosophy. The four philosophies I will discuss in this section are three classic philosophies—idealism, realism, and pragmatism, and one modern philosophy—the ethic of care.

The father of philosophy, Plato, is the author of the original beliefs that fall under the category of idealism.[3] In this belief system, individuals have a firm conviction that we cannot see Truth—it is in the shadows or "out there someplace." The world is ever changing and therefore not Truth; Truth is only in the world of ideas.[4] Though we cannot directly interact with Truth, it exists as innate knowledge, separate from our sensory experiences.[5] The role of the teacher is to pull truth out of students using a strategy called the Socratic method.[6] You have probably experienced the Socratic method, though you may have heard it referred to as "playing the devil's advocate." If you have ever been in a class where, no matter what you said, the teacher responded with a question to challenge your position, you experienced the Socratic method. This practice is often used by teachers wanting their students to develop critical thinking skills, to analyze and apply content, and to recognize multiple dimensions in an issue.

Plato also believed in a hierarchy of people. He believed all children should go to school. After a few years, the majority of children would drop out of school and become the workers of society—do the laundry, cook food, wash clothes, dig holes, etc. The remaining students would stay in school for a few more years, and then the majority of those students would drop out also. Plato believed that this second class of dropouts should be the military of society. The last group of students in school would never drop out; they would be the philosopher kings who would rule society.[7]

The last key piece of Plato's idealism is the belief in universal Truth. Plato argued that, though we cannot interact with Truth directly or ever fully know it, Truth never changes. That which was Truth 2000 years ago is Truth today and will be in the future. That which was evil in ancient

3   Plato was the first idealist, but many famous philosophers followed in this tradition, and with their writing expanded on Plato's writings: Descartes, Berkeley, Kant, Hegel, Fichte, Royce, Bradley, and A. C. Ewing, to name a few. Retrieved March 16, 2012, from http://www.qcc.cuny.edu/SocialSciences/ppecorino/roark-textbook/Chapter-10.htm
4   Roark, Dallas. (1982). *Introduction to Philosophy*. Emporia: Dalmor Publishing, retrieved March 16, 2012, from http://www.qcc.cuny.edu/SocialSciences/ppecorino/roark-textbook/Chapter-10.htm
5   Markie, Peter. (2008). "Rationalism vs. Empiricism." *Stanford Encyclopedia of Philosophy*. Retrieved March 16, 2012, from http://plato.stanford.edu/entries/rationalism-empiricism/
6   Dye, James. (1996). *Socratic Method vs. Scientific Method*. Retrieved March 16, 2012, from http://www.niu.edu/~jdye/method.html
7   Wildman, Wesley. Plato (427–327 B.C.), retrieved March 16, 2012, from http://people.bu.edu/wwildman/WeirdWildWeb/courses/wphil/lectures/wphil_theme02.htm#Society

history is evil today and will be evil in the future. That which is beautiful in the past is beautiful today and will be beautiful in the future. Different understandings of Truth are not because Truth changes, but because the world changes, which is separate from the world of ideas; in the world of ideas, rather than this world, Truth exists.[8]

One may ask, "Who cares what a guy thought over 2000 years ago and what does it have to do with schools today?" The first significance of Plato is his influence on Christianity. Those who live their lives today based on whether or not they will go to heaven, nirvana, or whatever name one gives to the place one goes after death, live an idealist life as described by Plato. Truth for people of faith is in God or Allah or Vishnu, etc.; Truth is not of this world. Thus, they are guided by the principles of their faith and understanding of their Supreme Being. If one is not a person of faith, this is difficult to understand. Teachers, regardless of their own beliefs, will have students who are spiritual in their classes, and they need to understand what that means for their students. Idealism provides a road map to assist teachers in understanding their students of faith.

In our society we embrace the concept of equality, even if it does not play out in our politics. Thus, acknowledging a hierarchy of people does not come easily. Yet our education system is designed with Plato's idea of a hierarchy of people. We have levels in our K–12 system of education (elementary, middle, and high school), and we have levels in our overall system of education (high school, college, graduate school, and doctorate). We emphasize equality through high school and then we institute a meritocracy, in which individuals must prove (financially and in performance) that they are worthy of additional degrees. At the K–12 level, we have a variety of laws (IDEA, *Brown v. Board*, NCLB) in place, which are supposed to ensure equality of education—yet we do not fund schools equally, have equal pay for teachers, and have accelerated and gifted education programs. Thus, even at the K–12 level, though there is somewhat of an assumption of equality, we actually impose a hierarchy of students.

In regard to universal Truth, we teach the same subjects today in schools that have been taught for centuries. As will be discussed in the educational theory section of this chapter, a major belief exists that all-important knowledge already exists and has already been written about. The role of the teacher is to introduce students to this knowledge. Thus, idealism can be seen in the content and manner in which many teachers instruct.

Plato's student, Aristotle, is the author of ideas that fall under the category of the philosophy of realism. Aristotle also believed that Truth was universal; however, unlike his teacher, he believed Truth was something that could be known through our senses. We can see, hear, feel, touch, and smell the Truth. Whereas Plato emphasized fine-tuning students' contemplation skills, Aristotle believed that teachers should fine-tune students' skills of observation. Plato viewed Truth as in the world of ideas; Aristotle viewed truth as in the physical world.[9]

---

8 Markie, Peter. (2008). "Rationalism vs. Empiricism." *Stanford Encyclopedia of Philosophy*. Retrieved March 16, 2012, from http://plato.stanford.edu/entries/rationalism-empiricism/ , Roark, Dallas. (1982). *Introduction to Philosophy*. Emporia: Dalmor Publishing, retrieved March 16, 2012, from http://www.qcc.cuny.edu/SocialSciences/ppecorino/roark-textbook/Chapter-10.htm

9 Aristotle's writings, as with Plato's, are far too broad and complex to be addressed here. Nor is a comprehensive explanation necessary here. The purpose here is simply a very brief introduction into the field of philosophy. See the

The difference between Plato's view of Truth and Aristotle's view of Truth can be seen in politics today. Plato's Truth can be seen in those who argue for religious Truth. Aristotle's Truth can be seen in those who argue for scientific Truth. Examples of this can be seen in the abortion debate. Is a fetus a life? Should a woman control her own reproduction? Should religious Truths govern these decisions or is this a medical (science) Truth? Does a fetus feel pain (science or realism)? Is a fetus a human being with a soul (religion or idealism)?

The difference between Plato's view of Truth and Aristotle's view of Truth is also seen in debates regarding schooling. In the first decade of this century, Aristotle's view won the argument. What is knowledge and how should it be measured? Testing is an outcome of the belief that knowledge can and should be measured; measurement is a form of regulated observation. New voices are beginning to be heard on the political scene, which are asking, "What about knowledge beyond basic skills?" and "What about the development of critical thinking skills?" Heard among these discussions are the voices that ask, "How can we assess the development of critical thinking skills?" This question is basically asking, "How can we use Aristotle's view of Truth to evaluate the outcomes of Plato's view of Truth?" Understanding this could possibly lead to the question, "Should we continue to seek ways to measure and evaluate that which is immeasurable?"

The debates between religion and science, contemplation and measurement, the non-observable and the observable have a long history and will continue well into the future. Another philosophy, often referred to as the American philosophy, takes a very different view of Truth. Whereas idealists and realists view Truth as universal, pragmatists believe Truth changes. What was true two thousand years ago is interesting, but what does it have to do with today? What is Truth today will be different from Truth in the future.

Pragmatists also believe that one cannot know Truth unless one experiences Truth. Dewey argued that "Mere activity does not constitute experience."[10]

> When we experience something we act upon it, we do something with it; then we suffer or undergo the consequences. We do something to the thing and then it does something to us in return …When the activity is continued into the undergoing of consequences … It is not experience when a child merely sticks his finger into a flame; it is experience when the movement is connected with pain which he undergoes as a consequence.[11]

In other words, one cannot know love until one has been in love or perhaps lost love; one cannot know goodness until one is rewarded for good behavior; one cannot know evil until they

---

online resources for more information and a better understanding of these philosophies. The information obtained in this paragraph was obtained via a wide variety of readings; however, most recently I read Cohen, S. Marc, "Aristotle's Metaphysics," *Stanford Encyclopedia of Philosophy* (spring 2009 edition), Edward N. Zalta (ed.), retrieved March 16, 2012, from http://plato.stanford.edu/archives/spr2009/entries/aristotle-metaphysics

10   John Dewey. (1961). *Democracy and Education*. New York: Macmillan Co., pp. 139 –140, as cited in McDermott, John (ed.). (1981). *The Philosophy of John Dewey: Two Volumes in One: 1 "The Structure of Experience," and 2 "The Lived Experience"*. Chicago: Chicago University Press, p. 495.

11   Ibid.

have experienced the consequences. Truth is also not the same for everyone, because we experience consequences differently. What one person considers punishment could be experienced as a reward by another person. Take, for example, the punishment of a school detention. For a child who is going to miss a fun activity, a detention is a punishment; for a child who perhaps is from a volatile home, a detention could actually be viewed very positively, an escape from something negative.

The United States is viewed as the land of pragmatists; we are not mere thinkers or observers—we are doers. In many respects, the United States is anti-intellectual and anti-schooling, because intellectual work and schooling are not "doing"; rather, both involve contemplating and observing. John Dewey, whom I will discuss later in this chapter, is the father of pragmatic education, progressivism, yet his theory does not shape intellectualism or schooling in the United States. Perhaps this disconnect is one of the reasons for anti-intellectualism and the un-schooling movement in the United States. This point will be explored further in this chapter.

The Ethic of Care is a modern philosophy, authored by Nel Noddings.[12] This philosophy is also referred to as the feminist philosophy, the philosophy of mothers, and the philosophy of teachers. In this philosophy, there are two primary players: the-one-cared-for and the-one-caring. The-one-caring makes moral decisions based on what he or she concludes is best for the-one-cared-for. This philosophy is very similar to pragmatism in that Truth for one person is not Truth for another person.

One of the best ways for me to explain this philosophy is to share with the reader my interactions with my two granddaughters, Serena and Madison. Serena is eleven; Madison is five. When Serena does something I do not like, such as sitting within five inches of a television screen, all I need to do is say her name and she will say "Sorry, sorry, sorry," and correct her behavior. With Madison, I need to tell her what she is doing is wrong, why it is wrong, and why I want her to stop it, and she will proceed to explain to me why I am wrong. These two behavioral responses to my "corrections," are not the result of age differences. These are natural or nurtured personality differences. Since Madison could talk she has explained to me why I am usually wrong; from a very early age Serena did what she was told to do. I am "the-one-caring" for both of these children, but to care for each I must be different.

In conversations and interviews with teachers, the Ethic of Care is quite apparent. How information is presented to one child and is understood by that child is very different from how information must be presented for another child to understand. Getting one child engaged in the learning process is different from getting another child engaged. Gaining one child's attention is a different process than gaining another child's attention. Stopping destructive behavior from one child to the next requires different techniques. The Ethic of Care is the defense against large class sizes; the Ethic of Care recognizes individual differences among children.

---

12 *Caring: A Feminist Approach to Ethics and Moral Education.* Berkeley: University of California Press, 1984.

Ideologies

To reiterate, ideologies are all-encompassing belief systems with inherent contradictions. In this section, I will focus on four ideologies—Puritanism, Romanticism, Progressivism, and scientism. Philosophies can be used to address societal issues, but more often ideologies are in play.

Puritanism is the belief that children are born bad and that it is the job of adults to give them the structure and guidance necessary for them to understand what is good and what is bad.[13] A person with the Puritan ideology will assume that, if left to their own devices, children will make the wrong decisions. Another way to put this is that a classroom without an adult present will result in someone or something being hurt. School policy in which students may not be left in a classroom alone, without an adult present, are examples of Puritanism; playground attendants, lunchroom attendants, teachers supervising study halls, and the need for an adviser for all student groups are examples of the Puritan ideology.

The contradiction within Puritanism comes into play in the evaluation of parenting practices, teachers, and any adult who is responsible for children. The question posed is, can they be trusted? Thus, it is not that children need adults to supervise them; it is that children need a certain *type* of adult to supervise them. As a nation, we tend to trust parents much more than professional educators (teachers). We have an assumption that all parents love their children; that parents know what is best for their child's education. Thus, we have homeschooling, and as a result, parents are involved in such practices as the creation of IEPs. However, when it comes to health, we trust medical professionals (doctors and nurses) over the judgments of parents. Though parents may be present for most medical procedures, they do not have the final say on the medical treatment of their children. If parents do not take their child to a medical professional or refuse medical treatment for their child, the child may be taken from the parent and/or the parent is jailed. If parents do not take their child to school or make sure their child attends school, very few legal practices, if any, are enacted.[14]

The practice of standardized testing is another example of Puritanism at work in schooling. We cannot trust professional educators to properly teach children, so children must be tested via a standardized test, and educators must be punished for failure. We do not evaluate the medical profession similarly. We do not have a standardized test of the health of children in our nation; nor do we punish doctors who do not succeed in ensuring that their patients are healthy. With teachers, if a child does not come to school regularly or parents do not make sure the child does his or her homework, it is still the teacher's responsibility to ensure that learning will occur at a certain level. With doctors, if a child eats more candy and junk food than vegetables and fruits

---

13   Bernier, Norman and Williams, Jack E. *Beyond Beliefs: Ideological Foundations of American Education.* Englewood Cliffs, NJ: Prentice Hall.

14   Some states and municipalities have attempted to seek prosecution of parents for student truancy, the punishment being a fine or some jail time. See Ives, Millard. May 25, 2010, "Parents Jailed for Child's Truancy, *Daily Commercial*, retrieved March 18, 2012, from http://www.dailycommercial.com/052510parents ; Sarrios, Jaime. December 17, 2011. "Student Truancy Can Spell $1,000 Fine, Jail for Parents," *Atlanta Journal-Constitution*, retrieved March 18, 2012, from http://www.ajc.com/news/atlanta/student-truancy-can-spell-1262559.html

each day, we do not hold their pediatrician accountable if the child becomes obese, unhealthy, or his or her teeth rot. For such behaviors, we also do not hold parents accountable, for the most part. However, if a child's health deteriorates and the parent does not seek and utilize the advice of a doctor, they may be punished legally. Thus, some adults can be trusted and some cannot be trusted. Often the decision of whom to trust is tied to the Puritan ideology.

Romanticism is the complete opposite of Puritanism. The Romantic ideology is the belief that children are pure and innocent. If a child does something that is viewed as opposite to the norms of society, Romantics believe that the child was taught this negative behavior by society.[15] Thus, Romantics view all adults suspiciously and all children positively; it is rules and policies (made by adults) that corrupt children. Examples of Romanticism in schools are all attempts to censor books. The assumption is that the book will corrupt children, and no adult, perhaps especially a teacher, is qualified to guide children in seeing the wrongness of the book's message. Efforts to censor video games and television programming are Romantic attempts to protect children in and outside their homes. In contrast, computer programs that allow parents to censor their children's television viewing are Puritan, in the belief that children cannot be trusted with a television remote control and their parents will do what is necessary to supervise what is seen by the children. The way to differentiate Puritanism and Romanticism is whether or not a policy allows for the intervention by a responsible adult. Efforts to completely censor a product from society imply that no adults can be trusted.

In schools, Romanticism is most often evident when parents argue that their child deserves a higher grade on an assignment or a lesser punishment for breaking a school policy. However, the key to understanding Romanticism in schools is whether or not parents are opposed to policies or simply want exceptions made for their own children. When parents are opposed to a school policy that restricts student behavior, Romanticism is at play; when parents want an exception made for their own child, but agree with the rule or policy in general, it is not Romanticism. Another example of Romanticism in schools is when one believes that effort should be rewarded in grades. The assumption is that the child tried his or her best and therefore should be rewarded, regardless of performance. Again, however, this is Romanticism only if an individual applies this principle to all children, not simply their own children.

The contradiction of Romantics is that they view most—but not all—children as pure and innocent. The issue of school bullying has recently gained national attention due to school shootings and other tragic outcomes. Recently, in Chardon, Ohio, a male student pulled out a gun and shot five classmates. That day, as the media questioned students from Chardon High School, they repeatedly asked, "Was he (the shooter) bullied?"[16] One student after another said no. Yet the question was asked, again and again. When the prosecutor for the case involving the

---

15   Ibid.
16   Observations made while watching the coverage of the shootings on CNN, WEWS, WKYC, and Fox News Cleveland.

shooter first made an announcement he stated, "This is not an issue of bullying."[17] Why did the media and prosecutor even mention bullying? None of the witnesses mentioned bullying, but an assumption of media coverage was that something had to occur to make this child take a gun to school and shoot his classmates. Later it was revealed that both of the shooter's parents had been arrested for domestic abuse and he lived with his grandfather. Bullying has existed as long as schooling has existed, but children taking guns to school and shooting classmates is a relatively new phenomenon. Domestic violence also has a long history, but again, school shootings are a recent occurrence. Many children are bullied who never take a gun to school and many children in violent homes never take guns to school. Thus, blaming bullying or violence in the home is the Romantic ideology at work.

The ideology of Progressivism does not engage in the argument of whether children are good or bad, nor does it distinguish between good and bad adults. The premise of the Progressive ideology is that if everyone works together, societal problems will be resolved.[18] In the early 1900s, Progressivism was a very active ideology that begat an era of change known as the Progressive Movement.[19] Some of the causes addressed during this era were child labor, women's suffrage, the education of African Americans and immigrants, industrial monopolies, conservation, and political corruption.[20] Theodore Roosevelt, Jane Addams, Margaret Sanger, Booker T. Washington, W. E. B. Du Bois, and John Dewey were some of the more famous progressives who acted on their beliefs.[21] Some of the laws which resulted from the Progressive Movement in the United States are the Meat Inspection Act, the Clayton Antitrust Act, and the Federal Trade Act.[22]

Today, Progressivism is less evident on the national stage, especially among bipartisan politicians. It is evident, however, at the local level at food banks and soup kitchens, in crisis hotlines, and shelters for the abused. Progressivism is perhaps most visible after a tragedy. After the tragedy of 9/11, Americans united to help the families of those lost, a bucket brigade was organized to clean away the debris, and people even lined up to give blood, though 9/11 did not cause a blood shortage. After Hurricane Katrina, communities provided sanctuary for those who no longer had a home; blankets, food, and other supplies were sent from across the country, as well as financial donations. After tornados devastate a community, hundreds of volunteers are seen in the media helping those affected reestablish their lives.

In schools, Progressivism is apparent in organizations such as sports and band booster clubs, which have fund-raisers for the local sports teams and bands. Progressivism is also seen after school tragedies in candlelight vigils and counselors being brought in to help survivors. After the shooting at Chardon High School, a newscaster from Cleveland, Ohio (60 miles east of Chardon),

17 "Ohio Suspect Confesses, Prosecutor Says," *New York Times*, retrieved March 16, 2012, from http://www.ny-times.com/2012/02/29/us/ohio-school-shooting-suspect-confesses-prosecutor-says.html?pagewanted=all
18 Bernier, ibid.
19 Mintz, S. (2007). The Progressive Era. *Digital History*. Retrieved March 16, 2012, from http://www.digitalhistory. uh.edu/database/article_display.cfm?HHID=163 ; Rury, John. (2002). *Education and Social Change: Themes in the History of American Schooling*. Mahwah, NJ: Lawrence Erlbaum Associates, Publishers.
20 Retrieved March 15, 2012, from http://www.regentsprep.org/regents/ushisgov/themes/reform/progressive.htm
21 Ibid.
22 Ibid.

announced, "We are all citizens of Chardon."[23] Governor Kasich, who is seen more as a critic of teachers (especially teachers' unions), joined with teachers, administrators, students, parents, and community members to commemorate those who were killed or injured in the Chardon shootings.

One contradiction or weakness of this ideology is that it is short lived, and we tend to place time limits on helping others. Once an issue loses interest in the media, it also loses interest for most people. A second flaw is the assumption that people actually want to solve social issues, rather than blame others or prove to others that they are correct.

The last ideology, scientism, has dramatically changed schooling in the United States. Scientism is the belief that solutions to societal problems are found within science or come from scientists. This ideology does not distinguish between adults and children, like Puritanism and Romanticism, nor does it distinguish between working together or individually, like Progressivism. Instead, the key is the scientific method. If the scientific method is applied it can solve all societal problems; if it is not applied we can trust those who have training in the scientific method to make the right decisions for all of us.[24] Thus, we put medical doctors and rocket scientists in a higher status than teachers or social workers. Another example is that in our national budget, the National Science Foundation is a line item and received approximately $685 billion dollars. In contrast, the National Endowment for the Arts is not a line item in the federal budget. On the home page of the National Endowment for the Arts, they ask for donations and they report that only 9% of their budget is the result of federal tax dollars.[25] The National Science Foundation publicizes no such financial challenges on their home page.[26]

In schools, this ideology is very apparent with the emphasis on testing and the assumption that tests are true indicators of learning that is occurring in a school. We also see it in which programs are cut and teachers being let go when a school is financially strapped. In this nation, we have a shortage of science teachers, but not a shortage of art, music, or dance teachers. If we cut science from the curriculum in a time of school financial crises, instead of teachers of the arts perhaps we would have a shortage of arts teachers, not science teachers. Or if we as a nation paid as much for artistic endeavors outside of schools as we do for scientific endeavors outside of schools, perhaps those who elect to teach the arts would be less likely to go into teaching and those who enjoy science would be as likely to pursue a teaching career as any other scientific career.

23   Retrieved   March   16,   2012,   from   http://www.newsnet5.com/dpp/news/local_news/oh_geauga/cleve land-news-anchor-looks-at-the-murders-of-high-school-kids-in-chardon-and-reflects-on-the-crimes
24   Bernier, ibid.
25   Retrieved March 16, 2012, from http://www.nea.gov/
26   Retrieved March 16, 2012, from http://www.nsf.gov/

Theories of Education

When pre-service teachers take their methods classes regarding how to teach, or child development classes regarding why children act a certain way at a certain age, they learn many theories, which they will use in their future classrooms. The theories in this section will not help one determine how to teach or why children act as they do. The educational theories in this section answer the "What should be?" questions, and they all speak to the question "Why do we have public schools?"

- What should be the role of students in a classroom?
- What should be the role of teachers in a classroom?
- What should be taught in schools?
- How should teachers teach?

The last question sounds like it is a "how-to" question, but it is more of a discussion question than instructions, and it must be tied back to the previous three questions. This "how-to" question cannot stand in isolation of the "should be" questions. This "how-to" question is not a question regarding best practices; rather, it is a question which gets to the heart of why we have public schools. Are teachers authority figures or guides? Are students passive or active learners? What do we expect our teachers to know and convey to students? Given the answer to these three questions, how should teachers teach?

Theories of education fall into two broad categories—teacher-centered and student-centered. In teacher-centered classrooms, the basic assumption is that teachers have knowledge and students do not. Therefore, the primary task of teaching and learning is for teachers to give knowledge and students to receive knowledge; in this classroom the teacher is active, the student is passive. In student-centered classrooms, the basic assumption is that students come to classrooms with knowledge and it is the job of the teacher to build upon that knowledge. Thus, teachers and students both play an active role in teaching and learning.[27] In this section, I will begin the discussion of theories of education with student-centered Progressivism, as described by John Dewey, and then I will shift to perennialism, as characterized by Robert Hutchins. I end this section with a discussion of essentialism, as described by William Bagley

Progressivism is the first and most significant student-centered theory of education. The teacher is a guide, not an all-knowing authority figure. Three primary components exist in a progressive classroom: 1) It is child-centered; 2) It has a democratic community of learners; and 3) It focuses on the scientific method for all learning. In a child-centered class, the interests of students play a central role in all learning. An assumption is that learning occurs only when students are intrigued by a topic and chose to explore that topic; learning occurs when it follows the nature of a child. The progressive classroom is also democratic. Students learn what it means to be a citizen of a

---

27 Retrieved March 16, 2012, from http://assessment.uconn.edu/docs/TeacherCenteredVsLearnerCenteredParadigms.pdf

democracy by first becoming an active member of a classroom with a voice in what will be learned in that classroom. Lastly, all learning is discovery learning through application of the scientific method. Students are given problems to solve, and in order to solve those problems they must pose questions, test hypotheses, reformulate questions, and again test hypotheses.

The theory of progressivism originated from the writings of John Dewey, who argued in his pedagogical creed that education is both psychological and sociological.[28] In regard to the question, "What is a student?" Dewey argued that we must recognize students' individual "powers, tastes, and interests,"[29] and empower each student by giving "him command of himself."[30] Furthermore, this command is of little value if students do not recognize that they are social beings and that "society is an organic union of individuals."[31] As a pragmatist, Dewey argued that we cannot know the future; thus, "it is impossible to prepare the child for any precise set of conditions."[32]

Given this position, "What should be taught in schools?" Dewey maintained that "We violate the child's nature and render difficult the best ethical results by introducing the child too abruptly to a number of special studies of reading, writing, geography out of relation to his social life." Instead, "the true center of correlation on the school subjects is not science, nor literature, nor history, nor geography, but the child's own social life."[33]

Needless to say, Dewey's view of what is needed in education is very inconsistent with the current standards movement in education. He viewed teachers as guides and saw examinations as "of use only so far as they test a child's fitness for social life and reveal the place in which he can best be of service and where he can receive the most help."[34] He argued that students should be stimulated and controlled "through the life of the community" and that the school should "simplify existing social life" for students, but mirror life that "carries on in the home, in the neighborhood, or on the playground ... school life should grow gradually out of the home life; that it should take up and continue the activities with which the child is already familiar in the home."[35]

Progressivism is rarely seen in schools today, especially the democratic and scientific components. Standardized education negates this possibility. When it is legislated that children must learn certain information at certain grade levels, it is impossible for teachers to follow the nature of children as their guide, to allow children to have a voice in what they learn, and to give them the time necessary for the trial-and-error practices of utilizing the scientific method. Progressive education requires a great deal of patience on the part of the teacher; it requires teachers to not have a preconceived notion regarding what children will discover when they are permitted to

---

28 Dewey, John. (1897). *My Pedagogical Creed.* New York: E. L. Kellogg & Company.
29 Ibid., p. 6.
30 Ibid., Dewey wrote at a time when male pronouns dominated all writings. Thus, when quoting him I will use masculine pronouns, though the reader should recognize that I view this as applied to males and females.
31 Ibid.
32 Ibid.
33 Ibid., p. 10.
34 Ibid.
35 Ibid., pp. 7 and 8.

make mistakes and learn from those mistakes. It requires a teacher to be open-minded to the possibility—if not probability—that students will teach them new information and skills of which they were not aware. As will be discussed in the next chapter, progressivism is perhaps the best means for the development of critical thinking skills and global awareness among children, but given the current structure of schools, as a result of the standards movement, teachers do not have time for it.

Perennialism can be seen in any movie one has watched that includes an image of a college classroom. The teacher is at the front of the class talking, while students sit quietly writing as fast as they can every word the professor states. Perennialists view teachers in the classroom as all-knowing, all-powerful authority figures. Students in the classroom are sponges, empty vessels, just waiting to hear (and memorize) what the omniscient before them knows. Outside of the classroom, students are encouraged to be active when they read. Perennial teachers were trained in the liberal arts—history, philosophy, literature, etc.—the great works by great authors or scholars such as Plato, Shakespeare, Freud, Durkheim, etc.[36] More often than not the great works are in the Western tradition and do not include Eastern or African writings.[37] These writings are referred to as the Canon, a body of knowledge that all good teachers, according to perennialists, should know. The role of a teacher is to give students the knowledge one has; the role of the students is to absorb the knowledge. The assumption is that what is being taught to students is new information, that they have never heard this information previously. However, the information provided is not "new" information; it is perennial, unchanging information, that which is found in the great works.[38]

Key authors in the tradition of perennialism are Robert Maynard Hutchins and Mortimer Adler. Hutchins argued for educational reform that focused on the liberal arts:

The liberal arts are the arts of freedom. To be a free a man must understand the tradition in which he lives. A great book is one which yields up through the liberal arts a clear and important understanding of our tradition. An education which consisted of the liberal arts as understood through great books and of great books understood through the liberal arts would enable us to comprehend the tradition in which we live. It must follow that if we want to educate our students for freedom, we must educate them in the liberal arts and in the great books.[39]

---

36 Cohen, LeoNora and Gelbrich, Judy. (1999) "Section III: Philosophical Perspectives of Education." Foundational Perspectives of Education. retrieved March 16, 2012, from http://oregonstate.edu/instruct/ed416/PP3.html

37 For a list of books of the Western Canon see http://gutenberg.net.au/greatest-books-a.html ; http://www.westerncanon.com/

38 Ornstein, Allan C. and Levine, Daniel U. (2004). *Foundations of Education*, ninth edition. Boston: Houghton Mifflin Company.

39 Hutchins, Robert Maynard.(1965). *Education for Freedom*. Baton Rouge: Louisiana State University Press, p. 14, passages selected by Adam Kissel, retrieved March 17, 2012, from http://home.uchicago.edu/~ahkissel/hutchins/education.html

The first six chapters of this book are very much in the tradition of Adler's view of how to read a book, "You know you have to read 'between the lines' to get the most out of anything."[40] Adler also prescribed something that I advise my students to do when they read a book:

I want to persuade you to do something equally important in the course of your reading. I want to persuade you to "write between the lines." Unless you do, you are not likely to do the most efficient kind of reading … Why is marking up a book indispensable to reading? First, it keeps you awake (And I don't mean merely conscious; I mean wide wake). In the second place, reading is active, is thinking, and thinking tends to express itself in words, spoken or written. The marked book is usually the thought-through book. Finally, writing helps you remember thoughts you had, or the thoughts the author express … And that is exactly what reading a book should be: a conversation between you and the author.[41]

Like Adler, I instruct my students to read with a pencil in hand, to write in the margins of the book, and throw away their highlighters. Students should develop a coding system of underlines, vertical lines, stars, circled words, and other markings. Much like solving a mystery and collecting evidence, coding information that one reads "preserves them better in your memory," and "your grasp of the book would be surer."[42]

Like perennialism, the theory of essentialism views teachers as all-knowing authority figures; however, what should be taught, how to teach it, and why differ greatly. As can be seen in the statements of Hutchins, the perennialism theory of education posits that studying the liberal arts will lead to the "art of freedom."[43] It is believed among those from this tradition that knowledge of the great books will lead to an understanding of our heritage and shape the minds of leaders. Instead of teaching the great works, essentialists believe that the basics are most important and stray away from the idea of schools playing a role in shaping our nation. The Back to Basics movement is an essentialist educational reform in opposition to progressivism. As stated by William Bagley, the first proponent of essentialism:

A primary emphasis has been the alleged need of building the program of instruction around local communities … In so far as we can learn, this theory has never explicitly recognized that the state or the nation has a stake in the content of school instruction.

---

40   Adler, Mortimer J. "How to Mark a Book," *Saturday Review of Literature*, July 6, 1941, pp. 268–272, from Loomis, Roger Sherman and Clark, Donald Lemen (eds.) (1942), *Modern English Readings*. Princeton, NJ: Farrar and Rinehart Inc.
41   Ibid.
42   Ibid.
43   Ibid., Hutchins.

The need of common elements in the basic culture of all people, especially in a democracy, has in effect been denied.[44]

Bagley called for a "system and sequence of learning," and accused progressives of "a dogmatic denial of any value in, even of the possibility of learning through, the logical, chronological and casual relationships of learning materials."[45]

The purpose of schools is to teach reading, writing, and arithmetic: the basic skills necessary to function in our nation. As stated by Bagley:

> There can be little question as to the essentials. It is by no means a mere accident that the arts of recording, computing and measuring have been among the first concerns of organized education. They are basic social arts. Every civilized society has been founded upon these arts, and when these arts have been lost, civilization is invariably and inevitably collapsed.[46]

Thus, nothing short of the collapse of democracy is at risk if we do not teach children basic skills. As will be discussed in the next chapter, *A Nation at Risk*, the document most often attributed as initiating the current standards movement, has a very similar ring to it. For now it is clear that No Child Left Behind, and especially its implementation, falls squarely in this tradition.

CONCLUSION

Perennialism is consistent with the first six chapters of this text, but do not assume that my educational theory is perennialism. In my courses, the first third of the class is perennialism, the last two thirds are progressive. As discussed in the introduction of this text, I take my students on a journey from an extremely teacher-centered classroom to an extremely student- centered classroom. I believe that each of these are of value in a classroom and that there is a time and place for each. The key is to have a professional teacher who can explain at any point why he or she is utilizing a theory of education in his or her pedagogy and can do so by answering each of the questions above, as well as using professional language to do so.

Ultimately, what will give philosophies, ideologies, and theories power is when they are used by teachers to describe what, why, and how they introduce students to knowledge and skills; what will give teachers power is using a professional language. This chapter is an introduction to that language. The bashing of teachers has become sport in America. Politicians often state that teachers deserve more respect, and then proceed to criticize their ineptness. Doing so has assisted

---

44 Bagley, William. (1938). "An Essentialist Platform for the Advancement of American Education, 1938," p. 559 as cited in Milson, Andrew J., et al. (ed.) (2009). Essays from 1640–1940. Charlotte: Information Age Publishing
45 Ibid., p. 556.
46 Ibid., p. 562.

many politicians in winning elections; it has also helped tremendously to profit companies that contribute to political campaigns.[47] This trend will not end until teachers' voices take prominence in political debates regarding schooling in the United States. Teachers will never gain a higher reputation until they begin speaking professionally. This chapter, in addition to giving teachers a way to analyze political debates, also provides the beginning of a professional language for teachers.

Four characteristics are commonly tied to professions: 1) professional autonomy, a clearly defined, highly developed, specialized theoretical knowledge base; 2) control of training, certification, and licensing of new entrants; 3) self-governing and self-policing authority, especially in regard to professional ethics; and 4) a commitment to public service.[48] Teachers do not have autonomy or power, but they do have a commitment to public service. Whether or not teaching has a clearly defined, highly developed, specialized theoretical knowledge base is debatable. In interviews with teachers, they repeatedly express a desire for respect and to be viewed as a professional.[49] Such desire is consistent with what Pratte and Rury identify as the characteristics of professionals: remuneration, social status, autonomy, authoritative power, and service.[50]

If teachers hope to gain more social status, more respect, perhaps more power and autonomy, I believe they must demand it. The first step to that demand, I believe, is utilizing professional

47   For examples of this in Ohio, see: Leonard, Timothy, March 6, 2012, "Kasich Could Save money with Charter School," Cincinnati.com retrieved March 17, 2012, from http://cincinnati.com/blogs/letters/tag/white-hat-management/ ; "Kasich Guest Rhee Draws Focus to Education Scam," Ohio Federation of Teachers, retrieved March 17, 2012, from http://oh.aft.org/index.cfm?action=article&articleID=c0c1729c-016f-4f91-9ec8-e78180803fbb ; Joseph, May 9, 2011, "Meet the Lobbyist Responsible for Ohio's New Charter School Wild West," Plunderbund.com, retrieved March 17, 2012, from http://www.plunderbund.com/2011/05/09/meet-the-lobbyist-responsible-for-ohios-new-charter-school-wild-west/ ; Dick, Denise, April 10, 2010, "Southside Academy Chief: Law Is on White Hat's Side," retrieved March 17, 2012, from http://www.vindy.com/news/2011/apr/10/southside-academy-chief-law-is-on-white-/ ; "White Hat Management Political Contributions," Join the Future, retrieved March 17, 2012, from http://www.jointhefuture.org/blog/245-white-hat-management-political-contributions ; Madfloidian, June 7, 2010, "Ohio White Hat Charter Management Refuses to Testify Before State Legislature," retrieved March 17, 2012, from http://www.democraticunderground.com/discuss/duboard.php?az=view_all&address=389x8509704 ; Manic, Madrigal, "Kasich Ignores Campaign Promise Again: Yes There's More," May 27, 2011, The Madrigal Maniac, retrieved March 17, 2012, from http://www.madrigalmaniac.com/2011/05/27/kasich-ignores-campaign-promise-again-yes-theres-more/ ; Dave, "Brennan's Bonanza: Kasich Expands Vouchers for Failing Charter School as Record $5.2 Million Fine Imposed on Charter Group Goes Unpaid," ProgressiveOhio.org, retrieved March 17, 2012, from http://www.progressohio.org/blog/2011/03/brennans-bonanza-kasich-expands-vouchers-for-failing-charter-schools-as-record-52m-fine-imposed-on-c.html

48   Ismat, Abudal-Haqq, July 7, 2000, "Professionalizing Teaching: Is There a Role for Professional Development Schools," Washington, DC: ERIC Clearinghouse on Teacher Education, retrieved March 17, 2012, from http://www.ericdigests.org/1992-3/teaching.htm ; also see Shon, Christopher, (2006). "Teacher Professionalism," Faculty Publications and Presentations, Paper 46, retrieved March 17, 2012, from http://digitalcommons.liberty.edu/cgi/viewcontent.cgi?article=1053&context=educ_fac_pubs

49   Clark, Debra L. (2003). "The Perceptions of Teachers as Regarding Their Role as Moral Agents in the Classroom" (Unpublished Doctoral Dissertation). Kent State University, Kent Ohio, see http://www.kent.edu/ehhs/oaa/dissertations/upload/clarkdeborah.pdf

50   Pratte, R. and Rury, J. L. (1991) "Teachers, Professionalism, and Craft." Teachers College Record, 93, 59–72. EJ 438 554 as cited in Ismat, Abudal-Haqq, July 7, 2000, "Professionalizing Teaching: Is There a Role for Professional Development Schools," Washington, DC: ERIC Clearinghouse on Teacher Education, retrieved March 17, 2012, from http://www.ericdigests.org/1992-3/teaching.htm

language to explain what they practice. When asked to explain how they made moral decisions in a classroom, the teachers I interviewed often stated they used intuitive decisions or went with what they "felt" was correct. Imagine going to a doctor or lawyer and being told that their professional judgment was based on how they felt. One expects doctors to provide scientific evidence to defend their professional judgments; one expects lawyers to cite case law. Those two professions, just like teaching, require intuitive decision making, but individuals in those professions do not publicize that side of their professional decision making; teachers do.

DISCUSSION QUESTIONS

1. Are you an idealist, realist or pragmatist? Identify five ways in which your philosophy has played a role in your decision making thus far in your life. If you cannot pick just one, identify five ways in which each philosophy you use has influenced your life decisions. For example, if you are an idealist as well as a pragmatist, list different decisions you have made for each philosophy.
2. In what ways have you experienced each ideology in the following classroom/schooling practices:
    a. Classroom management or discipline;
    b. Teacher/student relationships;
    c. Teacher versus student spaces (bathrooms, lockers, playgrounds, classrooms, teachers' lounge);
    d. Extracurricular activities (particularly coaching or advising styles);
    e. Parent/teacher conferences;
    f. Test taking;
    g. Homework assignments and grading.
3. Use the information and language from this chapter to describe your beliefs regarding each of the following questions:
    a. What is a student?
    b. What is a teacher?
    c. What should be taught?
    d. How should it be taught (and why)?

ACTIVITIES

1. Read John Dewey's *Pedagogic Creed* and rewrite it to represent what occurred in the K–12 experiences of students in the class.
2. Are you a feminist? Using the links below, determine if you are a feminist. If so, what type of feminist?

3. Write a canon. In small groups, create a non-Western literature canon. This canon need not be books. For example, create a canon of alternate music songs or a canon of children's books or of movies with female leads. Upon completion of each canon, have a discussion regarding the criteria of each canon, as well as how it was developed.

ONLINE RESOURCES

1. Feminist Theory:
   Center for Digital Discourse   http://www.cddc.vt.edu/feminism/enin.html
   Women Studies Resources   http://bailiwick.lib.uiowa.edu/wstudies/theory.html
2. Philosophy:
   Stanford Encyclopedia of Philosophy   http://plato.stanford.edu/
   Internet Encyclopedia of Philosophy   http://www.iep.utm.edu/
3. _My Pedagogic Creed_, by John Dewey: http://dewey.pragmatism.org/creed.htm
4. Western Canon: http://gutenberg.edu/resources/great-books/

CHAPTER EIGHT
TEACHER PROFESSIONALIZATION

WHY DO I NEED TO KNOW THIS?

What is a teacher? Hansen describes teaching as a vocation rather than a job, career, or profession and argues that a key ingredient is the length of time a teacher is employed:

> The sense of vocation finds its expression at the crossroads of public obligation and personal fulfillment. It takes shape through involvement in work that has social meaning and value. This means that a great many occupations can have a vocational dimension. Medicine, law, and teaching come promptly to mind as examples. However, other activities such as athletics and gardening can be vocations too ... In principle, a person can serve the public and feel pleased in doing so by merely holding a door open for a few colleagues on the way into work. Such an act may take five seconds. But a vocation emerges over a far longer period of time ... a person with a vocational orientation toward teaching may wait and prepare for teaching before actually entering the ranks. Moreover, the person might engage in the practice for years before he or she genuinely begins to feel it to be a vocation and to treat it as such while working in the school and classroom. Many teachers, doctors, nurses, and ministers can attest to the fact that it takes a considerable time to appreciate both what their work requires of them and how they can best fulfill it.[1]

Thus, for Hansen, a teacher is someone with a service orientation, but that orientation develops over time. Noddings describes teachers as "the ones-caring" who model the ethic of caring:

---

1   Hansen, *The Call to Teach*, 3–4.

Besides engaging the student in dialogue, the teacher also provides a model. To support her students as ones-caring, hence she is not content to enforce rules—and may even refuse occasionally to do so—but she continually refers the rules to their ground in caring. If she confronts a student who is cheating, she may begin by saying, *I know you want to do well, I know you want to help your friend ...* What matters is the student, the cared-for, and how he will approach ethical problems as a result of his relation to her. Will he refer his ethical decisions to an ethic of caring or to rules and the likelihood of apprehension and punishment? Will he ask what his act means in terms of the feelings, needs, and projects of others, or will he be content with a catalogue of rules of the game?[2]

Thus, for Noddings, a teacher must also have a service orientation, but only in regard to the students in her classroom. Hansen's description is more of a service orientation to all of society. Goodman and Lesnick also describe teachers as having a service orientation, but they argue that this orientation is limited by the lack of authority they have regarding independence of professional judgment:

The competing paradigm sees a teacher as a professional. As such, a teacher stands in a fiduciary relationship to his or her students, to whom primary accountability is owing, just as a physician's primary accountability is to the patient, and the lawyer's to the client. In those professions, the fact that someone else may at times sign the check or pay the bill is, under professional codes of ethics, not supposed to dilute that loyalty. It is systemic obligations of a professional that can limit responsiveness to client, patient, or student desires: In a lawyer, the obligation is to the law itself; in the doctor, to the primary principal, *do no harm*; in a teacher, to pedagogic practices that support the intellectual and moral growth of students ... A professional can carry out these obligations only if his or her independent professional judgment is honored.[3]

In direct contrast to Goodman and Lesnick, Biklen argues that the movement to professionalize teaching is actually hindering teachers:

The professional model ... interferes with the construction of cooperative relationships with the lay community (parents, particularly mothers), so that it feeds the tensions that, for many teachers, become adversaries rather than partners. Second, it feeds the tensions that, for many teachers, arise out of the uneasy coexistence of love, concern for, and interest in their students on the one hand, and on the other, feeling of dissatisfaction

---

2   Noddings, Nel (1984). *Caring: A Feminine Approach to Ethics & Moral Education*, Berkeley: University of California Press, p. 178.
3   Goodman, Joan and Lesnick, Howard. (2001). *The Moral Stake in Education*. New York: Longman, 2001 168–169.

with certain working conditions of schools, particularly bureaucracy, and teachers' vulnerability and powerlessness.[4]

Though opposed to the professional model for teachers, in her argument, Biklen does view teachers as having a service orientation. There are, of course, countless definitions of what it means to be a teacher. For this study, these definitions are most applicable to teachers in that they project the image of a teacher as an individual motivated to nurture others. This image was in some way provided by each of the participants in both the first and second studies. Not only did they seem to have a propensity to nurture others, but they are also dedicated to do this task. Though every teacher spoke with a sense of dedication, they define moral agency differently. Perhaps as Hansen explains, "a vocation emerges over a far longer period of time."[5]

Ultimately, teachers must decide what a teacher is. This chapter is designed to assist pre-service teachers in that defining process:

WHAT IS A PROFESSIONAL TEACHER?

Step 1: Examine the websites of both teachers' unions, three professional associations, and three independent special interest groups. During this examination, determine how that group describes a professional teacher.

You are very unlikely to find a page on the any of these sites that says "qualifications of a professional teacher." You probably will not even find the phrase "professional teacher." This is a "read between the lines" activity. How is the organization criticizing schools? What are the assumptions behind the criticism? Is there a place for the role of teacher in that criticism? For example, with the independent special interest groups, are they arguing for religious freedom in schools? If so, the assumption is that religious freedom does not exist in schools. Is there evidence of this, and does that evidence—or lack of evidence—lead one to an assumption about what teachers may or may not be doing in the classroom? For example, is there evidence of a story of one child's experience in one school, or are there many stories? What is the role of the teacher in that story? If there does not appear to be a role for a teacher, why do you think this is?

Teachers' Unions:

» American Federation of Teachers[6]
» National Education Association[7]

---

4   Biklen, Sari Knopp. (1995). *School Work: Gender and the Cultural Construction of Teaching*. New York: Teachers College Press, p. 45.
5   Hansen, David (1995). *The Call to Teach*. New York: Teachers College Press, p. 3.
6   Retrieved March 21, 2012, from http://www.aft.org/
7   Retrieved March 21, 2012, from http://www.nea.org/

Professional Associations (SPA):

» CEC (Council for Exceptional Children)[8]
» ISTE (International Society for Technology in Education)[9]
» NAEYC (National Association for the Education of Young Children)[10]
» NMSA (National Middle School Association)[11]
» ACTFL (American Council on the Teaching of Foreign Languages)[12]
» AAHPERD/AAHE (American Alliance for Health, Physical Education, Recreation and Dance/American Association for Health Education)[13]
» AAHPERD/NASPE (American Alliance for Health, Physical Education, Recreation and Dance/National Association for Sport and Physical Education)[14]
» ALA (American Library Association)[15]
» TESOL (Teaching English to Speakers of Other Languages)[16]
» ITEA/CTTE (International Technology Education Association)[17]
» NCTE (National Council of Teachers of English)[18]
» NCSS (National Council for the Social Studies)[19]
» NCTM (National Council of Teachers of Mathematics)[20]
» NSTA (National Science Teachers Association)[21]
» NASP (National Association of School Psychologists)[22]
» NAEA (National Art Education Association)[23]
» OAEA (Ohio Art Education Association)[24]
» OMEA (Ohio Music Educators Association)[25]
» National School Board Association[26]
» The Council of Educators for Students with Disabilities[27]

---

8   Retrieved March 21, 2012, from http://www.cec.sped.org/am/template.cfm?section=Home
9   Retrieved March 21, 2012, from http://www.iste.org/welcome.aspx
10 Retrieved March 21, 2012, from http://www.naeyc.org/
11 Retrieved March 21, 2012, from http://www.amle.org/
12 Retrieved March 21, 2012, from http://www.amle.org/
13 Retrieved March 21, 2012, from http://www.aahperd.org/aahe
14 Retrieved March 21, 2012, from http://www.aahperd.org/NASPE/
15 Retrieved March 21, 2012, from http://www.ala.org/
16 Retrieved March 21, 2012, from http://www.tesol.org/s_tesol/index.asp
17 Retrieved March 21, 2012, from http://www.iteaconnect.org/
18 Retrieved March 21, 2012, from http://www.ncte.org/
19 Retrieved March 21, 2012, from http://www.tesol.org/s_tesol/index.asp
20 Retrieved March 21, 2012, from http://www.ncte.org/
21 Retrieved March 21, 2012, from http://www.nsta.org/
22 Retrieved March 21, 2012, from http://www.nasponline.org/
23 Retrieved March 21, 2012, from http://www.arteducators.org/
24 Retrieved March 21, 2012, from http://www.oaea.org/
25 Retrieved March 21, 2012, from https://www.omea-ohio2.org/Default.html
26 Retrieved March 21, 2012, from http://www.nsba.org/default.aspx
27 Retrieved March 21, 2012, from http://www.504idea.org/Council_Of_Educators/Welcome.html

» NABE (National Association for Bilingual Education)[28]
» American Indian Education Foundation[29]
» National Indian Education Association[30]
» National Board for Professional Teacher Standards[31]

Independent Special Interest Groups

» The Center for Effective Discipline[32]
» Focus Adolescent Services[33]
» Stop Bullying Now[34]
» No Child Left[35]
» Education Commission of the States[36]
» Learning First Alliance[37]
» Hoover Institution[38]
» Sound Vision[39]
» Christian Answers[40]
» Anti-Defamation League[41]
» American Civil Liberties Union[42]
» Family Research Council[43]
» National Center for Learning Disabilities[44]
» NAACP[45]
» Bully Police[46]
» Resource Center for Adolescent Pregnancy Prevention[47]

28 Retrieved March 21, 2012, from http://www.nabe.org/
29 Retrieved March 21, 2012, from http://www.nrcprograms.org/site/PageServer?pagename=aief_index
30 Retrieved March 21, 2012, from http://www.niea.org/
31 Retrieved March 21, 2012 from http://www.nbpts.org/
32 Retrieved March 21, 2012, from http://www.stophitting.com/
33 Retrieved March 21, 2012, from http://www.focusas.com/
34 Retrieved March 21, 2012, from http://www.stopbullyingnow.com/index.htm
35 Retrieved March 21, 2012, from http://nochildleft.com/
36 Retrieved March 21, 2012, from http://www.ecs.org/html/aboutECS/mission.asp
37 Retrieved March 21, 2012, from http://www.learningfirst.org/
38 Retrieved March 21, 2012, from http://www.hoover.org/taskforces/education
39 Retrieved March 21, 2012, from http://www.soundvision.com/Info/education/pubschool/pub.free.asp
40 Retrieved March 21, 2012, from http://www.christiananswers.net/q-wall/wal-g010.html
41 Retrieved March 21, 2012, from http://www.adl.org/issue_religious_freedom/faith-freedom/faith_freedom_schools.asp
42 Retrieved March 21, 2012, from http://www.aclu.org/
43 Retrieved March 21, 2012, from http://www.frc.org/
44 Retrieved March 21, 2012, from http://www.ncld.org/
45 Retrieved March 21, 2012, from http://www.naacp.org/
46 Retrieved March 21, 2012, from http://www.bullypolice.org/grade.html
47 Retrieved March 21, 2012, from http://recapp.etr.org/recapp/

» Americans United for Separation of Church and State[48]
» Keep Schools Safe[49]
» National School Safety and Security Services[50]
» Eagle Forum[51]
» National Youth Violence Prevention Campaign[52]
» Islam for Today[53]
» Atheist Parents[54]
» Jews on First![55]
» Stop the ACLU[56]
» ProEnglish[57]

Small Group Discussion Questions

1. Which organizations did each person in the group examine?
2. What are the differences and similarities between teachers' unions, professional associations, and independent special interest groups? To answer this question, examine the history of each organization, their membership and mission statement, as well as what other organizations say about that particular organization.
3. What patterns were observed regarding how teachers' unions, professional associations, and independent special interest groups described teachers (i.e., teacher as victim, teacher as responsible, teacher as guilty party)?
4. What were the primary concerns or issues of each website examined? Most, if not all, websites are created to convince readers of something; often they have a link to issues or topics.
5. What was each website trying to convince readers to believe about teachers?

Step 2: Compare your findings from Step 1 to the description of a professional teacher by the National Council for the Accreditation of Teacher Education[58] (NCATE), the U.S. Department of Education's[59] description of a highly qualified teacher, the Interstate New Teacher Assessment and Support Consortiums'[60] (INTASC) description of a professional teacher and the way in

---

48   Retrieved March 21, 2012, from http://www.au.org/
49   Retrieved March 21, 2012, from http://www.keepschoolssafe.org/
50   Retrieved March 21, 2012, from http://www.schoolsecurity.org/
51   Retrieved March 21, 2012, from http://www.eagleforum.org/education/
52   Retrieved March 21, 2012, from http://www.nyvpw.org/
53   Retrieved March 21, 2012, from http://www.islamfortoday.com/schools.htm#Young%20Adults
54   Retrieved March 21, 2012, from http://www.atheistparents.org/
55   Retrieved March 21, 2012, from http://www.jewsonfirst.org/06b/indianriver.html
56   Retrieved March 21, 2012, from http://www.stoptheaclu.com/
57   Retrieved March 21, 2012, from http://www.proenglish.org/
58   Retrieved March 21, 2012, from http://www.ncate.org/
59   Retrieved March 21, 2012, from http://www2.ed.gov/nclb/methods/teachers/teachers-faq.html#5
60   Retrieved March 21, 2012, from http://www.ccsso.org/resources/programs/interstate_teacher_assessment_consortium_(intasc).html

which teacher professionalism is measured by the Praxis Series.[61] NCATE, the Department of Education, INTASC, and the Educational Testing Service (creators of the Praxis Series) are special interest groups, but they are special interest groups with the power of accreditation and laws backing them. The power of the other special interest groups is in their ability to persuade.

Small Group Discussion Questions:

1. What is NCATE and what is its history? From where does the power of NCATE originate?
2. What is the Department of Education and what is its history? From where does it get its power?
3. What is INTASC, its history, and its source of power?
4. What is the Educational Testing Service, its history, and its source of power?
5. How does NCATE describe a professional teacher?
6. How does the Department of Education describe a professional teacher?
7. How do these descriptions differ from those of the teachers' unions, SPAs, and "other" special interest groups?

Step 3: Go to the Ohio Department of Education website and read about the Licensure Code of Professional Conduct for Ohio Educators,[62] Value Added (Module 1),[63] and the Ohio Educator License System.[64]
Small Group Discussion Questions:

1. NCATE stands for the _____ _____ for the _____ of _____ _____ and is responsible for policing and evaluating teacher education programs.
2. Standard 1 of NCATE identifies the _____, _____, and _____ pre-service teachers must possess upon completion of their academic program.
3. Standard 4 of NCATE identifies the _____, _____, and _____ pre-service teachers must possess upon completion of their academic program regarding _____.
4. The role of the federal government in teacher licensure is defining what it means to be a _____ _____ _____, which consists of a _____ degree, state _____, and prove they know their _____.
5. INTASC stands for the _____ ___ _____ _____ and _____ _____ and consists of _____ education agencies and _____ educational organizations.
6. Praxis 1 measures basic skills in _____, _____, and _____ and at Kent must be passed to obtain upper division status.

61 Retrieved March 21, 2012, from http://www.ets.org/praxis/
62 Retrieved March 21, 2012, from http://www.ode.state.oh.us/GD/Templates/Pages/ODE/ODEDetail.aspx?page=3&TopicRelationID=520&ContentID=41492&Content=122396Retrieved March 21, 2012 from
63 Retrieved March 21, 2012, from http://www.ohiorc.org/value-added/
64 Retrieved March 21, 2012, from http://education.ohio.gov/GD/Templates/Pages/ODE/ODEPrimary.aspx?page=2&TopicRelationID=515

7. Praxis II measures general and subject specific _____ _____ and _____, principles of teaching and learning, which are tied to _____ _____, as well as _____ _____ _____.

8. Making fun of another teacher's weight is a violation of _ _ of the Licensure Code of Professional Conduct for Ohio Educators.

9. Posting naked pictures, pictures of underage drinking, or smoking from a bong are examples of violations of _ _ of the Licensure Code of Professional Conduct for Ohio Educators.

10. Providing false information on a résumé is a violation of _ _ of the Licensure Code of Professional Conduct for Ohio Educators.

11. Getting a speeding ticket when a student or school personnel are in the car is a violation of _ _ of the Licensure Code of Professional Conduct for Ohio Educators.

12. Smoking is a violation of _ _ of the Licensure Code of Professional Conduct for Ohio Educators.

13. Encouraging booster clubs to purchase sports equipment is a violation of _ _ of the Licensure Code of Professional Conduct for Ohio Educators.

14. Resigning from a teaching post prior to the end date of the contract is a violation of _ _ of the Licensure Code of Professional Conduct for Ohio Educators.

15. Violation of the Licensure Code of Professional Conduct for Ohio Educators can result in _____, _____, or _____ one's teaching license.

16. A BCII criminal background check remains valid for ___ _____ after the date the report was completed.

17. True or False: If one has a conviction expunged from their record,. he or she is not required to admit that prior conviction in the BCII.

18. The three types of reports on school report cards are _____ reporting, _____ _____ _____, and _____-_____ progress.

19. _____ reporting summarizes overall performance on achievement tests, attendance, and graduation rates for the district and school (as applicable—for example, elementary schools do not have a "graduation rate" calculated into their performance, and high schools do not have test scores for elementary or middle grades).

20. _____ _____ _____ indicates how the school and district are helping each specific subgroup of children progress academically.

21. _____-_____ progress will look at the academic growth of each individual student to better understand the support that schools and districts are providing for student progress.

22. How will the Ohio Transition Resident Educator Program change the training of newly hired teachers? Cite four examples.

23. Does the licensure code bring more professionalism to teaching or does it reduce teacher professionalism?

24. The code was written by the state legislature. Does the fact that it was written by elected officials, rather than teachers, bring more professionalism to teaching, or does it reduce teacher professionalism?

25. How will the policy of value added change the work environment of teachers and learning experiences of students?
26. Does the licensure code and/or value added policy change the definition of a professional teacher that resulted from Steps One and Two above?
27. What is the Ohio Transition Resident Educator Program and how will it change teacher licensure in Ohio?

Step 4: Watch the PBS video series *School: The Story of American Education*. [65] If you are a school in Ohio and/or have access to Ohio Link, you can access the video by clicking on the following link: *School: The Story of American Education*.[66]

Small Group Discussion Questions:

1. On most school days _____ Americans are in school as students; if teachers and administrators are included, it is approximately _____ percent of the population.
2. The _____ _____ _____ was the first textbook used in Puritan Massachusetts schools, though in _____ schools, children were more likely to use a hornbook.
3. In 1776 the average attendance length was __ days.
4. ____ _____ is often referred to as the schoolmaster of America because he believed that we needed a national _____ based on the legends of the Founding Fathers.
5. ____ _____ Speller created an American language separate from the English language.
6. According to _____ _____, the survival of the nation depended on educating all Americans. Education had two purposes: to educate all Americans on the principles of _____ and as a staging ground for identifying the _____ aristocracy.
7. Over _____ years, Horace Mann visited approximately _____ schools; his reports on what he witnessed became the primary argument for a common school for all children.
8. According to _____ _____, schools should be the great equalizer of the nation.
9. Bishop _____ _____ initiated the protest against the Protestant influence in schools and argued for public money for a Catholic school system.
10. The Great School Debate was actually a group of Protestant ministers against one man, Bishop _____ _____.
11. Though Bishop _____ _____ was unsuccessful in getting public funds for Catholic schools, his arguments and the Philadelphia Bible Riot led to a secularization of public education. He also is primarily responsible for the Catholic school system, which became known as the _____ school system in America.
12. Prior to the Civil War, _____ of blacks lived in the South and most were slaves. Educating blacks was illegal in the South, but not in the North; however, blacks were _____ in schools.

---

65   Retrieved March 21, 2012, from http://www.pbs.org/kcet/publicschool/about_the_series/program.html
66   Retrieved March 21, 2012, from http://dmc.ohiolink.edu/cgi/i/image/image-idx?q1=School%3A+the+Story+of+American+Education&rgn1=ic_all&type=boolean&c=dvc&view=reslist

13. Blacks tied together the fight for _____ with the fight for freedom.

14. The argument for segregation of schools was that it benefited _____ children due to their special needs and characteristics.

15. In _____ the first desegregation law was passed in Massachusetts, primarily due to the efforts of _____ _____ on behalf of his daughter, Sarah. The national desegregation case law, *Brown v. Board of Education*, did not occur until _____.

16. In the expansion of the West, schooling played such a key role that it resulted in a _____ _____ crisis. This led to the hiring of female teachers primarily because they were _____.

17. _____ _____ saw teaching as a moral undertaking for _____. Later she acknowledged that her primary goal was to create a profession for _____.

18. _____ _____ were textbooks specifically written for children in the West. A primary focus of these textbooks were _____ education.

19. The annual _____ _____ was a time when a town gathered to evaluate the local teacher and school curriculum based on student performance.

20. By 1870 school expenditures were ___ _____ and school enrollment reached __ _____; by 1890 school expenditures were ___ _____ and school enrollment reached ____ _____.

21. In the early 1900s approximately _____ children did not attend school because they were required to go to work every day.

22. In 1900, ____ percent of children attended public school and average schooling was ____ years.

23. How did the saying "toe the line," originate?

24. _____ _____ became known as the father of progressive education.

25. The most progressive school system in the United States in the early 1900s was located in _____ _____.

26. What is an example of "school is a panacea for everything?"

27. Why did riots break out in New York over the Gary Plan?

28. When did the English language–only movement begin?

29. _____ percent of 17-year-olds graduated from school in 1920.

30. What was the "science of school management," who created it, and how did this change the view of the purpose of education?

31. Who was Lewis Terman, and what was his view of a utopian society and schools?

32. What was the problem with the IQ movement?

33. Why were Hispanic, black, Native American, and female students given a vocational education?

34. What was life adjustment education?

35. Why do Americans, particularly immigrants, shun progressive education?

36. How did Sputnik and the Cold War change education?

37. In the 1950s schools kept children safe by preparing them for a _____ _____ and by preventing _____ via _____.

38. In the 1950s approximately _____ of students graduated from high school and __ went on to college.

39. _____ states segregated African American students in 1950; the average schooling for _____ _____ was 5.4 years; __ percent of disabled children were not enrolled in school.

40. Why did the fight for equality begin in Topeka, Kansas?

41. _____ Brown was the plaintiff in *Brown v. Board of Education*.

42. How did black students receive a superior education to white students? How did white students receive a superior education to black students?

43. I believe that the number one reason for the achievement gap today is because of the greatest error made when schools were desegregated. What was that error (Hint: teachers)?

44. What roles did Presidents Eisenhower and Johnson play in bringing equality to schools?

45. What were the carrot-and-stick of civil rights in schools?

46. In 1968, __ percent of Mexican Americans dropped out of school at the ___ grade.

47. What happened when Severita Lara attempted to present a list of student demands to her school board? What happened the next day? What happened to the school board, and how did white parents and students react?

48. In *Lau v. Nichols*, the Supreme Court ruled that when children are different, treating them the same is actually an act of inequality. This decision made bilingual education in the United States mandatory in public schools. What is the debate that continues today regarding the purpose of bilingual education?

49. In 1970, __ percent of law and medical degrees were awarded to women; ___ percent of high school athletes were female.

50. What was the "battering ram" that opened the door for women in education?

51. What was President Richard Nixon's position on busing?

52. African Americans with high school diplomas in1950: _____ percent

    African Americans with high school diplomas in 1980: _____ percent

    Medical and law degrees awarded to women in 1950: ____ percent

    Medical and law degrees awarded to women in 1980: ____ percent

    Average school attendance in 1950: ____ years

    Average school attendance in 1980: ____ years

53. What was President Ronald Reagan's position on civil rights in education?

54. How were the fights for racial, cultural, gender, and disability equality in schools similar, and how were they different?

55. By 1980 approximately what percent of school age children attended school, and what percentage graduated?

56. According to Diane Ravitch, do the majority of Americans think schools are doing a good job or bad job?

57. _____ declared that "America has committed unilateral educational disarmament."
58. Was *A Nation at Risk*, which initiated the standards movement, accurate or misleading?
59. What initiated the "era for high-stakes testing?"
60. Between 1983 and 1984, the annual cost of standardized testing was ____ _____.
61. What was the educational experiment in Spanish Harlem?
62. What is the marketplace model of education?
63. What are the advantages and disadvantages of magnet schools?
64. What is a voucher?
65. What is a charter school?
66. What is school choice, whom does it mostly affect, and what are its primary flaws as currently implemented?
67. How could choice, vouchers, and charter schools "rip apart the fabric of this nation?"
68. How have vouchers reversed decisions made after the Bible riots of Philadelphia in the late 1800s?
69. What group worked to make homeschooling legal in all 50 states?
70. In 2000 and 2001, ___ percent of school children were educated solely at home.
71. In 2000 and 2001, limited voucher plans were available in _____, _____, and _____.
72. In 2000 and 2001, what percent of school children used vouchers?
73. What was the Baltimore educational experiment? Did it fail or succeed?
74. What is Channel One, and why did schools give it access to schoolchildren?
75. Compare and contrast Core Knowledge schools, progressive schools, and charter schools?
76. Between 2000 and 2001, what was the enrollment in public schools in numbers and percentage?
77. Excellence without equity leads to _____.
78. How has the purpose of education in the United States changed? Cite three examples from each video to support your answer.
79. How has the role of teachers changed throughout the history of the United States?
80. What were the educational debates discussed in the videos?
81. What role should a teacher play in debates about public school?

Step 5: Using the questions in Steps 1 through 4, answer the question: What is a professional teacher?

Voting with Your Feet

For each of the following dilemmas, what is the best resolution?

Why I Want to Be a Teacher

When teaching a class similar to this class, a professor announced on the first day of class that he would not grade a student based on his or her opinion. Upon hearing this, one of the students replied, in a rather rude manner, that the professor was being disingenuous. She angrily stated, "Bull----. I have been in class after class and heard one professor after another state that I will not be graded on my opinion. Then the professor turns around and grades me on my opinion. This is the same crap I have gotten in other classes." To this the professor replied, "No, honest, I promise I will not grade you on your opinion."

The student, of course, did not believe the professor at first. However, as the course progressed, she came to the conclusion that, yes, this professor could be trusted. Because of this newfound trust, when the students were assigned the final paper of the course, entitled "Why I Want to Be a Teacher," she decided to actually be honest and tell him why she wanted to be a teacher.

This student wanted to be a teacher because she strongly believed that much of what she heard throughout her college years was simply liberal propaganda. She believed that European Americans were greatly superior to all other ethnicities. She wanted to become a teacher so that she could teach European Americans about their superior nature; she wanted to teach African American, Asian American, Hispanic/Latino, and Native American children that they are here "to serve the white man."

Should the professor pass or fail this student? If she passes, she will student teach next semester in an inner city school.

Figure 1

AYP

A local rural school district has repeatedly failed to meet the Adequate Yearly Progress (AYP) requirement of No Child Left Behind (NCLB). The school is at risk of being closed as a result. Though the majority of students in the school have passed the tests, students on an Individual Education Program (IEP) have not. The Individuals with Disabilities Education Act requires that students on an IEP be placed in the Least Restrictive Environment (LRE). Thus, the school is not permitted to segregate the students who are failing the tests into a specialized classroom, for the most part. The students by and large must be included in traditional classrooms.

In an effort to meet the AYP requirement of NCLB, in December last year, the decision was made to pull students out of the "extra" classes who are not passing the tests. Specifically, students not passing the tests would be pulled out of music, art, physical education, social studies, and science. Thus, some students experienced the full curriculum and some focused on reading, writing, and arithmetic exclusively. The policy has continued into this school year.

Is this school policy good or bad?

Figure 2

JUST RIGHT READING

A third grade teacher gave her students a half hour each day to do "just right reading." Just right reading is when students engage in silent readings of their choice, as long as they are able to read and understand 75 percent of the words in the text.

- One day during "just right reading," a little boy in her class pulled out a King James Bible and began "reading." Because she knew this child's reading level, she knew that the King James Bible did not fulfill the "just right requirement." When she told the boy this, he said "Are you telling me I am not allowed the read the Bible?" She replied that reading the Bible was permitted, but it had to be a Bible that met the "just right" criteria. He responded that in his church there is only one Bible, the King James Bible.
- This particular little boy and his religion were becoming an issue in the classroom in another way. He was telling other students in the class, particularly Jewish and Muslim children, that their religion was not real, and therefore they were children of the devil. Also, at the beginning of each day and at lunch, he insisted on praying aloud; when this occurred all other students stopped what they were doing to listen to him.

You are the teacher; what would you do?

Figure 3

THE FARM BOY

You are a school principal. A parent just called and told you that her son told her that his teacher, Mr. Sunny, found a weapon on a student today and did not report it. You call Mr. Sunny to the office and he tells you the following story:

As you know, in my middle school special education classroom we have a young man named Chris. Chris is a farm boy with whom I have been working hard. He does not like school and sees no purpose in going to school. His parents also see little value in schooling. They have done fine, and neither parent graduated from high school. In school, the other children did not play or socialize with Chris. Instead, he was a victim of bullying. I and other teachers have tried to stop the bullying, but also became frustrated with Chris. He did not come to school clean. He often smelled of horse manure. His hair was rarely washed. His clothes were missing a button or slightly torn. He walked around staring at the floor, with his hands in his pockets, his shoulders slumped. He shuffled instead of lifting his feet. Chris really had no incentive to go to school and many incentives to not come to school. Hence, Chris rarely came to school.

I decided on a strategy for getting Chris to come to class. I announced to the class that if everyone came to class every day for a week I would buy pizza for the entire class. The children started encouraging Chris to come to school. Chris came to school every day for a week and I bought the class pizza. Then I announced that if everyone came to class every day for two weeks I would again buy the entire class pizza. Chris became a very popular student in class. I noticed that Chris's hygiene was improving. He still walked with a bit of a shuffle and with his hands in his pockets, but he now held up his head and the slump was gone from his shoulders. Students invited him to sit with them at lunch; students chose to work with Chris on group projects; students welcomed Chris each morning and told him, at the end of the day, that they hoped to see him the next day in class.

This process continued until I promised the class that if they all came to class every day for an entire quarter I would take the class to Pizza Hut for lunch. During this process, the other students gradually gained a stronger and stronger appreciation for Chris. I felt that I achieved my goal, and as a result, Chris's present and future were looking more and more positive. Chris even became a class leader of sorts.

On the day of the incident, Chris was teaching the class how to put together a model airplane. All was going well when Chris whipped out his jackknife to demonstrate how to closely trim the decals for the model and the entire class froze. The students in the class knew that knives were not permitted in school; I knew I was required to turn Chris in, but if I did you would have expelled him. At first Chris did not understand why everyone froze. Then I watched as Chris slowly realized what was wrong. Chris hung his head and slumped his shoulders. He looked completely defeated. I wanted to cry. I knew all of my work, all of Chris's progress, was about to be reversed by "zero tolerance policies." I knew that if I followed school policy and federal law that Chris would be expelled and it was very likely that he would never return to school. I did what I believed was best for Chris.

Should this teacher be fired?

Figure 4

When My Heart Tugs

You are a school principal. A parent just called and told you he heard that a teacher named Ms. Moran was revealing private information about some students to other students. When you call her in to question her, this is her reply:

I am an eighth grade math teacher who did not go to school to be a teacher until both of my sons were in college. I love my students as if they were my own children. I know my children and know what is right for them.

Bobby and Billy are students in my class. As you know, Bobby has golden blond hair, deep blue eyes, and he is a charmer. Everyone loves Bobby. He is a leader among his classmates; always picked first for a team. He usually is teacher's pet, not only because he always gets good grades, but because he is a little gentleman with impeccable manners. Part of the reason why Bobby is so darn cute and nice is because Bobby's parents adore him. Because they are comfortable financially, Bobby always has the latest designer clothes as well as the coolest toys.

As you also know, Billy is not so cute or nice. He too has blond hair, but it is dirty blond hair in color and cleanliness. Billy also has blue eyes, but they do not sparkle like Bobby's; they tend to be hooded behind an angry stare. The children in my class do not like him, and it is hard to blame them. Billy usually smells not only of body odor, but often of other strange smells. Nobody wants Billy on their team. He is always the last one picked for a team and, more often than not, not even chosen. Instead, a team groans when I say, "Billy, you are on that team." Teachers tend to groan also when they find out that Billy is in their class. But I did not groan or complain. Even though he is frequently suspended for fighting and being usually behind everyone else, I work with him to keep him up with the other students. When he is in class, he does not do his homework. He does not participate in class discussions. He sits slumped in his desk in the back of the class, glaring and snickering at everyone. When I have tried to reach out to him, he just glares more and never reciprocates. And it is no wonder, given the way the other adults in the building treat him.

One day I was walking up the steps when I heard a commotion. Students were cheering on Bobby to do something. I do not know why, but I decided to tiptoe up the stairs and see what was happening, without the students seeing me. When I got to the top of the stairs I sneaked a peek around the corner and was shocked with what I saw. Four boys held down Billy, as Bobby kicked him repeatedly. When I stepped forward, the four boys let go of Billy very quickly. All of the students started telling me that Billy started the "fight." When I turned to Billy and asked what happened, he just shrugged. But I know what I saw: Bobby was assaulting Billy and no "fight" was occurring. Because of school policy, both of the boys were sent to the office, and you suspended Billy for repeated fighting and gave Bobby a detention because this was his first fight. I told you that this was unfair based on what I saw, but you would not listen.

After what I witnessed in the hall, I decided to keep a closer eye on Billy and Bobby. I had read all of my students' files and knew that Billy was taken from his biological parents because he was severely abused. I also knew that school personnel suspected that Billy was again being abused by his adoptive parents. Perhaps Billy was a victim in the school fights; perhaps he was being bullied. Because of his abusive background and the possibility that he was being abused again, perhaps he would be less likely to report being bullied. I also was a bit skeptical about Bobby's charming ways. I wondered if it was possible that Bobby was the bully, that Bobby was the instigator of the fights that caused Billy to repeatedly get suspended.

After a month of observing Billy and Bobby, I concluded that my suspicions were true. I witnessed Bobby knock Billy's books off of his desk one day. On another day, he pushed Billy out of the lunch line and took his place. To make matters worse, it appeared that Bobby was instigating other children to also pick on Billy. I repeatedly saw different children walk up behind Billy and whisper something. I could not hear what they were saying, but the look on Billy's face told me that what they were saying hurt Billy's feelings.

I was not sure what to do with what I was observing, so I talked to other teachers and you. All of you doubted my claims and said that you did not believe that Bobby was a bully and Billy a victim. All of you told me to stop mothering my students and let them work out their own problems. I did not feel comfortable talking to Bobby's or Billy's parents. If other teachers could not believe that Bobby was a bully, his parents, who absolutely adored him, also would not. If I spoke to Billy's parents, I was afraid they might use it to further abuse him.

After a great deal of thought, I decided to talk to Bobby and try to reach his heart. So one day I called Bobby out into the hall and told him that Billy had been a serious victim of child abuse and because of that he was taken from his parents. I also told Bobby that I knew he was bullying Billy and wanted him to realize that he was perpetuating the abuse Billy experienced from his parents. I told Bobby that I wanted him to become a more caring individual and to start with caring for Billy.

I know that you told me to "leave it alone," but when my heart tugs I must act, and my heart tugs for Billy.

Figure 5

THE TEST

Prior to debating this dilemma, you may want your students to first research the evolution/ creationism debate. I have used the following websites for this purpose:

> http://www.pbs.org/wgbh/evolution/
> http://plato.stanford.edu/entries/creationism/
> http://law2.umkc.edu/faculty/projects/ftrials/conlaw/evolution.htm
> http://www.pbs.org/faithandreason/stdweb/info.html
> http://www.intelligentdesign.org/

Imagine that you have graduated from college, applied for, and got the job of your dreams. You are teaching your favorite subject to your favorite age group in the school of your choice. You have been teaching in this school for three years, you are still on probation, and you love your job.

In the school recently, an issue developed that has caused conflict between teachers, parents, and the community. Teachers are arguing with each other in the teachers' lounge and the arguments are heated. Parents are attending school board meetings and fighting among each other.

The issue is tied to the topic of evolution. One day, a teacher, Ms. Maile, announced in her class that the subjects they would study next semester would be evolution, carbon dating, fossils, and the history of the earth. After class, one of her students, Jodi, came up to her and told her that her parents would not allow her to participate in any discussions, listen to any lectures, participate in any activities, and do any assignments tied to evolution. Jodi explained that as a Christian she knew that God created the earth and everything else is blasphemy. Though Ms. Maile was impressed that Jodi wanted to stand by her convictions, she explained to Jodi that not participating in anything tied to evolution would result in a failing grade for the semester, because evolution was a part of every lecture, activity, and assignment next semester.

Jodi was a very popular straight "A" student. She came from a very poor family, however. She was up for a full scholarship given to one student each year, if that individual graduated with straight A's and a perfect attendance record. Jodi had both. She did not want to lose her opportunity to go to college, so she spoke to her parents about what would happen if she avoided all mention of evolution. Her parents told her that if the teacher would allow her to pass out pamphlets on the topics of intelligent design or creationism, she could continue to participate in the class.

Jodi was excited that this was the solution to her dilemma when she spoke to Ms. Maile the next day. Unfortunately, as Ms. Maile explained to Jodi, she could not allow her to pass out the pamphlets in her class. If she wanted to do so on her own time that was fine, but not in her class. Because of Ms. Maile's response, Jodi's parents required her to get up and walk out of the class whenever the topic of evolution was present. Jodi failed the class, and as a result, did not get the scholarship she needed to go to college.

When the community found out what occurred, many were outraged and called for Ms. Maile to be fired; other parents supported Ms. Maile. Some teachers too thought that Ms. Maile should be fired; the union supported her. Tonight is the board meeting to determine whether or not Ms. Maile will be fired.

After one of your classes, one of your students comes up to you and asks you what you think about the topic. You try to avoid answering by saying something benign, but the student will not let you off the hook. Instead, the student pushes you until you actually give your true opinion on the subject.

Figure 6

SMALL GROUP DISCUSSION QUESTIONS

1. Examine each of the above dilemmas separately. Each person in the group should voice how they believe the dilemma should be resolved.
2. The group should then come to a consensus regarding the resolution of each dilemma.
3. Defend the decision of the group regarding each dilemma, using information from Chapters One and Two of this text. For example, given Horace Mann's position on the purpose of public schools, would he support the decision of the group? Is the group's decision consistent with Jefferson's argument for a natural aristocracy?
4. Use case law to defend the decision of the group. You may need to go beyond the content of Chapters Three and Four and use the online resources for this question.
5. Tie the requirements of IDEA and NCLB to the conclusion of your group.
6. Is the decision consistent with the policies of the following teacher professionalization groups?
    » Teachers' Unions
    » Professional Associations
    » NCATE
    » INTASC
7. If your decision cannot be defended using educational history, case law, and educational policy, is it indefensible? Should you reconsider your earlier decision?
8. What belief systems are apparent in the decisions of your group, as well as the discussion?

TRENDS IN EDUCATION

Analyzing teaching dilemmas is one way to utilize the content of this book. Another valuable intellectual activity is developing the ability to scrutinize trends in education. This section will assist pre-service teachers in developing those skills.

The Standards Movement

The standards movement began with the Reagan presidential campaign. Campaigning with the promise of ending the U.S. Department of Education and returning governance of schools to the state level, President Reagan ensured that taxpayers would save much money. At the beginning of the Reagan administration, disagreement occurred regarding how to address this issue. In particular, disagreement existed regarding the appointment of Terence Bell as secretary of education, who disagreed with Reagan's views on the elimination of the U.S. Department of Education.[67]

Against Reagan's advice, Bell appointed the National Commission on Educational Excellence, because "he thought that it would conclude that public schools were doing a satisfactory job and that this finding would end conservative calls for radical reform."[68] In contrast, Reagan gave the commission an opposing directive: "Focus on five fundamental points that would bring excellence back to education; bring God back into the classroom. Encourage tuition tax credits for families using private schools. Support vouchers. Leave the primary responsibility for responsibility for education to parents. And please abolish the abomination, the Department of Education."[69] By determining its problems, the assumption was that American people would agree that schools return to the jurisdiction of the states.[70] The outcome of this commission was the report, *A Nation at Risk*, which did not please Bell or Reagan, but did gain the public's attention with inflammatory language such as:

> If an unfriendly foreign power had attempted to impose on America the mediocre educational performance that exists today, we might view it as an act of war … We have, in effect, been committing an act of unthinking, unilateral educational disarmament.[71]

Using the language of war was very effective in gaining the nation's attention, as did other statements such as the following, which highlighted weaknesses of the school system:

---

67 McGuinn, Patrick J. (2006). *No Child Left Behind and the Transformation of Federal Education Policy, 1965–2005*. Wichita: Kansas State University Press; Vinovskis, Maris A. (2009). *From A Nation at Risk to No Child Left Behind*. New York: Teachers College Press.

68 McGuinn, pp. 42–43.

69 Ibid., p. 43.

70 Ibid.

71 National Commission on Excellence in Education, April 1983. *A Nation at Risk: The Imperative for Educational Reform*. Retrieved March 23, 2012, from http://www2.ed.gov/pubs/NatAtRisk/index.html

- International comparisons of student achievement, completed a decade ago, reveal that on 19 academic tests American students were never first or second and, in comparison with other industrialized nations, were last seven times.
- Some 23 percent of American adults are functionally illiterate by the simplest tests of every-day reading, writing and comprehension.
- About 13 percent of all 17-year-olds in the United States can be considered functionally illiterate. Functional illiteracy among minority youth may run as high as 40 percent.[72]

Initially, the public's reaction was a call for educational reform. The public's reaction to *A Nation at Risk* was not what President Reagan anticipated. Instead of agreeing with ending the U.S. Department of Education, the public initially demanded more accountability of schools. William Bennett, Reagan's second secretary of education, fueled the flames by highlighting the report and suggesting that it called for less of a federal role in education, support for local control, and to "shake up the education establishment and promote choice."[73]

Research/Discussion Questions:

1. What was the role of the federal government in the administrations of the presidents who followed Reagan?
2. What is meant by "choice" in discussions regarding educational reform?
3. What has been the change in the U.S. Department of Education since the publication of *A Nation at Risk*?
4. Two major federal policies have resulted from the standards reform movement, No Child Left Behind and a Race to the Top. How have each of these policies positively and negatively influenced schools?
5. Formulate an argument in support of or in opposition to the standards movement. Use educational history, case laws, and educational policies to defend your position.
6. Is the decision consistent with the policies of the following teacher professionalization groups?
   - » Teachers' Unions
   - » Professional Associations
   - » NCATE
   - » INTASC
7. If your decision cannot be defended using educational history, case law, and educational policy, is it indefensible? Should you reconsider your earlier decision?
8. What belief systems are apparent in the decisions of your group as well as the discussion?

---

72 Ibid.
73 McGuinn, p. 43.

Privatization of Public Education

A key word in debates regarding educational reform is "choice," which, in many respects, is code for privatization of public schools. No Child Left Behind and a Race to the Top have resulted in a dramatic increase in the role of the federal government in educational policy, as well as a notable increase in the federal funding of schools.[74] Key words in understanding privatization of public education are "vouchers," "charter schools," "supplemental educational services," and "for-profit schools."

Research/Discussion Questions

1. What is a charter school?
2. What is a school voucher?
3. According to No Child Left Behind, what are supplemental educational services? Who provides these services?
4. What role do charter schools play in No Child Left Behind?
5. What is Race to the Top, and how is it related to charter schools?
6. How are charter schools different in Ohio from other states?
7. How are charter schools funded in Ohio?
8. Are charter schools required to follow the same laws as public schools?
9. Does the Individuals with Disabilities Education Act apply to charter schools?
10. Is segregation permitted in charter schools?
11. How is regulation of charter schools different from regulation of public and private schools?
12. Formulate an argument in support of or in opposition to the standards movement; use educational history, case law, and educational policies to defend your position.
13. Is the decision consistent with the policies of the following teacher professionalization groups?
    » Teachers' Unions
    » Professional Associations
    » NCATE
    » INTASC
14. If your decision cannot be defended using educational history, case law, and educational policy, is it indefensible? Should you reconsider your earlier decision?
15. What belief systems are apparent in the decisions of your group, as well as the discussion?

Violence in Public Schools

Kent State University, Columbine, and Virginia Tech—three schools that will forever be associated with school violence, but they are not the only schools tainted by tragedy. Perhaps no topic gains the attention of educators and pre-service teachers more than the topic of school violence;

---

74 "The Federal Role in Education." U.S. Department of Education. Retrieved March 25, 2012, from http://www2.ed.gov/about/overview/fed/role.html,

perhaps no topic can more quickly garner media attention faster than school violence. With that stated, what we "know" about school shootings is not necessarily accurate. This topic, like all other topics, is tainted by bias.

Research/Discussion Questions

1. What is the history of violence in public schools?
2. Identify ten acts of violence in schools. What do these events have in common? How do they differ?
3. How does the media portray violent events in schools? Particularly focus on whom the media blames for acts of violence.
4. What has been the political response to violent events in schools?
5. What is the bias of the media and politicians regarding violence in schools?
6. Formulate an argument regarding violence in schools. Use educational history, case law, and educational policies to defend your position.
7. Is the decision consistent with the policies of the following teacher professionalization groups?
   » Teachers' Unions
   » Professional Associations
   » NCATE
   » INTASC
8. If your decision cannot be defended using educational history, case law, and educational policy, is it indefensible? Should you reconsider your earlier decision?
9. What belief systems are apparent in the decisions of your group, as well as the discussion?

ACTIVITY

1. As I finish writing this book a new educational policy was just passed regarding schooling in Ohio. The U.S. Department of Education exempted Ohio and a few other states from the requirements of No Child Left Behind. What that will mean for Ohio schools, I do not know. Using a search engine research "state exemptions from No Child Left Behind" to find out what this means. Which states are exempted? Why are they exempted? How will this change schooling in those states versus the states that were not exempted? Make sure to go to the department of education websites for states exempted and states without exemptions to see how schooling differs.
2. This chapter required locating additional sources than those provided. Who were the authors of the additional sources?
3. Was it Wikipedia? Everyone uses Wikipedia, even college professors, and it is a great place to start research. But NEVER read what is written in Wikipedia by starting at the top. Scroll

immediately to the end of the page and check the references the author cited before you read the article.

4. What are the credentials of the authors? Are the authors experts? How does one determine who is an expert and who is not?
5. What are the biases of the authors?
6. Do authors with opposing biases agree on anything?
7. Do the findings of this step in the process change your original findings? How so? Why or why not?

CHAPTER NINE

HUMAN DIVERSITY IN EDUCATION

WHY DO I NEED TO KNOW THIS?

According to the 2010 census, the Hispanic population in the United States increased by 15.2 million, or 43 percent. In contrast, the non-Hispanic white group grew at a 5 percent rate and dropped from 69 to 64 percent of the population.[1] By 2042 current ethnic minority groups in the United States will make up the majority of the population of the United States.[2] The foreign-born population is also diversifying. Prior to 2005, over half of all immigrants came from Latin America and the Caribbean. Since 2005, less than half of all immigrants came from that region. China and India are strongly represented in the population of new immigrants.[3]

Our nation, however, is not only diversifying in ethnicity and nationality. Family structures are also changing. In 2010, 19 percent of people were getting married for the second time; 5 percent were married three or more times.[4] Unmarried individuals over the age of 18 now make up approximately 43.6 percent of the population; 35 percent of all children in the United States were born to single, divorced, or widowed mothers.[5]

---

1   "Overview of Race and Hispanic Origin: 2010." 2010 U.S. Census Briefs, p. 3. Retrieved March 24, 2012, from http://www.census.gov/prod/cen2010/briefs/c2010br-02.pdf
2   "An Older, More Diverse Nation by Midcentury." August 14, 2008. News Release. U.S. Census Bureau. Retrieved March 23, 2012, from http://www.census.gov/newsroom/releases/archives/population/cb08-123.html
3   "The Newly Arrived Foreign-Born Population of the United States: 2010." November 2011. American Community Survey Briefs. U.S. Census Bureau Newsroom. Retrieved March 24, 2012, from http://www.census.gov/prod/2011pubs/acsbr10-16.pdf
4   "Valentine's Day 2012: Feb. 14." January 2, 2012. Profile America Facts for Features. U.S. Census Bureau Newsroom. Retrieved March 24, 2012, from http://www.census.gov/newsroom/releases/archives/facts_for_features_special_editions/cb12-ff02.html
5   "Unmarried and Single Americans," Week September 18–24, 2011, U.S. Census Newsroom. Retrieved March 24, 2012, from http://www.census.gov/newsroom/releases/archives/facts_for_features_special_editions/cb11-ff19.html

As for religion, 78.4 percent of Americans identify as Christian. However, the largest-growing populations in regard to religion are those with no affiliation: 16.1 percent.[6] More than one fourth of Americans have left the faith of their childhood. Blacks attend religious services more than any other ethnicity, and even those who self-describe as unaffiliated list religion as "somewhat or very important."[7] According to the Pew Forum, the United States is on the verge of becoming a "minority Protestant country," even though the Catholic faith "has experienced the greatest net losses of membership."[8]

These population changes are dramatically changing the demographics of students, at the same time that the demographics of teachers are not changing. The majority of teachers continue to be women (53 percent) and white (83 percent).[9] Though the religious beliefs of teachers are less well known, it is fair to assume that it is reflective of the nation as a whole.

Thus, the argument for why teachers must understand human diversity in education is that the student population is diversifying at a much higher rate than the teaching population. The first step in understanding issues of diversity is to understand one's own cultural identity. In the following section is an activity that will assist pre-service teachers in understanding their own cultural identity. Following that section is an activity, which will assist students in having a greater understanding of diversity at the national and international level.

HUMAN DIVERSITY IN EDUCATION

My views of human diversity in education are strongly influenced by my mentor, Averil McClelland, one of the coauthors of *Human Diversity in Education: An Integrative Approach*.[10] I wrote the instructor's manual for the first edition of their text. This activity is the evolution of some of the exercises in that manual.[11]

The first three steps of this activity are the result of a Longview Foundation Grant in which I served as a global learning scholar, 2011–2112. For this grant, I created a learning module to assist students in recognizing that they are cultural beings with specific cultural identities. This module is based on the Cushner, McClelland, and Safford Cultural Learning Process discussion tool and requires students to answer true or false about twelve sources of cultural knowledge (cultural identifiers) and twelve socialization agents. Though the authors of the Cultural Learning Process,

6 "Summary of Key Findings." U.S. Religious Landscape Survey. The Pew Forum. Retrieved March 24, 2012, from http://religions.pewforum.org/reports

7 Ibid.

8 Ibid.

9 "Characteristics of Full-Time Teachers." (2011). National Center for Education Statistics. Retrieved March 24, 2012, from http://nces.ed.gov/programs/coe/indicator_tsp.asp

10 Cushner, K., McClelland, A., and Safford, Philip. (2003) *Human Diversity in Education: An Integrative Approach*. Boston: McGraw Hill.

11 Clark, Debra (2000). Instructor Manual and Test Bank to Accompany Cushner, K., McClelland, A. and Safford, Philip. (2003) *Human Diversity in Education: An Integrative Approach*. Boston: McGraw Hill.

particularly McClelland,[12] point out that this is simply a discussion tool, I believe it can be used to assist students in visualizing their cultural identity. As a result, I created the online learning module for that purpose.[13]

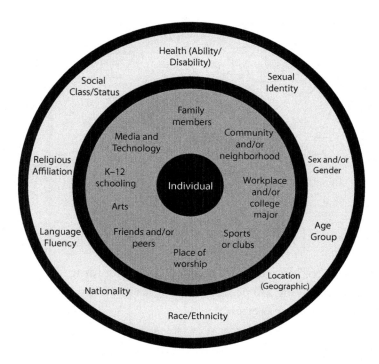

Figure 8[14]

The purpose of the learning module tied to the Cultural Learning Process is to give students a visual image of their own cultural identity that they can bring to class and share with their group.

---

12   Personal communications, November 2011–present.

13   In my class, I show my student the cultural learning process designed by Cushner, McClelland, and Safford and begin a discussion of how they might change the model. Figure 8 is the outcome of these discussions and is not the actual model designed by Cushner, McClelland, and Safford. The activity that follows is based on the adapted version visible in Figure 8; the online learning module uses the original model.

Throughout this text I have encouraged the reader to examine the footnotes in an effort to evaluate the biases of authors. Footnotes are also for the purpose of respecting intellectual property. Showing the actual model created by Cushner, McClelland, and Safford would violate copyright laws, which is illegal, as well as disrespectful of the intellectual property rights of the original authors.

For a more through explanation of the cultural learning process and the topic of human diversity in education, see Cushner, McClelland, and Safford. 2003. *Human Diversity in Education: An Integrative Approach*. Boston: McGraw Hill.

14   Adapted from McClelland, Averil, e-mail correspondence March 20, 2012.

Labeling statements as true or false will result in circles and pie pieces in the model getting larger or smaller, as well as the creation of a network image (see Figure 9).

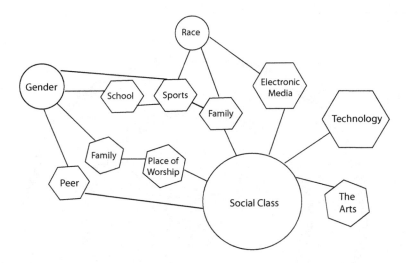

Figure 9

Step 1: The first step of this activity requires understanding the variables of the Cultural Learning Process. The following are personal examples from my life. As you read through these, compare them to your own life experience.

Cultural Identifier: Age
- We each have been on this earth for so many years and each of those years defines us. I have been on this earth for 51 years. If you have been on this earth for 20 years, we have different knowledge. I grew up when talking on the phone meant you had to be at home, standing next to a wall where the phone hung on the wall. Not only did each person in the family not have their own phone, when we picked up the phone someone who lived in another house might already be on the phone, and we would need to wait for a half hour or so to see if they were off the line. You grew up in a world where phones are mobile and everywhere.
- We also have expectations of behavior tied to age. The saying "act your age" is an example of this expectation. However, these expectations are tied to the other cultural identifiers. For example, in some countries girls as young as eight marry men in their 40s or 50s.[15] In the United States there is the expectation that children should be in school at least until the age of 18, if not until their 20s; in other countries children go to work at the age of five.

Cultural Identifier: Location (Geographic)

---

15   "Breaking Vows: Early and Forced Marriage and Girls' Education." Retrieved March 19, 2012, from http://www.plan-uk.org/resources/documents/Breaking-Vows-Early-and-Forced-Marriage-and-Girls-Education/

- Many of us were born into and grew up in one town. This town at least partially defines us. Others grew up moving from one community to another. This too defined those individuals. The community or communities where you grew up gave you knowledge, as well as ignorance. For example, I grew up in an <u>Old Order Amish</u> community.[16] I am not Amish, but I was <u>influenced</u> by this portion of our community. In graduate school I went to New York City with a friend who grew up there. After about an hour of walking around the city she yelled at me, "Would you stop looking around and for Pete's sake stop saying hello to everyone? We are going to get <u>mugged</u>!" I was living up to the "hick from the sticks" stereotype. I did not have the knowledge necessary to survive in a city.
- We each also lived in a specific region, state, or country; some grew up in multiple regions, states, or countries. This too gives one knowledge and ignorance, as well as <u>stereotypes</u> to shatter or live up to.[17] For example, what is someone from New York City like, what is someone from the South like? Whether from northeast Ohio, New York City, or Alabama, each person has specific knowledge and views of others.

<u>Cultural Identifier: Sexual Identity</u>
- I do not believe that I need to define the words gay or straight for you, nor do I believe that I need to define the stereotypes. Nonetheless, expand your thoughts on sexuality to include <u>polygamy</u>[18] and the role <u>religion plays in the topic of sexuality</u>[19]
- In the United States, our sexuality is also influenced by a religion that was prominent in the 1600s: Puritanism. However, the influence of Puritans on our culture is often the <u>myth of the Puritans.</u>
- Each of these cultural identifiers are also political issues. Sexuality is now on the national political landscape. Many degrade aspects of diversity by minimizing different cultural identifiers; sexuality gives us one of the clearest examples of this. For example: "<u>Sexuality is a choice</u>" or more recently, discussions of conversion or <u>reparative therapy.</u>[20]

<u>Cultural Identifier: Religious Affiliation</u>

---

16   "Origins of the Old Order Amish." Retrieved March 19, 2012, from <u>http://holycrosslivonia.org/amish/origin.htm</u>
17   For more information on stereotypes and knowledge associated with geographic regions, see "The United States of Mind," *Wall Street Journal*. Retrieved March 19, 2012, from <u>http://online.wsj.com/article/SB122211987961064719.html</u>
18   For more information, see Anderson, Scott, "The Polygamists," *National Geographic*. Retrieved May 20, 2012, from <u>http://ngm.nationalgeographic.com/2010/02/polygamists/anderson</u>-text
19   Also see "Religion and Sexual Ethics," *San Francisco Chronicle*, December 1994. Retrieved March 20, 2012, from <u>http://acme.com/jef/religion_sex/</u>
20   For more information, see "Attempts to Change Sexual Orientation," Psychology Department, UC–Davis, University of California. Retrieved March 19, 2012, from <u>http://psychology.ucdavis.edu/rainbow/html/facts_changing.html</u>; also see "Reparative Therapy, Homosexuality, and the Gospel of Jesus Christ." <u>AlbertHohler.com</u>. Retrieved March 19, 2012, from <u>http://www.albertmohler.com/2011/07/19/reparative-therapy-homosexuality-and-the-gospel-of-jesus-christ/</u>

- Religion is the belief in a higher power or not believing in a higher power; beliefs regarding what happens when one dies; a moral code.[21]
- Like all of the cultural identifiers, <u>religion</u> is not a choice. You were born and/or nurtured in a family that had religious beliefs, even if it was an antireligion belief. Though as adults we can choose what we believe, the messages we learned as a child stay with us and influence us. For example, did you attend participatory or solemn religious services as a child? Did people yell out words of praise to the preacher or sit silently in their pews? Regardless, if you have those same beliefs as an adult, you received the message that religious events should be solemn or participatory. Did men and women, children and adults sit together during religious services? Or were children sent off to a different service? Did men and women have different roles in your place of worship? Though you may have different religious beliefs now, you still have messages about the roles of <u>males and females</u>, <u>children, and adults</u> when it comes to the topic of religion.[22]

Cultural Identifier: Social Class/Status
- This is one of the more enjoyable cultural identifiers, if you are at the top. When I earned my PhD in December 2003, my family bought me a vanity license plate reading, "Dr. DLC." Prior to that date, I averaged approximately three speeding tickets per year. Since receiving my PhD, I have not received any speeding tickets, though my driving has not improved (it is probably much worse). I was stopped once for speeding and the officer asked me if I was a doctor. I told him that I am a professor, not a medical doctor. He asked me where I teach. I told him "Kent State University." His response was "I love Kent State," and gave me a warning.
- I believe this story exemplifies social status. I believe I have not received a speeding ticket—though I deserve approximately 20 each year—because my license has "Dr." on it. I am given more respect in an area in which I am not deserving, simply because of my title.
- The example I provided exemplifies the concept of social status, but it does not get to the often painful experiences of social status in schools. Bullying, emotional and physical violence by children to children, too often interferes with the learning experience. Sadly, adults rarely interfere with <u>bullying</u>; they view it as something the children have to work out for themselves.[23] The outcome of this view has too often been tragic. However, those are

---

21 For more information, see "Faith and Reason," Public Broadcasting Service. Retrieved March 19, 2012, from <u>http://www.pbs.org/faithandreason/</u>

22 For more information, see "Perspectives on Gender and Religion," Public Broadcasting Service. Retrieved March 19, 2012, from <u>http://www.pbs.org/moyers/faithandreason/perspectives3.html</u> ; also see "Religious Service Attendance." Child Trends Data Bank. Retrieved March 19, 2012, from <u>http://www.childtrendsdatabank.org/?q=node/303</u>

23 For more information on school bullying, see "Bullying at School and Online." Retrieved March 19, 2012, from <u>http://www.education.com/topic/school-bullying-teasing/</u>

extreme cases of social status. What were the <u>cliques</u> in your school—the jocks, the hoods, etc.? What group were you in?[24] That was your social status in school.

- Social class and social status are two identifiers that are often confused. Social status is the respect one is given; social class is the income of one's household. As a professor I have high social status, but middle social class. However, like all of the identifiers, what is most significant is the social class of one's parents. I was raised in a working-class home; thus, I have working-class values. For example, I put higher value on one's work than on one's income. This is a working-class value.
- Social class also shapes views about <u>parenting</u>.[25] It shapes which parents do homework with their children, which hire tutors, which assume education is the job of the school, and which send their children away for an education. Stereotypes are also given to different groups based on their social class. These stereotypes follow children into schools and <u>shape their education</u>.[26]

<u>Cultural Identifier: Language Fluency</u>
- Language is verbal and nonverbal, quiet and loud; it is guided by dialect and geographic region. In the United States, a commonly heard bias is voiced regarding language: "English should be our national language." Or "<u>Standard English</u> is proper English." This bias can be harmful to everyone. For example, for the purpose of improving test scores, one of the best reforms in education might be to begin teaching all children a second language. Some <u>research</u> suggests that bilingual and multilingual children are better at math, because math is the third or fourth language they learn.[27]
- Another bias is regarding a general view of "proper English." In the United States, there are three primary dialects of the American language: Ebonics, Rural English, and Standard English. Each has the same number of rules; they simply have different rules (such as what are plural and singular verbs.) <u>Ebonics</u> and <u>Rural English</u> are much closer to Shakespearean English than Standard English. Thus, one could argue that Standard English is the *least* proper English, and that Ebonics and Rural English are the most proper forms of English in the United States.[28]

---

24   For more information on school cliques, see "Cool Kids and Losers: The Psychology of High School Students in Peer Groups and Cliques." University of Michigan. Retrieved March 19, 2012, from <u>http://sitemaker.umich.edu/356. tran/true_clique</u>

25   For more information, see Gorman, Thomas. "Social Class and Parental Attitudes Toward Education," *Journal of Contemporary Ethnography*, April 1998, vol. 27, no. 1, pp. 10–44.

26   For more information, see Anyon, Jean, "Social Class and the Hidden Curriculum of Work." *Journal of Education*, vol. 162, no. 1, fall 1980, retrieved March 19, 2012, from <u>http://cuip.uchicago.edu/~cac/nlu/fnd504/anyon.htm</u>

27   Clarkson, Philip C. and Galbraith, Peter. "Bilingualism and Mathematics Learning." *Journal for Research in Mathematics Education*, vol. 23, no. 1, 34–44.

28   For more information on English dialects in the United States, see "The Dialects of American English," retrieved March 19, 2011, from <u>http://pandora.cii.wwu.edu/vajda/ling201/test3materials/AmericanDialects.htm</u> ; "Hooked on

Cultural Identifier: Health (Ability/Disability)

- This identifier is multidimensional. Each of us has a range of abilities and disabilities.
- Categories of abilities/disabilities are <u>physical</u>, <u>cognitive</u> (intellectual/learning), and <u>emotional</u>.[29] Abilities can be visible or invisible. Those with <u>invisible</u> abilities/disabilities often expend much energy determining when and where they should disclose their abilities/disabilities.[30]
- Another key point to remember about abilities and disabilities is that it is a range. My name is Dr. Clark; thus, the assumption might be that I am very intelligent. I have an average intelligence, but love to learn and I read a great deal, so one could argue that I am very smart, but only average intellectually. However, according to the <u>Individuals with Disabilities Education Act,</u> I am cognitively disabled.[31] I have <u>dyslexia</u>.[32] However, I was never on an <u>IEP</u>, though I went to school when the law was enacted. On my teaching evaluations, the item in which I always receive the most positive comments is "knowledge of content." So what am I: disabled, average, or gifted?
- In U.S. culture, we have given the right to declare who is healthy and who is not to the medical profession. Doctors have been given the right to provide medical care to children when parents oppose it. Parents have gone to jail for choosing to pray for their sick child rather than have medical personnel treat their child.
- When one has intestinal influenza or a cold, usually the last thing one wants to do is go in a car and visit a doctor. Once at a doctor's office, there is also little that can be done to stem the symptoms of influenza or a cold. Nonetheless, if one missed work or school, a doctor's note is required for an excused absence.
- In the United States, our view of health is strongly influenced by the ideology of <u>scientism</u>.[33]

Ebonics," Public Broadcasting Service, retrieved March 19, 2012, from <u>http://www.pbs.org/speak/seatosea/american-varieties/AAVE/hooked/</u> ; and "Dialects of the United States of America," International Dialects of English Archive, retrieved March 19, 2012, from <u>http://web.ku.edu/~idea/northamerica/usa/usa.htm</u>

29 For more information, see "Physical Disabilities," Special Ed Wiki. Retrieved March 19, 2012, from <u>http://sped.wikidot.com/physical-disabilities</u> ; "Cognitive Disabilities," Disabled World. Retrieved March 19, 2012, <u>from http://www.disabled-world.com/disability/types/cognitive/</u> ; and Smith, D. D. "Emotional or Behavioral Disorders Defined." <u>Education.com</u>, Pearson Allyn Bacon Prentice Hall. Retrieved March 19, 2012, from <u>http://www.education.com/reference/article/emotional-behavioral-disorders-defined/</u>

30 For more information, see "What Is an Invisible Disability?" Invisible Disabilities Association. Retrieved March 19, 2012, from <u>http://www.invisibledisabilities.org/what-is-an-invisible-disability/</u>

31 "Building the Legacy: IDEA 2004," U.S. Department of Education. Retrieved March 19, 2012, from <u>http://idea.ed.gov/explore/home</u>

32 Ibid., "Query: Dyslexia."

33 Ryder, Martin. (2005). "Scientism," *Encyclopedia of Science, Technology, and Ethics*, Micham, Carl (ed.). Retrieved March 20, 2012, from <u>http://carbon.ucdenver.edu/~mryder/scientism_este.html</u>

Cultural Identifier: Race/Ethnicity

- All of these identifiers are not real, so to speak; they are social constructions. They are part of our lived experiences, but they consist of categories we created and to which we attach hierarchy.
- Race is the best example of this. <u>There is no such thing as race</u>.[34] We created it. Various sciences from <u>biology</u>[35] to <u>anthropology</u>[36] can provide the technical proof that race does not exist.
- I believe, however, that the best proof that race is a social construction is that different cultures and different nations identify different races. For example, I had a friend from South Africa whom I mistakenly referred to as "black." He was deeply offended and explained to me that he was brown, not black. We do not have such a distinction in this country. If a person from Korea and a person from Japan walked down a sidewalk in this country, they would be commonly referred to as "Asian," and most Americans would view them as being from the same race. In Japan, <u>Korean</u> is a race.[37]

Cultural Identifier: Nationality

- <u>Nationality</u>[38] is where a person has citizenship and the rights and privileges, traditions, and values of that nation. <u>Ethnicity</u>[39] is the citizenship of one's ancestors. For example, I am a citizen of the United States, but my mother's family came from Germany. Thus, I am part German American.
- Just as we share traditions and values tied to our citizenship (nationality), we also share values as a result of our ancestry (ethnicity). For some Americans, ethnicity and nationality are of little importance; for others, it is central to all aspects of their life.
- The importance of one's nationality and/or ethnicity may be tied to the rights one has or does not have in this nation. For example, in <u>Arizona</u>, attempts have been made to force Hispanics to carry identification, which is not a requirement for other ethnic groups.[40]

---

34 "Is Race for Real?" Public Broadcasting Service. Retrieved March 20, 2012, from <u>http://www.pbs.org/race/001_WhatIsRace/001_00-home.htm</u>

35 Lee, Sandra Soo Lin, et al. "The Ethics of Characterizing Differences: Guiding Principles on Using Racial Categories in Human Genetics," Open Letter, July 15, 2008, *Genome Biology*, 2008, 9–404, BioMed Central, Ltd. Retrieved March 20, 2012, from <u>http://genomebiology.com/content/pdf/gb-2008-9-7-404.pdf</u>

36 O'Neil, Dennis, March 14, 2008, "Ethnicity and Race: An Introduction to the Nature of Social Group Differentiation and Inequality." Retrieved March 20, 2012, from <u>http://anthro.palomar.edu/ethnicity/Default.htm</u>

37 For more information, see Fukuoka, Yasunori. "Koreans in Japan: Past and Present." *Saitmama University Review*, vol. 31, no. 1. Retrieved March 20, 2011, from <u>http://www.han.org/a/fukuoka96a.html</u>

38 For more information on the extensive process one goes through to become a citizen in the United States, see the "Learners" link on the U.S. Citizenship and Immigration Services website. Retrieved May 20, 2012, from http://www. uscis.gov/portal/site/uscis/menuitem.2182d258012d5eb62b6859c7526e0aa0/?vgnextoid=37decf2351488210VgnVCM 10000025e6a00aRCRD&vgnextchannel=37decf2351488210VgnVCM10000025e6a00aRCRD

39 For more information on culture and ethnic groups in the United States, see "Culture and Ethnic Groups," <u>USA. gov</u>. Retrieved March 20, 2012, from <u>http://www.usa.gov/Citizen/Topics/History-Culture.shtml</u>,

40 Senate Bill 1070, State of Arizona, Senate, Forty-ninth Legislature, Second Regular Session, 2010. Retrieved March 20, 2012, from <u>http://www.azleg.gov/legtext/49leg/2r/bills/sb1070s.pdf</u>

<u>Cultural Identifier: Sex and/or Gender</u>

- How many genders are there? In U.S. culture, the standard answer to this question is two. However, there are many <u>more genders</u>[41] than two—masculine males, feminine females, masculine females, and feminine males, transvestites: male to female and female to male, androgynous individuals, and hermaphrodites.
- Expectations, stereotypes, rights and privileges are attached to each of the above. All of these are socially constructed.

<u>Step 2</u>: Return to the cultural learning model, and examine the messages you received from the socialization agents regarding each of the cultural identifiers. For example, were there chores for males in your family and different chores for females? If so, this was a message delivered to you regarding gender. In the model, technology is a reference to the Internet, mobile phones, and video games; electronic media refers to television, movies, and radio programs. Again, the authors of this model designed it as a discussion tool, but I believe it can also be used for each person to recognize his or her own cultural identity. The inside wheel of the model are socialization agents. Cultural identifiers (the outside circle) provide us with labels for recognizing different aspects of our and others' cultural identity. Socialization agents define for us what those labels mean.

<u>Step 3</u>: Go to _____ and complete the online learning module. *Under construction; online learning module will be available summer 2012.*

<u>Step 4</u>: Bring the printout of your cultural identity to class, and discuss in small groups similarities and differences in the images.

<u>Step 5</u>: Return to the adapted version of the Cultural Learning Process, and on a sheet of paper write all twelve cultural identifiers. Then indicate if you are a member of a minority group or a member of the majority for each variable (see Figure 10). Prior to beginning this list, select a point of reference: state level, national level, or globally. Also determine how to define the words "majority" and "minority." If necessary, use the Internet to determine a definition. If you complete this step and have one label for all items, select a different perspective (e.g., change from a national to a global level).

---

41   For more information, see Wilhelm, Amara Das, "Modern Third-Gender Types and Terms," The Gay and Lesbian Vaishnava Association, Inc. Retrieved March 20, 2012, from <u>http://www.galva108.org/modern_third_gender_types.html</u>

Age Group – Majority
Location (Geographic) – Minority/Majority
Sexual Identity – Majority
Religious Affiliation – Majority
Social Class/Status – Majority
Language Fluency – Minority
Health (Ability/Disability) – Minority
Race/Ethnicity – Majority
Nationality – Majority
Sex and/or Gender – Minority

Figure 10

Step 6: Upon completion of making the majority/minority list, examine Bennett's Model of Intercultural Sensitivity[42] and Spring's adaptation of the Cross Model of Ethnic and Racial Identity.[43] Bennett's model helps one understand the stages a majority member progresses through in becoming culturally aware. The Cross model consists of the stages of identity development undergone by a black person in the United States, as a stigmatized member of a minority group. Criticism of the Cross model is that it does not focus on the cultural aspects of being black. Though the Cross model has not stood the test of time to the degree that the Bennett model has, Spring adapted this model to apply to other groups, such as immigrants.[44] I believe this adaptation can be applied to individuals who are members of a minority group for each of the twelve cultural identifiers of the Cultural Learning Process.

Bennett's Model of Intercultural Sensitivity[45], [46]

Stage 1 – Denial: Inability to see cultural differences.
Stage 2 – Defense: Recognition of cultural differences, but negative evaluations of most.

---

42 Bennett, M. J. "Towards Ethnorelativism: A Developmental Model of Intercultural Sensitivity. In R. M. Paige (ed.), *Education* http://www.library.wisc.edu/edvrc/docs/public/pdfs/SEEDReadings/intCulSens.pdf ; also see Cushner, McClelland, and Safford (2003).
43 Ibid.; Cushner, McClelland, and Safford, pp. 122–130
44 Cushner, McClelland, and Safford, p. 110; also see Stith-Williams, Vivian and Haynes, Phyllis L. M. (Revised September 2007.) "For Cultural Competence: A Resource Manual for Developing Cultural Competence," Virginia Department of Education. Retrieved March 21, 2012, from http://www.doe.virginia.gov/special_ed/tech_asst_prof_dev/self_assessment/disproportionality/cultural_competence_manual.pdf
45 Bennett.
46 Cushner, McClelland, and Safford, online PowerPoint, Slides 11 and 12. Retrieved March 21, 2012, from www.lscc.edu/faculty/amanda_k_frye/.../cushner5_ppt_ch05.ppt

Stage 3 – <u>Minimization</u>: Acceptance of superficial cultural differences, but believe that all human beings are essentially the same.

Stage 4 – <u>Acceptance</u>: Ability to recognize and appreciate cultural differences on their own terms.

Stage 5 – <u>Adaptation</u>: Sees cultural categories as more flexible; becomes more competent in ability to communicate.

Stage 6 – <u>Integration</u> (rarely achieved): Moves easily among multiple perspectives.

<u>Criticisms of the Cross Model of the Racial and Ethnic Identity</u>[47]

Spring/Cross Model of Racial and Ethnic Identity[48]

Stage 1 – <u>Pre-Encounter</u>: Internalization of negative stereotypes by mainstream society.

Stage 2 – <u>Encounter</u>: Confrontation by an incident that forces questioning (i.e., racial profiling).

Stage 4 – <u>Immersion/Emersion</u>: Assumption of new ethnic identity, loss of self-hatred.

Stage 5 – <u>Immersion</u>: Total involvement in the ethnic culture; active in discussion, organization; highly ethnocentric.

Stage 6 – <u>Internalization</u>: Recognition of and comfort in living in two worlds; becoming bicultural or multicultural; can be both accepting and critical of mainstream culture.

<u>Step 7</u>: In small groups, identify statements for each stage of the Bennett model and each stage of the Spring/Cross model tied to the cultural identifiers of the Cultural Learning Process (See Figures 11 and 12).

<u>Step 8</u>: Each person should determine which stage they are at for each cultural identifier. Remember the Bennett model for the items in which one self-identifies as being a member of the majority culture, and the Spring/Cross model for items in which someone self-identified as a member of a minority group. If a person struggles with determining the stage of development, look at the opposite model and reconsider if the self-label is of a minority or majority member.

NATIONAL AND INTERNATIONAL DEMOGRAPHICS

Describe the lives of ten children who represent children in the United States and ten children representing the children of the world. Your description should be statistically accurate. For example, if one in five children lives in poverty in the United States, then two of the ten children on your list should be children living in poverty. When possible, use the resources below to research this activity. If you use other sources, make sure to identify those sources in your final report.

47 Sellers, Robert, et al. (1998). "Multidimensional Model of Racial Identity: A Reconceptualization of African American Racial Identity," *Personality and Social Psychology Review*, vol. 2, no. 1, 18–39. Retrieved March 21, 2012, from http://deepblue.lib.umich.edu/bitstream/2027.42/68695/2/10.1207_s15327957pspr0201_2.pdf

48 Cushner, McClelland, and Safford, online PowerPoint, Slides 4 and 5. Retrieved March 21, 2012, from www.lscc.edu/faculty/amanda_k_frye/.../cushner5_ppt_ch05.ppt

Bennett Model:	Denial	Defense	Minimization	Acceptance	Adaptation	Integration
Age Group	60 is the new 40					
Location (Geographic)						
Sexual Identity						Gay Marriage
Religious Affiliation						
Social Class/Status						
Language Fluency		English is the official U.S. language				
Health (Ability/ Disability)					Inclusion	
Race/Ethnicity						
Nationality				St. Patrick's Day		
Sex and/or Gender			Boys will be boys			

Figure 11

Spring/Cross Model	Pre-Encounter	Encounter	Immersion/ Emersion	Immersion	Adaptation
Age Group					
Location (Geographic)					
Sexual Identity		Anger over gay bashing			
Religious Affiliation				I am only friends with other Christians	
Social Class/ Status					
Language Fluency					Bilingual
Health (Ability/ Disability)	I am stupid because I am dyslexic				
Race/Ethnicity					
Nationality					
Sex and/or Gender			Boys have cooties		

Figure 12

Guiding Questions

1. What is the ethnicity/nationality of each child?
2. Does any child have a disability?
3. Where is the child living?
4. What are the ages of each child on each list?
5. What is the social class of each child?
6. What is the religion of each child?
7. What is the gender of each child?
8. What is the sexuality of each child?
9. How many languages does each child speak, and what are those languages?
10. What is the family of the child like (i.e., number of parents and siblings)?
11. Does the child attend school?
12. Does the child have access to electronic and print media? If so, what role does technology play in the child's life?
13. Does the child have access to technology? If so, what role does technology play in the child's life?
14. Does the child play sports or participate in the arts? If so, what sports and what types of arts?
15. What is the community and neighborhood of each child like?
16. Does the child work? If so, how much and where? Does the family of the child depend on the child's work for survival?
17. What is the religion of the child's family? What role does this faith play in the life of the child?

Online Resources

CIA World Fact Book   https://www.cia.gov/library/publications/the-world-factbook/
UNESCO   www.unesco.org
Library of Congress, Country Studies   http://lcweb2.loc.gov/frd/cs/
National Center for Educational Statistics   http://nces.ed.gov/
U.S. Census   http://www.census.gov/

CHAPTER TEN
APPLICATION OF BOOK CONTENT

WHY DO I NEED TO KNOW THIS?

Wxhat is the value of knowledge if it cannot be put to use? That is my pedagogical mantra. In this chapter, two large group activities are outlined which can be used to apply the information from the previous nine chapters of this text. The first activity is a charter school competition; the second is the creation of Web-Quests. Both activities require a lot of time set aside for in-class group meetings (lasting approximately two months), teamwork within student groups, and the course instructor serving as a resource, rather than an all-knowing authority figure.

CHARTER SCHOOL COMPETITION

The scenario for this activity is that the local public school is being restructured due to repeatedly failing to meet AYP. The community has created a selection committee that will grant one charter school contract to the winning proposal. This activity consists of three stages. The first stage is the research stage, in which class participants become experts in charter school history, laws, and politics, as well as the community in which their school will be located. The second stage is the creation stage. In this stage, further research will be necessary, but it is for the purpose of building a school, not simply becoming an expert. The last stage of this activity is a competition, where groups give a sales pitch to a committee that decides who will be awarded a charter school commission. Prior to these stages, however, charter school proposal committees should be formulated and positions assigned or chosen.

The **principal** is responsible for coordinating group meetings, both inside and outside of class, as well as electronic correspondence (e-mail, cell phones, chat rooms, etc.); liaison with the school superintendent (course instructor). Being liaison includes taking group attendance at each in-class and outside-of-class meeting and reporting the attendance to the superintendent. The principal will also be held accountable by the superintendent for holding other members of the group accountable for his or her charge, as well as resolving positively any conflicts that might occur in the group, and/or seeking the assistance of the superintendent, if necessary. The principal is also responsible for ensuring that each member of the group is given the necessary time to lead the group for his or her charge. In addition, the principal will lead the group in the selection of a community where their charter school will be located, as well as the mission of the school.

The **treasurer** is responsible for leading the group in the creation of the budget of the school. This is not a solo job, or even one that should be completed by one or two members of the group. Rather, the treasurer will lead the group in the process of researching how to create a charter school budget, for making decisions regarding the budget, and for the final writing and printing of the budget. The treasurer is also responsible for making sure the budget is consistent with school funding policies and laws in Ohio.

The **historian** of the charter school will keep a record of the group's processes, including the minutes of each meeting, identification of how research and tasks were completed in the group, and completing the final report submitted to the superintendent. The historian is not responsible for tracking down members to determine their involvement. Rather, each member of the group is responsible for making sure that the historian is aware of his or her engagement in the creation process. The historian is also responsible for making sure that the school mission, curriculum, and schedule can be defended utilizing educational history, as well as the history of the community in which the charter school is located.

The **director of curriculum** is responsible for leading the group in the creation of courses for the charter school that are consistent with John Dewey's theory of progressivism, but also meet the essentialist requirements of No Child Left Behind. In addition, the director of curriculum will lead the group in making sure laws regarding religion and schools are followed and understood by all personnel. The director of curriculum will also be responsible for the final writing and printing of the curriculum map for the charter school.

The **guidance counselor** will be responsible for leading the group in designing the calendar for the school. The calendar will cover one academic year, as well as a standard weekly and/or monthly schedule of courses. The guidance counselor will also be responsible for the final writing and printing of the school calendar. Further, the guidance counselor will lead the group in ensuring that the social needs of their students are met and that the school is consistent with laws about gender, segregation, sexual orientation, bullying, and other dimensions of human diversity and schooling.

<u>Step 1</u>: Research – "What is a charter school?"

1. What is No Child Left Behind?
2. What is meant by the achievement gap?
3. What is AYP?
4. What is a charter school?
5. What is a school voucher?
6. What role do charter schools play in No Child Left Behind?
7. What is Race to the Top, and how is it related to charter schools?
8. How are charter schools different in Ohio from those in other states?
9. Are charter schools required to follow the same laws as public schools?
10. Does the Individuals with Disabilities Education Act apply to charter schools?
11. Is segregation permitted in charter schools?
12. How is regulation of charter schools different from regulation of public and private schools?
13. What sources did you utilize to find answers to the above questions? What were the biases of the authors?

<u>Step 2</u>: Identify a town that might benefit from having a charter school. Be prepared to defend your reason for choosing this town.

1. Establish criteria for making this decision (i.e., based on school funding statistics, local violence statistics, a rich local history, state report cards).
2. Do not select a town in which anyone in the group is familiar.

<u>Step 3</u>: Thoroughly research the community where your charter school will be located. If possible, visit the community.

1. What is the history of the community?
   a. When and why was it founded?
   b. Was there any historical event in that community that you could possibly use as a theme?
   c. Does the community have a notable person or family who lived there?

    d. Does the community have a manufacturing history of note?

    e. Does the location of the community have historical significance?

    f. Was anything invented or pioneered in that community?

2. What are the demographics of the community?

    a. State the race and ethnic makeup of the community, and not just its statistical breakdown. Are there enclaves in the community (e.g., a Germantown)?

    b. Is there anything notable regarding gender and sexuality (e.g., Susan B. Anthony once lived there or there are five men to every woman or it has the third largest gay population in the nation or it has an ordinance that bans gays)?

    c. What are the languages spoken in the community?

    d. How many children attend school?

    e. What are the family compositions of the children who attend school?

    f. What is the religious composition of the community (places of worship, as well as attendance rates; number of bars to churches ratio)?

    g. What are the social classes of citizens? Do they have names? Or are they tied to an area of the town (i.e., the right or wrong side of the tracks)?

    h. Are there any health or disability patterns (e.g., a high number of cases of lung cancer or children with autism)?

3. Research local ordinances of the community and look for any that are nontraditional.

Step 4: Research the local public school. Some of this information may be available online; some of it will need to be extrapolated from general information at the state or federal level.

1. What is student enrollment?

2. How is the school funded?

3. What is the school budget?

4. How much money is spent on each student enrolled?

5. What are the demographics of the student population? Though this will be similar to the second item in Step 3, it will not necessarily be identical. For example, if a community was historically composed of native-born Americans, but has an influx of immigrants, it is possible that the older population of the community is white, but the younger population is more ethnically diverse.

6. What is the composition of the teaching population, as well as of the administration?

7. What are the demographics of school employees?

8. What is the curriculum of the school?

9. What extracurricular activities are available for students at the school?

Step 5: Write a mission statement and criteria for charter school

1. The mission must build upon the proud heritage of the community.
2. It must reflect the progressive theory of education.
3. The mission may not say anything about the economy, test scores, or anything that sounds traditional.

Step 6: Create the school curriculum.

1. Begin by creating grade levels and avoid traditional grade levels based on age.
2. Create classes tied directly to your school mission and avoid traditional classes, such as math, science, language arts, etc. Also, do not simply create fancy names for traditional content areas. Each course should not be available in traditional public schools.

Step 7: Staff your school.

1. Go beyond the traditional teacher/principal/superintendent hierarchical model of schooling.
2. Consider teams of employees and shared governance structures.
3. Write job listings for each position. You must include qualifications and a general job description, as well as salary and benefits.
4. Make sure that each position is competitive on the open market. For example, what is the average salary for a teacher, and is your starting salary and benefits package competitive?

Step 8: Create the school budget.

1. Start with the income of the school. What are the sources for income in your school (local, state, federal budgets, as well as private donations and grants)? How much will be received from each source?
2. Where will your charter school be located? Will you need to include rent or construction fees as part of your budget? Locate your school in an actual property of the community.
3. Include salaries and benefits in your budget, as well as whether or not you will include professional development funding (i.e., reimbursing teachers for items they buy for their classes and/or to attend conferences). Make sure to include salary increases or you will lose employees very quickly.

4. Furnish your school with equipment.

Step Nine: Create a school calendar that includes:

1. A typical weekly or biweekly schedule.
2. A typical monthly schedule.
3. Holidays.
4. Your school's schedule should not be a traditional school schedule. The traditional school schedule is an agricultural schedule; most communities are no longer agricultural.

Step Ten: Create a sales pitch for your charter school. Your sales pitch should be approximately a half hour in length. You should be prepared to answer questions from the following selected committee members[1]:

- The President of the Local Bank: This bank president is very frugal and believes that the major problem with the former local public school was their inability to manage their finances and resources, including personnel, well. This banker's primary concern is fiscal management of charter schools.
- The Former Coach of a High School Sports Team: Many of the former players had the potential to get a sports scholarship to college. Many of these same students will not be able to go to college if they do not play the sport in their senior year in high school. The coach's concern is the athletic program in a future charter school.
- Parent of an Autistic Son: This parent's primary concern is whether or not services will be provided for disabled students.
- Bishop of a Local Christian Denomination: The bishop's primary concern is that Christian principles are respected in the new charter school.
- Pro-American: This committee member's primary concern is that children will be taught proper English in the school, particularly students whose first language is not English.
- Successful Businessperson Who Was Raised in Poverty: If not for teachers who took a special interest in her future, that person would still be poor. This committee member is primarily concerned with the teacher selection process and qualifications.
- Garbage Collector: In the old public school, this man's daughter was continually bullied because of the social status of her family. His primary concern is how the charter school will handle student relations.

---

1 Because I teach five sections of this class each semester, students from different classes serve in the following roles and role play.

- <u>Parent of a Son Who Committed Suicide</u>: The son's suicide note indicated that he was bullied in school because students thought he was gay. In the suicide note, he admitted that he was gay. When alive, he had not come out to anyone. This parent believes suicide could have been prevented if the former school had done more to foster sexuality awareness and appreciation.
- <u>Former Teacher Who Is a Fundamental, Evangelical, Politically Active, Right-Wing Christian</u>: This teacher believes that the major problem in the old school was that teachers were not permitted to share their religious beliefs with students. He is primarily concerned that the charter school protect the religious practices of teachers as well as students, and that teachers will have the freedom to share their religious beliefs.
- <u>Former Janitor of the Public School</u>: This janitor saw firsthand the degree to which the students did not respect property. A major portion of his former job was fixing vandalism caused by the students. This committee member's major concern is that charter school personnel control the children and teach them respect.
- <u>Former Principal of the School</u>: One of the biggest hassles of the principal's former job was parents who continually complained. The majority of parents were helpful and supportive, but there were always one or two who wanted their child to have special treatment and believed their child could do no wrong. This former principal wants to know what the charter school will do to ensure positive parental involvement in the school.
- <u>Former Bullied Student</u>: This student had to go to work at an early age and could not afford pay-to-play. The former student's primary concerns are student-to-student relationships and elimination of pay-to-play.
- <u>Single Parent Who Works Second Shift</u>: If this parent does not keep a second shift job, the family will suffer financially as a result. This parent was never able to attend parent/teacher conferences or after-school sports or musical performances. This parent's primary concern is that the new charter school meet this family's unique needs.
- <u>Parent with a First-Shift Job</u>: This committee member did not accept a more lucrative second shift position so that she could attend all of her child's activities, but could not attend meetings during the school day. The primary concern is that the new charter school meet this family's unique needs.
- <u>Former Teacher Who Is a Liberal Atheist</u>: This former teacher believes that religions are destroying our nation and especially public schools, blaming the dismantling of the former school on right-wing, religious zealots. The primary concerns here are keeping religion out of schools and schools having comprehensive sex education.
- <u>Former ESL Teacher</u>: This former teacher is worried about those students whose second language is English. They are concerned that the charter school might not meet their needs.
- <u>Former Music Teacher</u>: This former teacher lost her job well before the school was dismantled due to the elimination of the music curriculum. When she lost her job, this teacher warned everyone that eventually all teachers would lose their job if NCLB was not fought. No one listened; she is still very bitter.

- <u>Parent</u>: No matter what is said, this parent does not agree and lets everyone know of the ensuing displeasure. This parent is thrilled that the former public school was dismantled and wants to make sure that none of the teachers from the former public school are hired in the new school.
- <u>Graduate Now Attending College</u>: This student's former teachers greatly helped and continue to help. Primary concern is that they be hired in the new charter school.
- <u>Parent of Child who Struggles in Math (or any subject)</u>: Because this parent struggled with math in school and did not see much value for math, he cannot help children in school. Now, this parent wants his children to get a strong background in math.
- <u>Elderly Member of the Community</u>: This community member believes far too much is being spent on schoolchildren, at the expense of caring for older citizens.
- <u>Retired College Professor</u>: The professor believes that children have it too easy in schools today, and that we have gotten too far away from classic literature, moral education, and self-responsibility.
- <u>Muslim Parent</u>: This parent is afraid her children may be discriminated against because of the backlash against Muslims in the United States. She is particularly concerned that if another attack on U.S. soil occurs, the children will be kept safe.

CREATE A WEB-QUEST

In this activity, students create a Web-Quest regarding an issue in education. The focus of the Web-Quest will be a global perspective and will be tied to the information located in Chapters One through Seven of this text. The stages of this activity are similar to those described above, with extensive research preceding the creation of a product.

Step 1: Identify a current issue in public education. The following are suggestions of possible topics:
  » The Arts and Schools
  » Sports and Schools
  » Violence in Schools
  » School Funding
  » Privatization of Public School
  » Bilingual Education
  » Educational Inequality
  » Brain Development
  » School Governance
  » Global Education
  » Parents and Schools
  » E-learning

- » Religion and Schools
- » Freedom of Speech and Education
- » National Core Academic Standards
- » Private Schools
- » Access to Schooling
- » Teacher Professionalization
- » Moral/Character Education
- » Tracking Students
- » Homeschooling
- » Gender and Education
- » Assessment
- » Special Education
- » Segregation
- » Bullying

<u>Step 2</u>: Research the history of the issue in the United States.

<u>Step 3</u>: Research case law and educational policies tied to the issue.

<u>Step 4</u>: Determine the role and/or obligations of teachers and administrators in the United States regarding the issue.

<u>Step 5</u>: Identify the diversity variables as outlined in Chapter Nine and their role in U.S. public schools. Make sure to examine each cultural identifier and each socialization agent to determine the role. For example, what role does technology play regarding school violence and/or the prevention of school violence? Where is technology likely to play a role (urban, suburban, or rural schools), and does this correlate with the locations where school shootings have occurred?

<u>Step 6</u>: What are the major debates within the United States regarding the issue under investigation? What belief systems, as described in Chapter Seven, play a role in these debates?

<u>Step 7</u>: Select two separate nations on two separate continents to research.

<u>Step 8</u>: Research the history of schooling in both nations.

<u>Step 9</u>: Research the structure of the legal and legislative structures of both nations.

<u>Step 10</u>: Determine at what level of governance are schools controlled (i.e., local or national level)?

Step 11: What are the demographics of the two nations? Make sure to refer to the variables in the Cultural Learning Process described in Chapter Nine.

Step 12: What is the quality of life for children in the other two nations?

- Do all children attend school?
- Are schools public?
- Are there child labor laws?
- Are child labor laws enforced for all children?
- Do families depend on the work of children for survival?

Step 13: Examine the role of teachers in the two nations.

How are they educated?
What are the qualifications of teachers?
What are the social class and/or social status of teachers in that nation?
Does the other nation have teachers' unions? And if so, what is the role of those unions?

Step 14: Compare your findings on the other two nations to the United States. Make sure to check all assumptions regarding the United States. For example, in this country, child labor laws are not the same and/or enforced equally. This is particularly the case when it comes to agriculture, where young migrant children often work at the side of their parents.[2]

Step 15: Create a Web-Quest

ONLINE RESOURCES

- Library Research Guide
- Web-Quests
- We-Quest Taxonomy
- Web-Quest Reception Scaffolds
- Web-Quest Production Scaffolds
- Seven Steps to Better Online Searches
- CIA: World Fact Book
- U.S. Census: People and Households

---

2   For more information see 2012http://www.pbs.org/now/politics/migrantchildren.html retrieved March 25.

Index

CPSIA information can be obtained
at www.ICGtesting.com
Printed in the USA
LVOW02s0748210116
471428LV00001B/4/P